STAND OUT!

OTHER BOOKS BY THE AUTHOR

❖

WINNING OFFICE POLITICS:
DuBrin's Guide for the 1990s

BOUNCING BACK:
How to Get Back in the Game When Your
Career Is on the Line

YOUR OWN WORST ENEMY:
How to Prevent Career Self-Sabotage

EFFECTIVE BUSINESS PSYCHOLOGY

HUMAN RELATIONS:
Job Oriented Approach

HUMAN RELATIONS FOR CAREER
AND PERSONAL SUCCESS

CONTEMPORARY APPLIED MANAGEMENT

THE PRACTICE OF SUPERVISION

ESSENTIALS OF MANAGEMENT

MANAGEMENT AND ORGANIZATION

WINNING AT OFFICE POLITICS

❖

STAND OUT!

330 WAYS FOR GAINING THE EDGE WITH BOSSES, CO-WORKERS, SUBORDINATES AND CUSTOMERS

ANDREW J. DuBRIN

PRENTICE HALL
Englewood Cliffs, New Jersey 07632

Prentice-Hall International (UK) Limited, *London*
Prentice-Hall of Australia Pty. Limited, *Sydney*
Prentice-Hall Canada, Inc., *Toronto*
Prentice-Hall Hispanoamericana, S.A., *Mexico*
Prentice-Hall of India Private Limited, *New Delhi*
Prentice-Hall of Japan, Inc., *Tokyo*
Simon & Schuster Asia Pte. Ltd., *Singapore*
Editora Prentice-Hall do Brasil, Ltda., *Rio de Janeiro*

10 9 8 7 6 5 4 3 2 1

Library of Congress Cataloging-in-Publication Data

DuBrin, Andrew J.
    Stand out! / Andrew J. DuBrin
      p. cm.
    Includes bibliographical references and index.
    ISBN 0-13-092842-9
    1. Career development. 2. Self-presentation.
    3. Interpersonal relations 4. Office politics.
    I. Title.
    HF5381.D813 1993   93-6606
    650.1—dc20   CIP

ISBN 0-13-092842-9

PRENTICE HALL
Career & Personal Development
Englewood Cliffs, NJ 07632

Simon & Schuster, A Paramount Communications Company

Printed in the United States of America

To Douglas

❖
ACKNOWLEDGMENTS
❖

My primary thanks on this project go to Tom Power, my editor at the Business Information Publishing Division of Simon & Schuster. Tom encouraged me to proceed with my book idea and avoided throwing even an inch of red tape in my path. The efforts of Roseann Wright, Tom Power's editorial assistant, and those of Eve Mossman my production editor are also much appreciated.

My students and researchers at the College of Business of the Rochester Institute of Technology made an important contribution to this project. These people dutifully collected hundreds of interviews about people who gained the edge in various situations. Thanks are also due the many people I have spoken to or observed who have impressed me with their winning tactics.

Carol Bowman, the woman in my life and significant other, receives my appreciation for her love and support. Thank you also to my family members Melanie, Douglas, Drew, Molly, and Rosemary for giving me an important identity outside of work. Carol's family members also contribute to this identity. Finally, I greatly appreciate my colleagues, friends, and acquaintances who have encouraged my past writing.

Andrew J. DuBrin

INTRODUCTION

On a recent vacation my eye was attracted to a junior-size T-shirt in a souvenir shop. On the front of the T-shirt was a drawing of a lion cub peering out from behind a tree camouflaging his den. With a concerned look on the cub's face, he proclaimed, "It's a jungle out there." The cub appeared hesitant to step out into the fierce, competitive world of the 1990s. Many humans face a similar problem, even when already involved in a career. To overcome worry, fear, and anxiety about beating or staving off the competition, most people need some way to stand out, or gain an edge. An *edge* in this context is any thought, action, tactic, or strategy that will put you at advantage in a work situation of consequence. Gaining an edge helps you stand out, and you stand out by gaining an edge.

Standing out is thus important in any situation where you want or need to gain advantage. Among these important situations are interactions with your boss, top-management, co-workers, lower-ranking people, customers, and prospective customers. Today, any person who uses your output is classified as a customer. Customers therefore include people who actually spend money for your product or service and anyone else who receives your help. If you analyze some statistics for a person in another department, he or she is your customer. Standing out is also important in dealing with people in your network and with prospective employers.

Gaining the edge is critically important during tough economic times. Under these circumstances, most people need an edge to survive. For at least the next decade, financial growth will be limited in the industrially developed world. This is especially true in North America. Because the manufacturing base is so small and organizations continue to be thinly staffed, good jobs and good customers will continue to be scarce. When prosperity strikes, standing out and gaining an edge is still important. Most people want to make sure they obtain at least their fair share of prosperity. Furthermore, during good economic times the people who prosper the most are those who know how to impress others. Prosperity for all has never existed.

The general approach to standing out presented in this book is to use the right tactic in a given situation to impress one or more other people. In a subtle yet important way, this book therefore differs from many other self-help business books. Instead of expounding on the virtues of one technique—such as being assertive, intimidating, or dressing smartly—we describe more than 330 related tactics. Most of the book is organized around situations in which you might need to gain the edge, such as relating to your boss or to a customer. All readers of this book already know something about coming out on top in a work situation. By carefully reading this book, however, you can improve your chances of achieving what you want. You stand out by adding to your repertoire some of the tactics recommended in this book for dealing with specific situations.

The tactics presented here are winners based on my long-term study of office politics, self-improvement, and overcoming adversity. In addition, the vast majority of these tactics are based on well-accepted principles of human behavior. Almost all the tactics are illustrated by an anecdote collected by me or by one of my researchers. You thus profit from the stand-out and edge-gaining methods of hundreds of people. The original cases are disguised to protect the identities of people who prefer not to let key people in their workplace know how they stood out. Only a handful of references are made to accounts of public figures.

The book begins by describing basic behaviors and skills for standing out and gaining the edge in most work situations—appearing self-confident and negotiating effectively. With self-confidence and negotiating skills as a foundation, the book then describes how to stand out with key people in the work place. The key people you might want to impress include superiors, co-workers, lower-ranking people, prospective customers, and existing customers. Added to this list are gaining the edge with people in your network and prospective employers.

This book has a rhythm and a format you should anticipate. First, I introduce a key idea about standing out, and then I present an illustrative case history or example. Where appropriate, I then offer an analysis of why the tactic worked. At various points in the book I ask you questions to help you think through how the edge might be gained in a difficult situation. Interspersed throughout the book are checklists or suggestions to help you sharpen your perceptions about coming out on top in a given situation.

CONTENTS

❖ 1 ❖

PROJECTING SELF-CONFIDENCE

The journey toward standing-out begins with projecting the right amount of self-confidence. The term "right amount" is chosen with considerable care. Usually the right amount of self-confidence is a moderate level. Projecting too much or too little self-confidence can put you at a disadvantage. At one extreme are people who project excessive self-confidence. They are usually perceived as egomaniacs with little concern for the thoughts or feelings of others. Bragging and boasting irritates and annoys the very people whom you are trying to impress. Another problem with people who project too much self-confidence is that they rarely listen to suggestions and criticisms. Bombastic and smug people are so convinced they are right that they dismiss even a hint of negative feedback.

At the other extreme are people who project too little self-confidence. They divert their gaze away from the listener; they cover their mouth with a hand while talking; and they speak in a whisper. The person who projects too little self-confidence is often perceived as ineffective, indecisive, and wimpish. The perception may be inaccurate, but other people act as if it were true.

Here we describe sensible techniques for projecting self-confidence. Learning to project self-confidence often pays enormous dividends. By developing a veneer of self-confidence, one becomes self-confident. Subtle changes take place in your psyche as you assume the role of a self-confident person. As people begin to relate to you as if you were self-confident, your self-confidence rises.

Even if you are satisfied with the level of self-confidence you project, reading this chapter could be beneficial. Use the information as a checklist to see if you have left anything out of your repertoire.

USE POSITIVE SELF-TALK

Negative self-talk, or putting yourself down with your own words, quickly establishes you as a person with low self-worth and self-confidence. A lack of self-confidence is projected in statements such as "I may be uninformed but . . .," "Nobody asked my opinion," "I know I'm usually wrong, but . . ." "I know I don't have as much education as some people, but . . ." Self-effacing statements like these serve to reinforce low self-confidence. The more you debase yourself, the further your self-confidence deteriorates. Negative self-talk thus becomes the proverbial self-fulfilling prophecy.

To appear self-confident, positive self-talk must replace the negative kind. Positive self-talk basically involves saying positive things about oneself to oneself. The biggest dividends in gaining the edge are forthcoming when positive self-talk takes place in front of others. In the method recommended here, the first step in using positive self-talk is to objectively state the incident that is casting doubt about self-worth.[1] The key word here is "objectively." Jackie, who is fearful of poorly executing a customer-survey assignment might say: "I've been asked to conduct a customer survey for the company, and I'm not good at conducting surveys."

The next step is to objectively interpret what the incident *does not* mean. Jackie might say, "Not being skilled at conducting a survey doesn't mean that I cannot figure out a way to do a useful survey, or that I'm an ineffective employee."

Next, the person should objectively state what the incident *does* mean. In doing this, the person should avoid put-down labels such as "incompetent," "stupid," "dumb," "jerk," or "airhead." All these terms are forms of negative self-talk. Jackie should state what the incident does mean: "I have a problem with one small aspect of this job, conducting a customer survey. This means I need to acquire skill in conducting a survey."

The fourth step is to objectively account for the cause of the incident. Jackie could say, "I'm really worried about conducting an accurate survey because I have very little experience of this nature."

The fifth step is to identify some positive ways to prevent the incident from happening again. Jackie might say, "I'll buy a basic book on conducting surveys and follow it carefully," or "I'll enroll in a seminar on conducting consumer surveys."

The final step is to use positive self-talk. Jackie imagines her boss saying, "This survey is really good. I'm proud of my decision to select you to conduct this important survey." When the opportunity arises Jackie will say to her boss something to the effect, "I'm glad you asked me to conduct the survey. I'm eager to take on new challenges, and I've done well with them in the past." Or she might say to her boss, "Thanks for the opportunity for professional growth."

Positive self-talk builds self-confidence and self-esteem because it programs the mind with positive messages.[2] Making frequent positive messages or affirmations about the self creates a more confident person and projects a more positive image. An example would be, "I know I can learn this new software rapidly enough to increase my productivity within five days." If you do make a mistake, the right positive self-talk (to yourself or in front of others) might be, "It's taken me more time than usual to learn how to use this new software. I know I'll have the problem licked in a few days."

USE POSITIVE VISUAL IMAGERY

Assume you have a situation in mind in which you would like to appear confident and in control. An example would be a meeting with a major customer who has told you over the telephone that he is considering switching suppliers. Your intuitive reaction is that if you cannot handle his objections without fumbling or appearing desperate, you will lose the account. An important technique in this situation is positive visual imagery. To apply this technique in this situation, imagine yourself engaging in a convincing argument about retaining your company as the primary supplier. Imagine yourself talking in positive terms about the good service your company offers and how you can rectify any problems.

Visualize yourself listening patiently to your customer's concerns and then talking confidently about how your company can handle these concerns. As you rehearse this moment of truth, create a mental picture of you and the client shaking hands over the fact that the account is still yours.

Positive mental imagery helps you appear self-confident because your mental rehearsal of the situation has helped you prepare for battle. If imagery works for you once, you will be even more effective in subsequent uses of the technique. Here is how one man used positive visual imagery to advantage.

Ed was a human resources specialist at a Silicon Valley manufacturer of computers. Because of his training background and his sensitivity to people, Ed received an assignment as the director of cultural diversity training. The assignment required Ed to establish training programs designed to help employees appreciate, and even celebrate, diverse ethnic and racial groups within the company. The training sessions involved such activities as a Vietnamese employee sitting in the center of a circle of both Caucasian and black employees. She would describe to the other members of the circle all the slights she thought she experienced as a company employee. As a result of dialogue with the person in the middle of the circle, other employees were supposed to become more sensitive to the feelings of culturally diverse employees.

Top-management support for the program was mixed. Cultural diversity training was thought to help the company move beyond equal employment opportunity and to encourage harmony. Some company executives were concerned, however, that the program was stirring up animosity that did not really exist.

The company announced a downsizing that included cutting back on "nonessential activities." Because of some of the negative sentiment expressed about his program, Ed was concerned about the downsizing. He thought it might mean the end of his cultural diversity program, and perhaps the end of his position. Instead of fretting needlessly, Ed applied positive mental imagery to the situation. (He had learned the technique in a self-improvement seminar.) For several days, Ed imagined himself striding confidently into a meeting with top management and extolling the cultural diversity program.

When Ed felt sufficiently confident, he requested a meeting with the vice president of human resources and the company president to review the status of his new training program. Ed approached the vice president first, and she arranged a 30-minute meeting with Ed, the president, and herself. During the meeting, Ed talked in glowing terms about the program and how it was perceived so positively by most employees. Ed also pointed out deftly how the Equal Employment Opportunity Commission looked favorably upon vendors who conducted cultural diversity training.

(Ed's company had a major contract with the federal government.) Furthermore, Ed talked confidently about future expansion of this vital program that was in the forefront of the industry.

Ed and his cultural diversity training program survived the downsizing. It is not absolutely certain that Ed's program was headed for the chopping block. Ed thinks, however, that his self-confident command performance may have helped avert disaster. Observe that Ed did two things right. He placed himself in a positive mental state, and he took the initiative to defend his program before an adverse decision was made.

BE SELF-DIRECTING

Self-confident people believe they can control their own fate. In this way they are self-directing. Such people do not blame the outside world for the good and bad things that happen to them. Instead, self-directing people take personal responsibility for external events. Because self-directing people believe that they control external circumstances, they are said to have an internal locus of control. Being self-directing contributes to an image of self-confidence. When you take responsibility for events around you, others regard you as being self-confident and in control. Such was the case with Jerry Andriak.

Jerry was a junior accountant working for a CPA firm in Boston. Most of the firm's clientele were small companies in the towns surrounding Boston. As the business downturn became more pronounced, many of the firm's clients began to cut back on the amount of service they requested. Many of the small and medium size firms began to perform some of the services for themselves that they had previously requested from Jerry's firm. For example, many of the accountants and bookkeepers working full time for the smaller firms now did most of the tax work. Legally required services, such as having the CPA firm help prepare the annual report, were retained.

Most of the professional staff in the CPA firm became convinced that their firm was headed toward a serious retrenchment. Several accountants and support staff who had left the firm voluntarily had not been replaced. Pessimism pervaded the firm. Staff members who had moaned about being overworked now expressed apprehension about not having enough to do.

Jerry took a different tack. He recommended to the partners that he organize a couple of free seminars for small-business owners. During the seminar, several CPAs would explain the full range of services offered by the firm. They would also describe how hiring outside accounting services was often more cost effective than having a full-time accountant on the payroll. Small-business owners interested in any of the services offered by the firm would be requested to write down their names, addresses, and phone numbers. The principals of the firm liked Jerry's idea, particularly because the firm would be making no unethical claims. Jerry was given a modest budget to implement his plans.

The seminars were a moderate success. About ten existing clients expanded their use of the firm, and the seminars attracted some new clientele. The principals in Jerry's firm were impressed with his initiative and ability to take control of a difficult situation. Jerry's self-directing approach resulted in an above-average year-end bonus. Of greater consequence to his career, Jerry was now under warm consideration to become a future partner at his firm.

People who are not self-directing look upon the outside world as the major controller of events. When victory comes their way, they often attribute their good fortune to luck. Another aspect of their behavior is even more damaging to projecting an image of self-confidence. People with an external locus of control typically blame their mistakes and misfortunes on others and on external circumstances. A person who makes statements such as the following will project an image of low self-confidence:

❖ I would have made the sale, but the competition decided to sell by price.

❖ If it were not for office politics, I would be a vice president in this company.

❖ I would be much more successful today if I weren't the victim of reverse discrimination.

❖ I would have finished college, but I ran out of money.

❖ The systems I have developed would definitely contribute to productivity, but nobody around here appreciates them.

❖ I would be making much more money today, but I'm stuck in a low-paying industry.

❖ The opportunities for a person in my field have shrunk to almost zero.

In each of the preceding situations, the person probably could have done something to be self-directing. For example, if the competition is selling by price alone, the self-directing person will emphasize service. The last two statements reflect the thinking of many dissatisfied career persons who have an external locus of control. A more impressive approach would be to say: "I'm in a low-paying industry, so I'm going to attempt to switch industries." Or, with an even stronger internal locus of control, a self-directing person might say: "Opportunities in my field have shrunk, so my plan is to switch fields."

EXHIBIT PERSONAL DYNAMISM

An especially effective way of appearing self-confident is to be perceived as dynamic, or filled with energy and vitality. If you are naturally energetic and effervescent, just be yourself. The energy you exude already contributes to the perception of you as self-confident and in control. If you are more subdued by nature, you still have the option of developing skills and behaviors that will make you appear more dynamic. Six such skills and behaviors are described next.

1. *Express your feelings assertively.* A vital tactic for appearing more dynamic is to express your feelings in an open, constructive, and candid manner. Visualize the scenario of a staff meeting in which the participants are weighing the pros and cons of a proposal. Most people make fact-oriented statements such as, "I see some merit in this idea. It could be cost-effective in the short range," or "This proposal has a lot of weaknesses. I doubt it will bring about a suitable return on investment."

   In contrast to the emotionally neutral statements just made, the dynamic person will project feelings about the proposals. To exhibit personal dynamism, make a statement such as, "Your proposed solution really excites [great feeling word] me. The idea would pay for itself in no time, and we would all be very proud [another great feeling word]. If you disliked the proposal you might state: "This proposal has a lot of weaknesses that really worry [a strong feeling word] me. It will most likely backfire [a word that provokes feelings in others], and lose money [an explicitly bad state of affairs]."

2. *Use animated facial expressions.* Facial blandness interferes with appearing dynamic and self-confident. To exhibit personal dynamism, it is essential to make frequent use of animated facial expressions. Use big smiles, little smiles, expressions of delight, frowns, scowls, looks of puzzlement and surprise, and reassuring nods. Animated facial expressions are also useful for purposes of projecting leadership characteristics.

   To develop animated facial expressions, practice in front of a mirror or a camcorder. Videotaping is slightly better than a mirror because many people find it difficult to modify their facial expressions when looking into a mirror. Think of various moods you want to project, and then do your best to match your facial expression to the mood.

If you need some guidelines for matching facial expressions to your mood, emulate television actors, actresses, newscasters, newsmakers, and especially comedians. Or model a business person who you think has effective facial expressions.

3. *Talk with optimism.* Optimistic people, almost by definition, project an image of self-confidence and dynamism. It will not be necessary to overhaul your personality if you are naturally pessimistic. Nevertheless, you can learn to keep some of your pessimistic thoughts to yourself and search for optimistic comments to fit each situation. When you have struggled through a rough assignment and finally completed it, talk about how you have benefited from the experience and will do even better next time. When you have barely met your quota, don't apologize. Talk positively about how you overcame unforeseen hurdles and squeaked through to accomplish your goals.

A key facet of projecting optimism is to look for the positives in what other people perceive to a negative event. Keep these examples in mind:

❖ You are the sales manager and sales have just plunged to a ten-year low. Instead of belaboring the misery, say: "We have finally hit bottom. From now on we can expect an upturn. My plans for a turnaround will be completed by next Monday."

❖ You are an administrative assistant and your boss is castigating you for having furnished her a report that was badly flawed. In a non-apologetic manner you say, "It is unfortunate that my report did not accomplish all it was intended to do. However, I've profited from the experience. I now have a clear picture of what you want in my next report."

❖ You are the company controller and your year-end analysis reveals that the company lost $350,000 for the year. Knowing that your boss likes to trample bearers of bad news, you point out: "We just missed our break-even point last year by $350,000. However, with just a 2 percent increase in market share we would have been in the black."

4. *Look and act powerful.* An indispensable part of projecting personal dynamism is to look and act powerful. Looking powerful is more subtle than would appear on the surface. If you take literally the advice of wardrobe consultants, you will look like a sales associate in a posh retail store or like a young professional in most metropolitan offices. On the other hand, if you ignore conventional wisdom about looking powerful you risk looking unimportant and lacking dynamism in the eyes of others. Specific ways of increasing your power look include:

❖ Dress with panache by adding a unique flair to your dress-for-success look, including carrying a luxury fountain pen, an expensive watch, or a thick silk tie or scarf. Opulent earrings and cuff links also add to panache, as does a freshly cleaned leather attaché case.

❖ Decorate your office with stainless steel, leather, and polished glass. Leave all family photos, mementos, and souvenirs home.

❖ Hair should be short for males with no sideburns or beard; it should be short and away from the face for females.

❖ On occasion, when standing, place hands on hip and place your feet apart about 18 inches.

❖ For emphasis when speaking, point the index finger parallel to the ground, and thumb at a right angle similar to aiming a gun.

5. *Move and act purposefully.* People who stride through the workplace as if they have an urgent purpose in mind project personal dynamism. Management consultant James R. Baehler observes that corporate officers, for example, move and act purposefully even when they're passing through a lobby. He provides an anecdote in support of his conclusion:

A few years ago I was standing in the lobby of an office building in Manhattan, waiting for a luncheon appointment. Waiting with me was a broadcast executive. We were making idle conversation and watching the flow of people in and out of the elevators. She turned to me and said, "I'll bet I can pick out every vice president who comes into this lobby. I can tell because they look like vice presidents."

She said she would show me what a vice president looks like. Turning to the bank of elevators, she studied the passersby for a moment and then said, "Here comes one now." She indicated a man in his late thirties, of average height and medium build, dressed in a dark suit, walking briskly toward us. As he came close to us he slowed to wait his turn through the revolving door.

I decided to take the opportunity to put my companion's claim to the test. I said to him, "My friend and I have made a bet, and I wonder if you could help us?"

"What's the bet," he asked without surprise or hesitation.

"My friend has bet that you are a vice president."

He laughed lightly and said, "Nope, wrong guess."

As he turned back to the revolving door my friend asked, "Do you mind telling us what your position is?"

"Not at all. I'm a chief corporate counsel." With that he turned and passed through the door.[3]

6. *Use a firm handshake.* Of no surprise, a firm handshake continues to be perceived by many people as a key indicator of self-confidence and dynamism. Gilda Carle, an image consultant, turned down a commercial artist whom she sought out to prepare advertising flyers for her company. Carle rejected him because "his handshake did not project the energy I wanted to have projected in my flyers." If your handshake is limp, you can strengthen your grip over time by daily use of an exercise spring. Frequent manual labor will also toughen your grip.

MAKE EFFECTIVE ORAL PRESENTATIONS

People who speak well while interacting with work associates project an image of self-confidence. Every reader of this book has either heard about, read about, or taken a course in effective communications. We all know that you should look at the listener, speak clearly, avoid mumbling, vary your pitch and tone, and make appropriate use of hand gestures. Here we look at several less-known aspects of spoken communications that will project self-confidence.

Use Heavy-Impact, Embellishing Languages

"It's important that I fill you in on my recent activities," said Megan Bloor to her boss, the vice president of commercial mortgages. "The bank's strategic plan is to get into the next generation of financial marketing. I've bought into the strategy, and it's working. Instead of simply selling commercial mortgages, I'm heavily into relationship banking. I've been building long-term symbiotic relations with some very big potential clients."

"So far, I haven't pinned down short-term results. But the long-term results could be mind boggling. We may soon become the dominant supplier of financial services to a key player in commercial real estate."

What Megan is really telling her boss is that she has been calling on a few potential large mortgage customers. So far no sales have been consummated, but she is on the right track. Her bank does want to establish long-term relationships with good customers. Megan embellishes her accomplishments by explaining how her rather mundane efforts support the corporate strategy. As perceived by her listener, Megan's language is powerful and upbeat, especially because it focuses on top-level company concerns.

During any given era, certain words used in the right context give power and force to your speech. Used comfortably and naturally, these words can help you project an appropriate degree of self-confidence. Eugene Fram, the J. McClure Warren professor of marketing at the Rochester Institute of Technology, advises that the following words and phrases will enhance your image:

❖ Talk about having attended a *prestigious* trade show rather than simply a trade show.

❖ Use the term *on the verge of* accomplishing something so long as a project is in process.

❖ Mention how an influential person (such as the company president or an important political figure) *knows of your work*. "Knowing of your work" is not untrue. The term does not necessarily mean that you have received his or her endorsement.

❖ Mention that you have *bonded* with your customers or your team members instead of simply stating that you have a good working relationship.

❖ Speak about being on the *verge of a breakthrough* when you have found even a minor way to improve a process. In truth, minor adaptations often do become breakthroughs.

❖ When referring to your position in the organization, casually mention that you are *close to the seat of power*.

Perhaps you work out of a cubicle 50 feet from the CEO's office, or you perform an occasional clerical task for him or her.

❖ When your department has won in an interdepartmental skirmish, or won a bid over a competitor, mention that you have *nuked* them. "Nuking" is more powerful than simply winning (except when it refers to using a microwave oven).

Minimize Junk Words and Vocalized Pauses

Using colorful, powerful words enhances the perception by others that you are self-confident. It is also important to minimize the use of words and phrases that dilute the impact of your speech. Such junk words and vocalized pauses convey the impression of low self-confidence—especially in a professional setting. Phrases such as "like," "you know," "you know what I mean," "he goes," (to mean he says), and "uhhhhhh," are *not* compelling. Using these junk words and vocalized pauses detracts from a sharp communications image.

An effective way of decreasing the use of these extraneous words is to tape-record your side of a phone conversation and then play it back. Once you hear how these words detract from your speech effectiveness, you can monitor your own speech for improvement.

Back up Conclusions with Data

You will appear and feel more self-confident if you back up your spoken presentations with solid data. One approach to obtaining data is to collect it yourself, such as conducting a telephone survey of your customers. Marty Del Prince, the sales manager of an office-supply company, wanted to start a delivery service for his many small customers, such as dental and real estate offices. He telephoned a good sampling of these accounts and found they would be willing to pay a premium price if delivery were included. Marty used these data to support his argument, thus convincing the company owner to approve his plan.

Convincing data for your arguments can also be obtained from published sources. Be specific about the source of your data, rather than say, "Research shows that . . ." Supporting data for hundreds of arguments can be found in the business pages of newspapers, business magazines and newspapers, and electronic data-retrieval services. An inexpensive yet trusted reference for thousands of arguments is the *Statistical Abstract of the United States.*

Susan Winters, a retailing executive, wanted to expand into Sacramento, California. At the time, other members of top management were reluctant to open new branches in smaller markets. Early in her presentation, Susan said, "As many of you know, Sacramento is the thirtieth largest market in the United States, with a population of close to 1.3 million people and growing." Her data-based comments created a climate of acceptance for the rest of her presentation, and Susan's expansion plans were approved.

One caution here, however, is not to rely on research so much that you appear to have no faith in your own intuition. For example, you may convey an impression of weakness if when asked your opinion, you typically say, "I can't answer until I collect some data."

USE IMPRESSIVE NONVERBAL BEHAVIOR

A self-confident person not only speaks and writes with assurance, but also projects confidence through body positioning, gestures, and manner of speech. Not everybody interprets the same body language and other nonverbal signals uniformly. Yet here are aspects of nonverbal behavior that will project an image of self-confidence in most work situations:[4]

1. Use erect posture when walking, standing, or sitting. Slouching and slumping are almost univer-

sally interpreted as an indicator of low self-confidence.

2. Exhibit dominant behavior such as standing up straight during a confrontation. Cowering will be interpreted as a sign of low self-confidence.

3. Pat other people on the back (not backside) and nod your head slightly during the patting.

4. Stand with your toes pointing outward rather than inward. Toes standing outward is usually perceived as an indicator of superior status, while toes pointed inward is perceived as inferior status.

5. Speak at a moderate pace and use a loud, confident tone. People lacking in self-confidence tend to speak too rapidly or very slowly. Whispering creates the image of a low-confidence person.

6. Smile frequently, in a relaxed, natural-appearing manner. At the same time maintain eye contact with those around you.

A general approach to using nonverbal behavior that makes you appear confident is to make appearing self-confident your goal. When this type of internal programming takes hold, you are likely automatically to carry out many of the behaviors mentioned here. By saying to yourself, "I am going to look confident in this meeting," you will have moved an important step toward appearing confident.

DRESS AND ACT PROFESSIONALLY

The usual purpose of dressing and acting professionally is to impress other people that you are willing to conform to codes of behavior favored by the organization. If you dress fashionably many people will assume that you are already successful or are striving for success. Similarly, if you act in a refined, mature manner people will assume that you are professional in your outlook. Dressing and acting professionally also makes a contribution to projecting self-confidence. If you are proud of your clothing and mannerisms, you will project more self-confidence than if you are self-conscious about how you are dressed and act.

An action tip here is to dress in a manner that makes you feel good about yourself to achieve a boost in self-confidence. But be careful not to choose a wardrobe that makes you think more about your clothing than about the situation you are facing. To find a confidence-building outfit, you may have to try on different outfits that you already own or purchase new clothing. Keep your confidence-building wardrobe on hand for days when projecting self-confidence is especially important.

Similarly, review your general behavior and mannerisms to decide which facets make you feel the most professional. Here is a sampling of the type of behavior we have discovered that makes many people feel professional:

❖ When somebody in the office makes an utterly gross and tasteless comment, you smile politely and say something to the effect, "Okay, let's move on to something else."

❖ When other people have gathered to gripe about the boss, you say, "Let's try to keep things in perspective. _____ has also made some important contributions to our department."

❖ A representative from a potential vendor says he bets you $500 in cash that your firm will not place an order for $25,000 worth of equipment from his company. (The representative, of course, "loses" if your company places the order.) You say politely, "Thanks for your offer but I do not gamble in making business decisions. Besides what you propose violates our policies about evaluating bids from vendors."

❖ You are bypassed for promotion and you think you should have received the nod. You write the person who was promoted a congratulatory note, promising him or her your full support.

The point of dressing and acting professionally is that if your clothing and behavior makes you feel inwardly confident, you will be better able to project a confident image to others. However mystical it seems, projecting outer confidence begins a process that makes you feel confident. As others respond to you positively because of the confidence you project, you will in fact become more self-confident.

STRENGTHEN YOUR FACIAL AND BODY APPEARANCE

Many people believe that a strong facial and body appearance are associated with success. They assume that successful people have more aesthetic faces and trimmer bodies than their less successful counterparts. This assumption has some merit. An attractive face and body will help you obtain some jobs and hold on to others. Yet the relationship between appearance and success is not as strong as commonly believed. As an experiment, carefully look at the facial features of the next fifty successful people in business or politics you see either in person, a photograph, or on television. You are likely to find that these people are no more physically attractive than are moderately successful people of comparable age.

Despite our comments so far, a good facial and body appearance can give you the winning edge. The most important reason is that a good appearance may help you feel better about yourself. Feeling better about yourself, in turn, heightens your self-confidence. A cosmetic surgeon we spoke to agreed strongly that his real contribution to patient welfare is not in making them more beautiful. He said instead, "I help people improve their self-image. Some of the people whose faces I lift, or whose noses I change, are really physically attractive people. Yet they feel self-conscious about some aspect of their appearance. By modifying that facial feature for them, their self-image improves."

Lana LeClerc, an industrial sales representative, explains how modifying her appearance led to changes in the amount of self-confidence she projected. "For five years, I was a telemarketer. My basic job was to take orders over the telephone and service existing accounts. I was rated as the top producer in my company. I knew the product line. I knew my customers, and I could sense when to ask for more business.

"Because of my good track record, the company asked me several times if I would like to try outside sales. I turned down the offer twice. My excuse was that I was truly happy in my present job. The truth was that I hated the way I looked. Telemarketing was ideal for me. My relationships with customers focused on my capabilities, my helpfulness, and my voice. Not on what I looked like.

"The second time I turned down the job became a last straw for me. I really wanted to prove to myself that I could make it as an outside sales representative. But I felt that my appearance was holding me back. So I plunged into a program of physical self-improvement. My goal was to lose fifteen pounds and have a better looking facial appearance.

"I worked out compulsively every day. The most helpful method I found for burning off calories and fat was to carry heavy weights for short distances. I rearranged furniture in my house. I took over my husband's jobs like carrying logs from the yard to our fireplace. I helped two friends move. I reduced my fat intake down to 20 percent of my total calories. My only snack food became raw carrots. A glass of wine became a once-a-week treat. I demanded more sex from my husband and went about it with more physical intensity.

"Next came my facial appearance. I signed up with a beauty consultant for a 'glamour transformation.' She changed my hairdo and showed me how to apply makeup to dramatize my best features.

"I really liked the new physical me when I looked in the mirror. When work associates and friends told me I looked great, I felt great. A new courage came over me. I felt I was at my prime. One day I walked into the sales manager's office and told her I was ready to apply for the sales rep position. I am doing very well in outside sales. Already I exceeded my quota. My career has changed in a positive direction."

The explanation for Lana's success is straightforward. The improvements in her physical appearance led to an improved self-image, which allowed her to project more self-confidence. The majority of her success as an outside sales representative is largely attributable to the same factors that helped her in telemarketing. She is pleasant, intelligent, and responsive to customer needs. Yet before she boosted her self-confidence, Lana would not allow herself to compete in outside sales.

DEVELOP A SOLID KNOWLEDGE BASE

A bedrock for projecting self-confidence is to develop a base of knowledge that enables you to provide sensible alternative solutions to problems. Intuition is very important, but working from a base of facts helps you project a confident image. Formal education is an obvious source of information for your knowledge base. Day-by-day absorption of information directly and indirectly related to your job is even more important. A major purpose of education is to get you in the right frame of mind to continue your quest for knowledge.

In your quest for developing a solid knowledge base to project self-confidence, be sensitive to abusing this technique. If you bombard people with quotes, facts, and figures, you are likely to be perceived as an annoying pedant.

Stuart Davidson is an example of a person whose use of a solid knowledge base projected the right image. Stuart is the owner and operator of a franchise for a national moving and storage company in El Paso, Texas. When he visits the home office he often discusses his views on world events. He also expresses his opinion on national and regional events.

Stuart's awareness of current events and demographic changes gained him the reputation of being an intelligent, well-rounded and confident franchise operator. The dispatcher based in national headquarters entrusts him with the most valuable and profitable accounts because of his impressive image. Aside from having good business skills, Stuart's image is enhanced by his solid base of knowledge about relevant topics.

DEVELOP AND PUBLICIZE NEW SKILLS

An important survival tactic in today's workplace is to continually develop job-related skills. Developing such skills pays a double dividend if you let others know of your new prowess. You will also come across to others as being self-confident. The reason is that most people realize it takes courage and confidence to learn a new complex skill. Bruce Craig, an engineering technician, provides a deft application of this tactic. In his words:

> Several years ago a new piece of testing equipment was installed in our lab. While the installation was being performed, I purposely watched. Immediately, everyone assumed that I knew all about the equipment because I had watched the installation. Also, many made casual references to the fact that I could operate the new equipment.

> Running the new equipment became a grudging task at times because it contained so many parts. Nevertheless, my efforts paid off. My worth to the organization increased because everyone else knew less about the equipment than I did. At one point I fixed the equipment when it broke down. I could tell how people admired my confidence.

> For my efforts, I received a certificate for a dinner for two. While giving me the award, our manager stated how important it was to have an in-house expert on the equipment. We therefore were not dependent upon help from outside the department. My next salary increase was above average.

Learning how to operate and repair the new equipment helped me earn the big increase.

STRIVE FOR PEAK PERFORMANCE

A key strategy for projecting self-confidence is to display peak performance. The term refers to much more than attempting to do your best. To achieve peak performance you must be totally focused on what you are doing. When you are in the state of peak performance you are mentally calm and physically at ease. Intense concentration is required to achieve this state. You are so focused on the task at hand that you are not distracted by extraneous events or thoughts.

The mental state achieved during peak performance is akin to a person's sense of deep concentration when immersed in a sport or hobby. For example, on days tennis players perform way above their usual game, they typically comment: "The ball looked so large today. I could read the label as I hit it." On the job, the focus and concentration allow the person to sense and respond to relevant information coming both from within the mind and from outside stimuli. When you are at your peak, you impress others by responding intelligently to their input.

Psychologist Charles Garfield says it is easy to detect those who have achieved or will achieve peak performance. Based on his study of more than 1,500 successful people, he concludes that peak performers have a mission in their work and lives. They have something they deeply care about to which they are fully committed.[5]

Turning in peak performance helps you develop superior self-confidence, which projects through to others. Tony Alvarez, a quality manager in a hospital, explains how peak performance helped him project self-confidence: "It was my day to make a presentation to the hospital administrators and medical chiefs about our new Total Quality Management program. I had done my homework, including researching the usual objections to this type of program in a hospital. I rehearsed my presentation alone three times in the conference room where it would take place. I had my slides and my flip charts ready, and they were beautiful.

"I woke up on the morning of my presentation feeling great. My body tingled with excitement, and my vision and hearing were sharper than usual. I knew it was going to be a good day. The presentation went more smoothly than I could have imagined. I was on stage; this was my day. Both the administrators and the medical chiefs were nodding their head in agreement. I knew my program was headed for approval.

"People congratulated me on my presentation. Two of them mentioned how confident and assured I was. I definitely think that exuding so much confidence helped my program get approved."

SHOW INTENSE PRIDE IN YOUR WORK

The aphorism, "Every piece of work you complete [or service your provide] is a self-portrait," is truer than ever. Programs such as Total Quality Management or Total Customer Satisfaction can make a contribution only when people take pride in their work. A by-product of being proud is that you project self-confidence. The process works in this manner: You complete a tangible project such as writing a report, designing a project, or hammering out a contract with a customer. You are able to say to yourself honestly, "I've done my best, this is an excellent piece of work, and I take pride in the result." Feeling proud creates a warm inner glow that leads to facial expressions and posture that project self-confidence.

BE TIDY AND FASTIDIOUS

Having a neat and clean desk and work area often enhances productivity. You spend less time looking for documents so you do not waste productive time and suffer from rages of self-hatred for being so absent-minded. Neatness and cleanliness also enhance promotability because your superiors are impressed with your efficiency. Large, bureaucratic organizations particularly favor the clean-desk, power look.

Being tidy and fastidious about your work area also contributes to an image of self-confidence. When you are tidy and fastidious you project an image of being in control and therefore self-confident. One reason for this perception is that top executives—who most people think are self-confident—appear to the public as being unusually neat and orderly. When photographed, their offices are impeccable and so is their attire. Successful entrepreneurs, scientists, professors, and people in the arts place much less value on neatness and orderliness. Being tidy and fastidious is therefore much less important in such settings.

We attempted to check out the relationship between tidiness and fastidiousness and the projection of self-confidence. We studied the results of a batch of performance evaluations conducted in a large company. Managers and individual workers who were given high ratings on self-confidence were typically those were are also rated as being neat and orderly. A little further digging also revealed that being fastidious about personal appearance also contributed to ratings of high self-confidence.

TAKE RISKS

Taking risks is associated with self-confidence. The risk taker consequently projects an image of self-confidence. One doesn't have to be a corporate bungie jumper, however, to receive the accolade of being confident. Taking sensible risks, such as offering an offbeat solution to a problem, will make one appear self-confident. Being a creative problem-solver projects self-confidence for two reasons. First, others will realize that offering the solution runs the risk of ridicule. Second, others will also realize that one's suggestion could be adopted and then fail. The person who offers the creative alternative to a problem thus must have the courage to risk rejection and be associated with a failed idea.

Larry Evans was the manager of data processing at a market research company located in Chicago. A couple of years ago he was involved in a problem-solving session about the need for more office space. After about five sensible alternatives were suggested, Larry took a risk and suggested something radical. He proposed that instead of renting more space, the company should begin a work-at-home program. The company would hire part-time employees who would perform data-entry work in their homes. Larry's firm would lend the employee the necessary equipment, but the company would actually be getting office space free.

The company followed through, and the work-at-home program proved to be a big success. High-quality applicants were in abundant supply, and productivity was better than expected. Colleagues admired Larry for his gutsy idea, and he became perceived as a very self-confident problem solver.

BE FLEXIBLE AND ADAPTABLE

Self-confident people can adapt to change quickly for the good of the organization. Low-confidence people, in contrast, want to preserve the status quo. Often they lack the mental flexibility and adaptability to cope with change. If you show a willingness to accept change readily, you will project an image of self-confidence. Of greater significance, adapting to change will enhance your self-confidence.

Margot Camilleri is a case in point about projecting self-confidence by being flexible and adaptable. She was a newly appointed regional manager in a retail chain, with jurisdiction over ten department stores. Margot enjoyed her new position. She also liked the condominium in Atlanta she had just purchased as part of her relocation. Five weeks into her new position, she received an urgent call from the home office. The store in Charlotte, North Carolina, was in trouble, and the company wanted Margot to manage the store for the intermediate future. With a sinking feeling in her stomach, Margot said yes. Her action plan for her second relocation in several months involved renting out her new home and finding an apartment in Charlotte.

Sudden changes in positions and cities created some temporary chaos for Margot. Nevertheless, she further cemented her claim to big things with her company. Top management admired her willingness to relocate twice for the good of the organization. Margot also projected the image of a retailing executive with a can-do, flexible, confident attitude.

BUILD YOUR SELF-ESTEEM

The ultimate solution to projecting self-confidence is to feel good about yourself. If you see yourself as worthy you will come across to others as having a positive self-concept. Building self-esteem, however, cannot be done in isolation. Self-esteem is derived in large measure from the feedback one receives from others. If you receive oodles of positive feedback from others for your accomplishments, your self-esteem will most probably increase. A practical approach to building your self-esteem would be to accomplish all the tactics and strategies described in this chapter. In summary, your self-esteem will be enhanced if you implement the following:

1. Use positive self-talk.
2. Use positive visual imagery.
3. Be self-directing.
4. Exhibit personal dynamism.
5. Make effective oral presentations.
6. Use impressive nonverbal behavior.

7. Dress and act professionally.
8. Strengthen your facial and body appearance.
9. Develop a solid knowledge base.
10. Develop and publicize new skills.
11. Strive for peak performance.
12. Show intense pride in your work.
13. Be tidy and fastidious.
14. Take risks.
15. Be flexible and adaptable.
16. Build your self-esteem.

❖ 2 ❖

EFFECTIVE
NEGOTIATING
TACTICS

Gaining the edge often depends on your ability to negotiate successfully for yourself or your group. Negotiation skill is either necessary or handy in many business situations. These include coming to terms on a salary, obtaining a budget for your department, obtaining office equipment and furniture, and getting a family or parental leave of absence. Added to this list are people for whom negotiation is a key aspect of their job. Among them are sales representatives, customer service representatives, labor relations specialists, insurance claims adjusters, and lawyers. Furthermore, specialists such as sports agents, literary agents, and talent agents would have little to offer to their clients if they lacked negotiating skill.

People study and practice for years to become skilled negotiators. Nevertheless, acquiring skill in the fourteen tactics presented here should give you the edge in most negotiating situations. When involved in negotiations, select the tactics that appear most relevant to the situation. Practice these tactics at every real or contrived opportunity. A contrived opportunity refers to negotiating for fun in such low-stakes situations as purchasing something in a garage sale or from a street vendor. Negotiation, like any other complex mental skill, requires substantial practice. Before reading further, take the accompanying quiz.

THE NEGOTIATOR QUIZ

Directions: The following quiz is designed to give you tentative insight into your tendencies toward being an effective negotiator. Answer each statement *Mostly True* or *Mostly False* as it applies to you.

	Mostly True	Mostly False
1. Settling differences of opinion with people is a lot of fun.	_____	_____
2. I try to avoid conflict and confrontation with others as much as possible.	_____	_____
3. I am self-conscious about asking people for favors they have not offered to me spontaneously.	_____	_____
4. I am generally unwilling to compromise.	_____	_____
5. How the other side feels about the results of our negotiation is of little consequence to me.	_____	_____
6. I think very well under pressure.	_____	_____
7. People say that I am tactful and diplomatic.	_____	_____
8. I'm known for my ability to express my viewpoint clearly.	_____	_____

	Mostly True	Mostly False
9. Very few things in life are not negotiable.	_____	_____
10. I always accept whatever salary increase is offered to me.	_____	_____
11. A person's facial expression often reveals as much as does what the person actually says.	_____	_____
12. I wouldn't mind taking a few short-range losses to win a long-range battle.	_____	_____
13. I'm willing to work long and hard to win a small advantage.	_____	_____
14. I'm usually too busy talking to do much listening.	_____	_____
15. It's fun to haggle over price when buying a car.	_____	_____
16. I almost always prepare in advance for a negotiating session.	_____	_____
17. When there is something I need from another person, I usually get it.	_____	_____
18. It would make me feel cheap if I offered somebody only two thirds of his or her asking price.	_____	_____
19. People are usually paid what they are worth, so no use haggling over starting salaries.	_____	_____
20. I rarely take what people say at face value.	_____	_____

(continued)

	Mostly True	Mostly False
21. It's easy for me to smile when involved in a serious discussion.	_____	_____
22. For one side to win in negotiation, the other side has to lose.	_____	_____
23. Once you start making concessions, the other side is bound to get more than you.	_____	_____
24. A good negotiating session gets my competitive juices flowing.	_____	_____
25. When negotiations are completed, both sides should walk away with something valuable.	_____	_____

Scoring and interpretation. Score yourself plus one for each of your answers that agrees with the scoring key. The higher your score, the more likely it is that you currently have good negotiating skills, *providing your self-assessment is accurate.* It might prove useful to have somebody who has observed you negotiate on several occasions also answer the Negotiator Quiz for you. Scores of 7 or below and 20 or higher are probably the most indicative of weak or strong negotiating potential. Here is the scoring key:

1. Mostly true	10. Mostly false	19. Mostly false
2. Mostly false	11. Mostly true	20. Mostly true
3. Mostly false	12. Mostly true	21. Mostly true
4. Mostly false	13. Mostly true	22. Mostly false
5. Mostly false	14. Mostly false	23. Mostly false
6. Mostly true	15. Mostly true	24. Mostly true
7. Mostly true	16. Mostly true	25. Mostly true
8. Mostly true	17. Mostly true	
9. Mostly true	18. Mostly false	

PREPARE THOROUGHLY

A negotiation session is a meeting. As such it will proceed more smoothly if both sides agree on an agenda and make other necessary preparations. An especially important form of preparation is to develop creative options ahead of the negotiating session. The person who steps forward first with a plausible compromise gains the offense.

Plan in advance what major and minor points you want to negotiate. Your opponent should do the same. Ideally, the two sides should agree on what items will be dealt with during the formal negotiating session. The agenda places control on what will be said and not said. Plan for the negotiating session by role playing the opponent's most likely response to your suggestions.

Successful sports agent Leigh Steinberg prepares obsessively before negotiating a contract for a client. He gathers extensive facts about his young clients, including their athletic strengths and weaknesses and their family and personal situation. Steinberg also researches the negotiating style of the opposition as well as the team's short- and long-term goals.[1] Steinberg's thoroughness adds to his confidence and can intimidate the negotiator for the professional sports team.

CREATE A POSITIVE NEGOTIATING CLIMATE

Negotiation proceeds much more swiftly if a positive tone surrounds the session. Take the initiative to show a positive outlook about the negotiation meeting. Nonverbal behavior such as smiling and making friendly gestures help you create a positive climate and gain the edge by disarming the other side. Gerard I. Nierenberg, a world-class negotiator, maintains that by staying positive, you will stop a negative person cold. "It will be like a child who throws a tantrum until the child sees that it's not working, that nobody's giving in. Then he or she will move on to something else."[2]

Many tough-minded negotiators play a standoff game in which they become bullheaded, entrenched, and committed to a win-lose conception of the outcome. Perhaps this game of macho-chicken worked in the past. But today, people know enough about good human relations not to submit to the demands of a bullheaded negotiator. Sean Bosworth was the president of a "network company." A network company has no operations of its own but subcontracts such vital activities as manufacturing, engineering, and marketing. Some of these companies even hire people to think of something for their company to manufacture.

Sean's company was successful in obtaining a million dollar contract to supply a fire-detection system for a new office building. He calculated that his company needed a gross profit margin of $400,000 on this deal to stay in business for a while longer. Sean therefore called a meeting with the small manufacturing firm who had agreed to supply the fire-detection system for his company. Sean began the meeting with an outburst of abuse: "To keep our contract, you have to cut your price by $100,000. I won't listen to any excuses. If you can't meet our budget, we don't need you. There are dozens of suppliers out there eager to do business with us."

The president of the small firm, along with the director of manufacturing, explained that they too needed to make a profit. Furthermore, they expected to be treated with dignity. Sean retorted, "I'm in business to make a profit. Treating people with dignity is way down on my list of priorities." The president of the manufacturing firm said, "We're leaving. Call us when you think it is fair for us to make a profit also and when you can treat your suppliers like human beings."

Sean miscalculated. He could not find another company to supply the detection system at the price he was willing to pay. Sean's company wound up supplying the detection system at a loss and three months behind schedule. His firm now faced the dual problem of pending bankruptcy and having to overcome a bad delivery reputation. By creating a negative negotiating climate, Sean had pushed his fledgling company toward collapse.

FOCUS ON INTERESTS, NOT POSITIONS

The true object of a negotiation is to satisfy your interests and those of the other party. If you cling rigidly to a particular position, your broad interests may be sacrificed. A negotiating position often obscures the nature of what a person is really trying to achieve. Assume that you are negotiating with your boss for a bigger budget for next year. Your position is that you want more money in your budget. Your true interest, however, is in being able to accomplish your job with the amount of money in your budget. If you negotiate with a focus on your interests, you have broadened your options.

One creative alternative facing you would be to suggest that if your budget cannot be increased, how about allocating some of your expenses to a central budget? In this way you would have enough funds available to accomplish your mission. And accomplishing your mission is your *true interest*. Such a negotiating posture might not only help you gain the edge in negotiations over the budget, it could readily give you a political edge by demonstrating that you have the good of the organization in mind.

BEGIN WITH A PLAUSIBLE DEMAND OR OFFER

The common-sense approach to negotiation suggests that you begin with an extreme, almost fanciful demand or offer. The final compromise will therefore be closer to your true demand or offer than if you opened the negotiations more realistically. Yet there is a substantial disadvantage to the common-sense approach to bargaining. To begin with, an unreasonable and potentially destructive demand will often be interpreted by the other side as bargaining in poor faith. Serious negotiations may therefore be delayed or canceled. Also, many people in our society are tired of gluttony and greed on the part of others.

Al Herman, a vice president of acquisitions at a Fortune 500 company, was well paid and quite content. His most recent compensation package was $350,000, composed of a $250,000 salary and a $100,000 performance bonus. Equally important, Al's job was filled with excitement, and he enjoyed working with the executive team. Al's exceptional intuition in choosing the right acquisitions for his company had become well known in the industry. With his reputation established, Al attracted the attention of a headhunter whose client needed a star acquisitions executive.

When the headhunter called, Al insisted that he was happy where he was but would at least have dinner with him. The headhunter described the vacancy in glowing terms. Among the pluses of the position in question were a much bigger staff and an emphasis on global acquisitions. After the dinner, Al casually mentioned that he was entrenched in his present position but he was curious enough to explore the position at least one step further.

Al met the president and the chairman of the board of the firm for a three-hour session. Both were interested in Al and authorized the headhunter to talk in terms of a total compensation package of a maximum of $425,000 for the first year. Al's interest was piqued when he learned of what the client was willing to pay, especially because he would be running a bigger operation. Al responded, "Four hundred and twenty-five thousand dollars is very fair. But for me to give up a wonderful job at a fine company, I would need $500,000. Besides that, I can more than earn back my compensation on the first good deal I complete for the company."

"It sounds as if you might be pushing things to the outer limit, but let me get back with my client," said the headhunter. When the headhunter talked to the president and chairman, both agreed that Al was not being unreasonable. He was asking for less than 20 percent beyond their initial offer. They also thought that the board of directors would go along with a $500,000 compensation package for an executive with such a fine reputation. The president and chairman arranged to have another meeting with Al to discuss the job further and get to know more about his mode of operation. After this successful meeting, Al then had the opportunity to tour a few of the company facilities the following week.

After getting to know Al better, the company was prepared to make Al an offer. They offered Al a salary of $400,000 plus a first year guaranteed bonus of $100,000. In addition they threw in a $15,000 signing bonus "just to make things interesting."

Al surprised himself by accepting the offer and resigning his current position. Al left his old firm on good terms and was told to reapply should his new situation sour. Al's sensible negotiating strategy of making a demand of less than 20 percent beyond the initial offer paid off handsomely. He had established such good faith that he was finally offered *more* than he requested.

BASE YOUR DEMANDS AND OFFERS ON A SOLID RATIONALE

In addition to being plausible, your demand should be based on a solid rationale. A solid rationale buttresses a negotiating demand because it enhances your credibility. You gain the edge because you are fact oriented rather than entirely subjective. A typical setting for applying this tactic is when asking for a raise. A weak rationale is to demand an above-average raise because you need more money. It is tactically sounder to provide a valid reason why you deserve a big raise. Here is a list of solid rationales for demanding a raise—even during mediocre economic times:

❖ According to my analysis, my work gives the company a 500 percent return on investment.

❖ Last year, my suggestions for improving operations saved the company $872,500. (A number such as 872,500 sounds more accurate than a number such as 850,000 or 900,000. Numbers ending in 50 or 100 sound like approximations. The last three digits can be rounded, however, to avoid sounding too per-fectionistic.)

❖ I checked a salary survey of our industry conducted by American Institute of Industrial Engineers. It shows that I am receiving below-average pay for a person of my experience and education.

❖ Adjusted for inflation I am making virtually the same salary I made when I started with the company five years ago. I therefore need at least a 5 percent salary increase to receive a true raise.

❖ I would like an above-average raise because I have been rated "outstanding" on my last four perfor-mance evaluations.

❖ I want a 7 percent raise because if you cannot give me one, I will be forced to accept a competitive offer at 10 percent more than I am making now. (Make sure this is truthful because you might be placed on the hit list for the next downsizing.)

In contrast to the businesslike rationales for demanding a raise just listed, observe these much more irrational and wimpy reasons for demanding a raise:

❖ My youngest child will be starting college this year. I simply cannot handle college expenses on my present salary.

❖ I would be happier if you gave me a raise.

❖ My spouse was just laid off. Without my receiving a 10 percent raise, we'll be sinking into heavy debt.

❖ My divorce settlement just came through. Without a raise, I won't be able to make all my child-support payments.

BE TRUTHFUL

Basing your demand or offer on a solid rationale is even more effective if you are telling the truth. In many instances, laying all the cards out on the table communicates that you are not game playing and that you respect the intelligence of the opponent. It may also encourage the other side to make more honest demands because their distorted demands will be contrasted to more honest ones. Jill Washington, a beauty-shop owner, lost a civil suit against a client who claimed her hair was ruined by improper treatment at Jill's salon. After two years of haggling by lawyers, a judge's verdict ordered Jill to pay the woman $5,000 in damages plus $6,500 of her legal fees. The judge declared that both payments be made within 30 days.

Jill knew that if she paid $11,500 at once, there would not be enough cash left to operate the business. She paid the plaintiff her $5,000 and attempted to borrow $6,500 to pay the legal fees because the lawyer demanded payment within 30 days. Jill applied for a loan at both a finance company and a bank. Both institutions turned her down. Jill brought photocopies of these rejections and a statement of her financial worth to the opposing lawyer. She pleaded with the lawyer to let her pay the $6,500 with payments of $270 per month for 36 months. When the lawyer demanded why Jill could not comply with the court order, Jill showed her the loan rejection letters and the analysis of her net worth. Angrily, the lawyer said, "Make your payments on time or you'll be hearing from me."

Jill gained the edge in this situation. Spreading payments for the legal fees over 36 months enabled Jill to keep operating her beauty salon. Without disclosing the truth to the opposing lawyer, Jill might have found herself in contempt of court and being hounded for the money. With her lawsuit behind her, Jill could focus better on tending her business.

REGARD THE OTHER PARTY AS A PARTNER

A constructive negotiating attitude is that you and other side are helpmates in achieving your goals. Rather than the typical adversarial outlook, each party in a negotiation needs to understand what he or she will gain from the other party's being successful. This partnership attitude has gained strength in industry because many manufacturers and suppliers realize they have a common stake. Neither side can prosper without the other side also prospering. In the short range, a given manufacturer can squeeze the profit out of a supplier. Yet if all manufacturers did the same, the suppliers would vanish or the manufacturers would have to produce their own supplies.

The partnership principle also applies within the same company. If you are negotiating with the human resources department to obtain temporary workers, you are both partners in the deal. To get your work accomplished, you need the office temporaries. If other departments throughout the organization do not make demands on the human resources department, the department will be deemed superfluous.

The president of a training and consulting firm recommends that you and the other side openly discuss what you can gain from each other's successes. Openly discussing these gains can help foster the positive negotiating climate needed for success.[3] Let's stop to look at the partnership aspects of a scenario that is being repeated in many places of work.

Assume that you have developed a manual for some company software. You want 500 copies of the manual distributed throughout the organization. Your vendor is a desktop publishing department within the company. According to company procedures, although you do not pay in cash, funds from your department are transferred to the other department. If the desktop publishing department charges more than you think is fair, you are prompted to respond: "The heck with you people. I can get this done on the outside for much less money." In turn, they can respond: "Use an outside vendor. Our departmental mission states that we are a profit center. We cannot take on jobs that force us to operate at a loss."

On the surface, it would appear that you two should part company. You can get a better price on the outside. At the same time, the internal group will not be forced to take on unprofitable business. If the issues are examined more closely, a different conclusion might be reached.

You and the desktop publishing group are really partners. The reason the other group has to charge you such a high price is that they are forced to tag on their fair share of administrative costs. They must help pay such overhead as the salary of the company president, company advertising, costs for planting shrubs at company headquarters, and the annual holiday party. Not being burdened with such bureaucratic costs, the local print shop can produce your manuals more cheaply.

Although this type of financial analysis sounds reasonable, it is based on spurious logic. If you get your manuals printed on the outside, *real* money will flow from your company to the outside. The desktop group is already being paid its salary, and all the other overhead costs will still be there no matter who prints your manuals. So the two of you should find a way of doing business. Recognizing that you are both partners in trying to help the company save money, you can create some workable compromises. Maybe the job can be printed on a lower grade of paper. Maybe you can get by with less fancy binders. And perhaps the desktop group can work more rapidly to reduce the labor costs charged to your department.

The underlying principle here is that if both sides regard each other as partners whose survival depends one on the other, some workable compromises will emerge. You can even overcome cost-accounting procedures that pit company departments against outside vendors.

DEVELOP OPTIONS FOR MUTUAL GAIN

The ultimate way to gain the edge in negotiating is to arrive at alternative solutions to the problem that will benefit both sides. The so called, "options for mutual gain" represent the new look in effective negotiation. In traditional negotiating approaches, one side rams through or sneaks by with a short-range win that creates long-range hostility. The purpose of developing options for mutual gain is to find a solution that will allow you to work peacefully with the other side in the future.

An effective negotiating tactic is to generate several workable options for mutual gain before you enter into the heat of the actual negotiating session. Trying to select a good option in the presence of your adversary may create emotional interference with your thinking. When the stakes are high, the stress created by the negotiating session may be so intense that creativity is dampened. You therefore run the risk of not arriving at creative alternatives to the points at issue.

Under ideal circumstances, you and the other side can join in a brainstorming session to arrive at options that will satisfy both your needs. A major hurdle must be overcome, however, before a systematic search for options is possible. You and the other side must realize that the outcome of negotiation is not inevitably one position winning over the other.

Another reason people do not naturally look for options for mutual gain is that they believe the amount of resources is fixed. The parties involved assume that what each one grants to the other side represents a loss for him or her. Negotiating professionals call this the "fixed-pie assumption." To move negotiation away from the fixed-pie assumption, an option for mutual gain must be chosen. Here is an example:

Keith Conti and Bob Mancini were partners in a food-supply business for restaurants. Business expanded enough to warrant moving into larger headquarters. A dispute developed between them over who should get which office in their new headquarters. To get another opinion on their problem, Keith and Bob asked their lawyer how they should settle. The lawyer wanted to remain neutral, but also wanted to help the partners settle their dispute. He asked each partner which features of an office were the most important. It worked out that Keith valued status, while Bob favored ample space. The solution chosen was to give Keith the corner office and to give Bob the central office. The corner office afforded high status, while the central office was 50 square feet larger than the corner office.

Keith and Bob were both happy with this solution. The major contributing factor is that both men had now achieved something important—both were winners. Keith achieved the status he wanted, and Bob had more space. Because both sides won, mutual antagonisms are not likely to arise. If money were not an issue, the partners could have rented office space with two spacious corner offices. However, in the food-supply business profit margins are thin.

Because inventing options for mutual gains is so important, another example is in order. In one company, the employees wanted a 5 percent cost-of-living adjustment (COLA), but management believed it was unaffordable this year. A representative group of employees was chosen to negotiate with management. The company proposed that the employees would be granted their cost-of-living adjustment if they promised to increase productivity by 5 percent for the year. If productivity was not increased, there would be no COLA the following year.

The employees accepted the challenge, and productivity actually increased by 6 percent. A creative option for mutual gain had been developed: Employees would receive the extra money they wanted and needed if they promised to earn it. In this unusual situation, both management and employees gained the edge.

An effective approach to arrive at options for mutual gain is to frame your demands in terms of the other party's needs. The alternative solution you suggest should clearly indicate how the other side will benefit. Visualize the situation in which you spot a file cabinet being underused in another person's office. Because the file cabinet is in that person's office, he or she is likely to feel some sense of ownership—even if it is company property. You have a critical need for that cabinet. If you say, "Might I have this cabinet that you don't seem to be using?" you have struck a one-sided deal.

Your demand can be framed in terms of the other person's needs, by stating, "I would like to make a deal with you. I am willing to help you unclutter your office by moving your unused file cabinet to my office. My thoughts are that you could use the space, and I could use the file cabinet."

Sara Fulford, the director of quality (an emerging position in many places of work) at an optical lens company needed two more quality technicians to handle her department's workload. Unfortunately, demand for the company's products was flat, and very few people were being hired. Sara met with her boss, the Vice President of Operations, to make her plea for the additional staff. The pedestrian approach would have been for Sara to say, "I can't get all our work done without additional help." Certainly, this is a legitimate and sensible, but not very effective, negotiating point.

To frame her request in terms of the other party's needs, Sara said, "I am confident that our company can achieve the 99.996 percent error-free work we are striving for. In order to hit this target, however, I will have to hire two more technicians. The investment in these two people will more than pay for itself." Framed in terms of achieving an important company goal, Sara's boss approved the request. Note that Sara was not manipulating her boss to achieve self-centered ends. She gained the edge by explaining how the company could satisfy its quest to produce optical lenses of extraordinary quality.

GRANT NO-COST AND LOW-COST CONCESSIONS

A simple yet effective negotiating tactic is to grant the other side concessions that are of no cost, or of low cost to you. Robert J. Laser, a negotiating specialist, concludes: "In nearly every negotiation, there are opportunities for you to give concessions to the other party that are valuable to him or her but of little value to you."[4]

Giveaways are important because they have the psychological effect of making the other side feel rewarded and appreciated. It is also possible that what is useless or unimportant to you is valued by the other side. Several years ago I conducted a house-contents sale of household items I wanted to replace or discard. Whatever I could sell was so much cash to the good. What I couldn't sell would serve the needs of charity and provide me a modest income tax deduction. Dozens of people flocked to my house in search of extra room furniture and hidden treasures. I was pleasantly surprised at how well the sale was progressing and how uncluttered my house was becoming.

Several of what I thought were hidden treasures were creating very little interest: four Italian Renaissance stone cherubs and two copper-and-glass chandeliers. I had taken down the chandeliers several years ago, and they were in basement storage. Finally, an antique dealer who specialized in kitsch eyed the cherubs fondly. As his head move right to left and back again I could tell he was vacillating. I said to the dealer, "Give me $150 for the four cherubs and you can have the two chandeliers as a bonus. I know if you polish them, they will have good resale value."

"I assume a check is okay," said the dealer.

"Of course," I replied. "Let me help you up the stairs with the chandeliers."

Experiments conducted by negotiating researchers provide useful clues to the manner in which concessions should be granted. The most effective technique in most situations is to grant small concessions throughout the bargaining session. Granting concessions works from both the standpoint of the buyer and the seller. If you are a buyer, and therefore leading from strength, start with a low bid and give in very slowly over a long period of time. If you are a seller, and therefore leading from weakness, just turn it around. You begin with a high, but plausible, price and lower your price gradually over a long period.

An alternative to lowering one's price is to grant low-cost, or no-cost concessions. As the buyer, you might offer to finance the purchase through the company if they meet your price. Also, you might offer to buy in larger quantities at a lower price. Still further, you might offer to purchase supplies in addition to the equipment. As the seller, you might offer to grant additional service or giveaway merchandise that you plan to dispose of at drastic reductions anyway. Giving additional service is only a no-cost or low-cost item if the workers providing the service are not already fully occupied.

Judy Preston, a credit supervisor, applied for a one-step promotion as a credit manager at another company. The prospective employer thought highly of Judy's qualifications and made her a job offer of 5 percent more than her current salary. Judy calculated that she needed another $1,500 per year beyond the offer to match her upcoming financial requirements. Judy granted a series of small concessions until she finally reached an agreement on a $1,250 increase beyond the company's initial offer:

1. "I'm willing to work at least three hours of volunteer overtime per week. This should almost recapture the extra $1,500 per year."

2. "Keep in mind that I have taken only two sick days in my career. If you hire me, you'll be getting more productivity from me than from a credit manager who takes an average number of sick days."

3. "I require very little staff support. I do all my own letters on the word processor. This will be another tangible savings for you."

The last concession Judy granted tipped the hiring decision in her favor. She was given a take-it-or-leave-it offer of $1,250 beyond the company's initial offer. Both parties made a wise decision because Judy performed outstandingly in her new position, and she enjoyed it immensely.

BE IN NO HURRY

Slow down and give yourself the edge in negotiations. A patient negotiator is often successful. If negotiations proceed at a deliberate pace, both sides learn more about the real issues involved. Another value of patience is that it enables the negotiator to probe more carefully before taking a stand. Negotiators from Asian countries, particularly the Japanese, are masters at deliberate negotiations. As they proceed deliberately, negotiators from the United States and Canada often become impatient. To bring the session to a close, they are willing to grant major concessions.

Howard Raiffa conducted a negotiation experiment in which Israeli subjects played against Americans. It was found that the Israelis fared better because they were less impatient to arrive at negotiated settlements. Many Americans became anxious with long pauses in the give-and-take of negotiations. Instead, they preferred to say something or do something to move negotiations forward.[5]

Taking your time in negotiations can give you the edge in another notable way. A hasty decision made while negotiating is often a poor one. Although it may seem that you are pressed to make a fast decision, there are many legitimate and ethical stalling tactics that will enable you to reflect on the proposition coming from the other side. You might call for a lunch break or request time to obtain some backup information from your files. Also, you might demand that you consult an expert advisor before committing yourself, or suggest that both sides resume negotiation in the morning.

Jeanne Farlow was a merchandise buyer for a chain of retail stores that catered to the youth market. Her company was interested in expanding its offering of leather coats. While on a buying trip to New York City, Jeanne met with the representative of an import firm that specialized in goods made in China. Jeanne liked the sampling of leather jackets and coats on display. The initial price offered to Jeanne's company seemed fair. It would probably allow for a 40 percent retail markup. Also, the quality of the samples was quite good.

The head of the import firm politely suggested that Jeanne sign quickly a contract for 500 coats and jackets. At the same time she would be given an option to buy another 500 at the same price should the first shipment sell quickly. Jeanne envisioned the accolades she would receive upon reporting back to headquarters in Cincinnati. But then a sudden insight flashed through Jeanne's mind. She thought she should conduct a little research about the origin of these goods.

Back in her hotel room, Jeanne made a series of phone calls to customs officials, the U.S. Chamber of Commerce, and the National Association of Manufacturers. Jeanne's intuition paid off. The import firm she was dealing with had been accused of trading with Chinese firms who used political prisoners for labor. Jeanne did not know for sure if the merchandise in question was made by prisoners. Yet she did know that an importer tainted with the reputation of trading in prisoner-made goods would be in a poor negotiating position. He would therefore not be able to command top price for his clients.

Having done her homework, Jeanne called the importer and made an appointment at ten-thirty the following morning. She told the importer emphatically, "There is some uncertainty in the market place about whether all leather jackets imported from China are made with prison labor. Because of this fact, I can offer you only 75 percent of the price I offered you yesterday." The importer assured Jeanne that he would never intentionally deal in goods made in the Gulag. Because his client was anxious to improve his cash flow, however, he would accept Jeanne's offer.

Jeanne thus gained the edge in this negotiation because she allowed herself time to do her homework. The first price she was offered was a good one. But the information she collected that afternoon from her hotel room enabled her to get an even better price. Furthermore, the leather jackets and coats were a success. Jeanne did buy another shipment at the same favorable price she paid for the first lot.

As mentioned in passing earlier, part of being in no hurry during negotiations is making good use of silence. Use the silent stare in this manner: You allow the other side to make his or her best offer or demand. Say nothing, but still maintain eye contact. Most people feel uncomfortable when faced with silence. To fill the void, he or she is likely to start talking more about the offer. Furthermore, the other side may interpret your silence as indicating disapproval. Consequently, the other side might lower the demand or increase the offer.

Aside from perhaps getting better terms, the silence offers another advantage. You can use it to assess the worth of the demand or offer up to this point.[6] Using this technique, you get the edge by silence and contemplation.

PLAY HARD TO GET

A common-sense, but still effective negotiating tactic is to make it appear that you will not readily accept the other side's proposition. Playing hard to get can also take the form of not granting concessions to the other side. Job finding is one aspect of work in which playing hard to get is very important. The applicant who is overly anxious to land employment may meet with less success than the applicant who remains mildly aloof. "I might be interested under the right circumstances," is a more effective tactic than, "Please let me have the job. I'll begin as soon as you want."

Does playing hard to get work in an era when pleasing the customer has become more important than ever? Playing hard to get is still effective because it capitalizes on a basic principle of human nature. People typically are drawn to objects they cannot readily obtain. If you maintain a mystique about your product or service it can often give you the edge. Pete Kroll sells life insurance and other investments. He continues to be a top producer in life insurance although people today are faced with a baffling array of investment opportunities. Pete has been using the same hard-to-get tactic for thirty years and it still works.

When Pete finds an individual or couple interested in one of the several types of life insurance offered by his firm, he begins his hard-to-get routine. His typical pitch takes this form: "I see that you are interested in a $100,000 whole life policy. I can understand why you would be. Not only does it provide good financial security for your family, it pays an unusually high rate of return. But don't get too excited yet. Our underwriters are very particular about who is eligible to receive such a policy."

At this point the prospect usually inquires about what could possibly disqualify him or her. Pete continues, "Our company turns down people for many reasons. Of course, the physical exams are more thorough than ever today. You would be surprised how many upstanding people have contracted blood diseases they never imagined they had. The credit check is also pretty thorough. We only insure good credit risks. I have also seen people turned down for various 'bad habits' that a background investigation might reveal.

"From the information you have given me so far, you appear to be a good risk. But I can't guarantee that. I can only forward your application to the home office. Let's all keep our fingers crossed."

Pete may sound corny to you, but his tactic works. He is wealthy, and much of the edge he has gained comes from keeping others on edge. He casts self-doubts in his prospects. Pete claims that when their application is approved, they often breathe a sigh of relief. They feel fortunate to be declared a good medical risk and to have a good credit rating.

Many prospects are also relieved to know that some dark secret from their past has not blocked their application for life insurance.

Playing hard to get can also be accomplished through body language. A recommended tactic along these lines is to flinch at the first demand or offer. Flinching puts the other side on notice that the person's demand or offer is unacceptable. The other side is then put on the defensive and will often move toward a more flexible negotiating posture.[7]

MAKE A LAST AND FINAL OFFER

In many instances you can get the edge in negotiating by offering the other side your final offer, or "doorknob price." A key part of this tactic is to exit from negotiations shortly after making your offer. If you look sincere and confident when making your last and final offer, the technique will be even more effective.

Mike Prince, a partner in a management consulting firm, used this technique to advantage in negotiating a completion date for a study requested by a potential client. The potential client wanted a study done in one month of how to reach new customers for its computerized home-shopping services. Mike wanted the assignment but did not have the resources to do the study immediately. After some thought he said, "We would very much like to conduct this study for you. However, the fastest turnaround we can offer is sixty days. If another firm can do a satisfactory job for you in less than sixty days, have them do it. You know where to reach me." The potential client called Mike two days later to sign a contract for the study to be completed in sixty days."

The tactic used by Mike Prince was effective for several reasons. Because the potential client was the buyer, he or she should be negotiating from strength. However, Mike as the seller had plenty of strength also. If the company wanting the study conducted immediately rejects Mike, they must now search out and interview other potential consultants. The process could be time consuming and confusing. Mike also had an edge because stating a last and final offer appears valid if stated openly and sincerely. Finally, stating a last and final offer contains an element of playing hard to get.

A variation of the last-and-final-offer technique is to make a first and final offer. You enter negotiations with an outer limit to what you can spend or offer. Visualize yourself shopping for a new car. After a careful budget analysis, you conclude that you can spend a maximum of $17,500 on a new automobile, including extra options, taxes, license, and fees. A potentially valuable negotiating tactic is to walk into the showroom and declare: "I've come here to buy a new car. What is the best car you can sell me for $17,500, including all costs? I've stopped here first, but if need be, I will do some comparison shopping."

The scenario just mentioned has a positive shock value. Instead of haggling over price, the dealer will be haggling over which car to sell you. Cars are not sold in precise dollar and cents amounts like chocolate or sliced turkey. The dealer may therefore have to mark a car down to meet your limit or throw in some extra options on a car below your limit.

USE DEADLINES

Many deadlines imposed on us are fictitious. You can still obtain the same deal after the deadline is passed, such as a special price on office furniture. Despite these fictitious deadlines, many deadlines do force people into action. This is true even when there is no specific penalty attached to not meeting the deadline. Examples include the date posted on the car windshield indicating the next service date, check-out times at hotels and motels, and starting times at work. Here are several examples of deadlines that will often move the negotiation in your favor:

❖ Will I be receiving that promotion to senior accountant by June 30? If not, I will feel impelled to act on this job offer from another firm. It has become a matter of pride.

❖ If we don't receive your order by March 1, we will not be able to ship your supplies for 45 days after your order date.

❖ My boss has to approve this deal, and she'll be leaving for the East Coast tomorrow.

Deadlines are effective negotiating tools for several reasons. One reason is that people in most developed countries are conditioned to accept deadlines. Early in life, we learn that many events are framed in terms of starting and stopping times. The bank opens at 10 A.M., school begins at 8:30 A.M., and church services, athletic events, and movies have specific starting times. A deeper reason is that most people want structure and cannot work without deadlines imposed by others. When you give another person a deadline, it therefore provides the structure he or she might need to function well.

NIBBLE

Nibblers treat themselves to small concessions after the larger deal has been agreed upon. The nibbler gets the concession because the other side does not want to undo a done deal. My view is that nibbling gives you the edge in a small way, but discredits your reputation. Nibbling, however, is widely practiced. For instance, the small-business owner has just agreed on a price of $2,500 to paint the exterior of a building. The owner then says, "Okay, we have agreed on the price. But before I make a deposit, will you please include painting the entrance way to the office on the inside?" The painting contractor might say silently, "Why take the chance on losing the whole deal? I had better paint the entrance way also."

If you are the one being nibbled, and you hate nibblers, there is an antidote. Have confidence in yourself and your side of the deal. Respond to the nibbler with something of this nature, depending on what is being nibbled: "I'm willing to rent you this machine at the agreed-on price. But you are not entitled to two free replacement parts. You will be billed for them at our standard prices." Few people enjoy undoing deals—even chronic nibblers. You therefore gain back the edge.

We have described thirteen tactics for helping you become a more effective negotiator. Negotiating skill is a major part of gaining the edge because so many transactions in business involve negotiations. Review the following checklist of tactics before entering into negotiations. For the ones that seem particularly relevant to your situation, consult the chapter for more details. When entering into negotiations, remember to:

1. Prepare thoroughly.
2. Create a positive negotiating climate.
3. Focus on interests, not positions.
4. Begin with a plausible demand or offer.
5. Base your demands and offers on a solid rationale.
6. Be truthful.
7. Regard the other party as a partner.
8. Develop options for mutual gain.
9. Grant no-cost and low-cost concessions.
10. Be in no hurry.
11. Play hard to get.
12. Make a last and final offer.
13. Use deadlines.
14. Nibble (least recommended).

❖ 3 ❖

IMPRESSING
YOUR BOSS

Self-confidence and negotiating skill are two major building blocks for gaining a winning edge in many situations.
With these attitudes and skills as a bedrock, the career-
minded person can move on to a major requirement for
success—impressing the boss. If you fail to gain the edge in
relationships with your boss, your other efforts toward survival and advancement will be largely wasted. Even if you
are adored by co-workers and customers, they do not write
your performance evaluation. Your fine reputation with others may help shape your boss's impression of you, but you
also have to impress the boss directly.

Here we describe both familiar and novel approaches
to impressing the boss. Because an approach is familiar, do
not dismiss its importance. People often neglect to use a tactic
they should be using simply because it is familiar. For example, you may have heard somewhere about the importance
of listening to constructive criticism. Reading about the tactic

here may prompt you to incorporate it into your game plan. For a less familiar tactic, ask yourself if your chances for success would improve if you used the tactic. If the answer is affirmative, try out the tactic at the next opportunity.

As with most of the suggestions in this book, the tactics you decide to use from this chapter should be slowly incorporated into your repertoire. The majority of tactics work best when used repeatedly and involve changes in attitudes and outlook. A minority of the tactics are geared toward occasional or one-time use. An example would be the tactics described in Chapter 10 about impressing prospective employers.

DISPLAY A STRONG WORK ETHIC

The best way to impress your boss is the old-fashioned way, through hard work. All other strategies and tactics for achieving success are supplements to having a strong work ethic and performing well on your job. A strong work ethic is in more demand today than ever because organizations are thinly staffed. Managers and professionals are under more heat than lower-ranking workers to produce more than in years past. Although employers may encourage people to lead a balanced life, they still expect evidence of an intense work ethic. The ten tactics described next are characteristic of people with a strong work ethic. Using them will therefore impress almost any rational boss.

Demonstrate Competence Even on Minor Tasks

Attack each assignment with the recognition that each task performed well, however minor, is one more career credit. A minor task performed well paves the way for your being given more consequential tasks. Many managers will test out new team members by assigning them minor tasks. If the team member performs well, he or she is then given more consequential tasks. Michelle Elliot, a telecommunications analyst, provides an example:

"My first day on the job, my boss Alice asked me to figure out why a computer program wouldn't boot. It took me two minutes to figure out that she wasn't putting it in the right computer drive. I showed Alice the nature of the problem. She was so appreciative. The next day she asked me to design a small telecommunications system."

Assume Personal Responsibility for Problems

An employee with a problem will often approach the boss and say, "We have a tough problem to deal with." The connotation is that the boss should be helping you resolve the problem. A better impression is created when the employee says, "I have a tough problem to deal with, and I would like your advice." This statement implies that you are willing to assume responsibility for the problem and for any mistake you may have made that led to the problem.

Assume Responsibility for Free-Floating Problems

A natural way to display a strong work ethic is to assume responsibility for free-floating (nonassigned) problems. The person who picks up the free-floating responsibility will often gain the edge by being perceived as responsible. Assuming even a minor task, such as ordering lunch for a meeting that is running late, can enhance the impression one makes on a boss.

Get Your Projects Completed Promptly

A by-product of a strong work ethic is an eagerness to get projects completed promptly. People with a strong work ethic respect deadlines imposed by others. Furthermore, they typically set deadlines of their own more tightly than those imposed by their boss. Becky Hartwell, a manager of consumer loans at a bank, described why she recommended a particular subordinate for a promotion to consumer loan supervisor:

"Kent was not the most creative person in the group. Also, his formal education was borderline for the job. Yet I recommended Kent because he always gets his work done ahead of schedule. Even if I have his input sitting in my in basket, it still serves a useful purpose before I get to it. I know that the information I requested from him is there in good shape whenever I need it."

Accept Undesirable Assignments Willingly

Another way of expressing a strong work ethic is to accept undesirable assignments willingly. Look for ways to express the attitude, "Whether or not this assignment is glamorous and exciting is a secondary issue. What counts is that it is something that needs doing for the good of the organization." Cliff Anderson was a financial aid officer at a university. A student group had organized a protest at what they perceived to be discourteous, insensitive, and inhumane service from the financial aid office. In addition to their on-campus protest, the group was attempting to get media coverage of their battle.

The director of financial aid requested that Cliff meet with the group, listen to their problems, and somehow mollify them without making false promises. Cliff knew that as spokesperson for the office, he would be the target of the students' hostilities. Nevertheless, Cliff's strong work ethic (and keen sense of office politics) propelled him to take on the assignment willingly. He met with the group for two and one half hours, and encouraged them to get every complaint out on the table. Cliff agreed with some complaints and simply noted all the others. He told the group he would do the best he could to have some of these problems rectified.

After Cliff's meeting, the protests subsided, and the financial aid office began a program of treating students more courteously. Cliff's boss was so impressed that he promoted Cliff to senior financial aid officer several months later.

Follow Through On Tasks

A distinguishing characteristic of a person with a strong work ethic is seeing a task through to completion. Many people express eagerness to assume responsibility. A smaller number of people follow the entire assignment through to completion. Effective follow-through can often be demonstrated in relation to items discussed during a meeting. The head of a meeting might ask, "Who would be able to check out the service warranties on competitive products?" One of the participants will volunteer even though he or she thinks the request is of low priority. The person will then make one or two half-hearted phone calls about competitive warranties. Nothing else happens to the request.

In contrast to the lax approach just described, the person with a strong work ethic will conduct the investigation. Next, he or she will surprise the boss by asking to have the results of the investigation placed on the next agenda. Displaying a strong work ethic in this manner is impressive because such follow-through is rare.

Submit Timely Information

An honest and constructive way of demonstrating a strong work ethic is to submit timely information. Because timely information is so important in a competitive business environment, the person who expends effort to be timely creates a positive impression. Rhonda Allport is part of a six-member regional sales support staff. Her group provides a variety of support services to district sales offices. Rhonda spends one half her time on the road and one half in the regional office. She is required to submit a written report to her manager after each trip.

Rhonda stands out among the six-person staff. She takes a lap-top computer on her trips and records extensive notes daily. Upon the completion of each trip Rhonda either prints a report and submits a fax or electronically submits a report to her boss. Rhonda's manager has the relevant information he needs even before she returns home. Her timely submission of information adds to his perception of her as a professional with a strong work ethic. Rhonda's timeliness also creates a positive impression because it is done with panache.

Work Long Hours

Work weeks exceeding 55 hours have become the norm for managers and professionals in many private and public firms. You may therefore need to work 60 hours per week to avoid being perceived as having a weak work ethic. Going beyond the standard work week thus becomes a defensive tactic. Working long hours is an effective offensive tactic only when it distinguishes you from others.

Jack Newcomb is the vice president of sales at an air freight company. He joined the company twenty years ago as a part-time driver. Jack attributes some of his success to the positive impression he created using the "unpaid half-hour." He began this routine after he attained full-time status. When drivers returned from their routes they completed their paperwork as quickly as possible, punched out, and left the premises.

Jack established a different work pattern from the other drivers. After completing his paperwork and punching out, he hung around an additional half hour. Jack would talk to the supervisors or the salesmen and offer whatever useful input he could. Jack would casually mention that he had already punched out so his supervisor would know he was working gratis. Jack's strong work ethic paid off in a promotion to supervisor in three years, much to the surprise of the other drivers.

Snoop for Details

In some occupations snooping for details is characteristic of thoroughness, devotion to duty, and a strong work ethic.

Auditors, defense attorneys, prosecuting attorneys, and tax examiners all gain points by being super snoops. Melissa Rothchild, an Internal Revenue Service examiner, describes what needs to be done to impress management in her agency: "Finding money that people owe the government is what I'm paid to do. When I conduct an audit, I have to thoroughly analyze all the information the taxpayer gives me. One area in which I have to really dig for details is when I audit checking accounts. It's a messy but important job to cross-check every bill presumably paid with checks drawn on the account.

"My investigation has to be the most thorough in uncovering the origin of funds for all deposits. For some reason tax cheats think the government is unlikely to uncover unreported income earned in small amounts. Business owners who get paid in cash face the biggest temptation of underreporting. My supervisor gets the most excited when my digging turns up unreported income. She always says how devoted and hard working I am."

Melissa's snooping legitimately reflects a strong work ethic. It requires superior effort to dig through somebody else's records and find irregularities. The good impression Melissa creates will help her gain the edge in receiving good performance evaluations at the IRS.

Look Busy

The most productive people can sometimes be seen with a clean desk, staring out the window. Such behavior may be conducive to planning or arriving at creative solutions to problems. Nevertheless, image is still important in creating the impression of having a strong work ethic. Try these suggestions for looking busy when you need time to think yet are in view of others:

- ❖ Leave your personal computer running with an open file on the screen.

- ❖ Keep a yellow tablet on your desk with a long To Do list.

- ❖ If you have a telephone answering machine, call yourself from another phone and leave the message light flashing.

- ❖ Keep a copy of *The Wall Street Journal* on your desk with an article circled with red underliner.

- ❖ Should you be on a schmoozing tour of the office, leave a jacket draped over the back of your chair. The jacket sends the message that you will be right back, but were called away from your work area.

STEP OUTSIDE YOUR JOB DESCRIPTION

Job descriptions are characteristic of a well-organized firm. If everybody knows what he or she is supposed to be doing there will be much less confusion, and goals will be achieved. This logic sounds impressive, but job descriptions have a major downside. If people engage only in work included in their job description, an "It's not my job" mentality pervades. A good way to impress your boss is therefore to demonstrate that you are not constrained by a job description. If something needs doing, you will get it done whether or not it is your formal responsibility.

Ben McClean is a human resources specialist at a meat-processing company. His company was being pressured by the local and federal government to take more drastic steps to reduce work-place hazards. A task force was appointed by the president to study the problem. Ben was not assigned as one of the task force members. Nevertheless, he thought he could make a contribution to the study of the problem. Without being given the assignment, Ben prepared a 25-page report on current trends in work-place accidents in the food-processing industry.

Ben submitted his report to the task force, simply stating that his findings might be of use to the group. The report made the job of the task force much easier, and Ben's efforts were widely praised. In recognition of his hard work and interest, the president then appointed Ben to the task force. Ben's boss, the vice president of human resources, also received praise for having such a helpful professional on the staff.

Ben stepped outside his job description in the sense that he had not been assigned to the task force, but yet contributed to its work. Particularly impressive was the fact that Ben did not dabble in areas where his professional skills were of little consequence. Instead, Ben used his ability to synthesize and analyze published information to help the firm.

PRODUCE CREATIVE IDEAS

Creativity no longer refers to any wild idea that is somebody else's problem to implement. Instead, a creative idea is novel and capable of being put to use. Creativity is not restricted to breakthrough ideas that create a new industry or a major new product. Your creative suggestion could relate to such matters as earning more money, saving money, improving customer service, or enhancing quality. A creative idea impresses the boss because it solves a real problem facing the firm.

The sales manager at a videotape distributor made a suggestion that has proved to be a financial success for the firm. She suggested that the company produce a catalog in video format. The catalog would contain brief clips from 50 videotapes distributed by the firm. Customers would be charged $19.95 for the catalog, plus $3.50 for shipping and handling. The video catalog has become a stable source of revenue for the firm as a hot-selling item by itself. It also generates sales of other videos because it is an attractive medium for ordering films.

Creativity can be improved with the right kind of practice. If you want to become more creative, try these time-tested suggestions.[1]

1. *Push for more than one solution to your problem.* The essence of creativity is to explore alternative solutions to a problem until you find a workable one.

2. *Keep an idea notebook at hand.* It will help you to capture a permanent record of flashes of insights and good ideas borrowed from others.

3. *Pose new questions every day.* Creativity requires a questioning, inquiring mind.

4. *Keep current facts in your field in mind.* Having current facts in mind gives you the raw material to form creative links among bits of material.

5. *Read widely in fields not directly related to your field of interest.* Maintaining a balanced, cultural media diet enables you to cross-reference bits of information.

6. *Avoid rigid patterns of doing things.* Try to overcome fixed ideas and look for new viewpoints. Attempt to push for more than one solution to your problem. Develop the ability to let go of one idea in favor of another.

7. *Be open and receptive to your own as well as to others' ideas.* Be alert to seize on tentative, half-formed ideas and possibilities. Entertain and generate your own far-fetched or seemingly silly ideas. If you are receptive to the ideas of others, you will learn new things that will help you creatively.

8. *Be alert in observations.* Look for the subtle aspects of objects, situations, products, processes, and ideas. The greater the number of new associations and relationships you form, the greater your chances of arriving at creative and original combinations and solutions. Many breakthrough products are a combination of other products, such as a fax machine that combines a photocopying machine and a telephone.

9. *Engage in creative hobbies.* Included here are manual hobbies such as arts and crafts and mental hobbies such as crossword puzzles. Creative hobbies are

important because active use of your mind enhances creativity.

10. *Improve your sense of humor and laugh easily.* Humor
helps relieve tensions, and most people are more
productive when they are reasonably relaxed.
Humor also helps develop creativity thinking because jokes and humorous comments are creative
acts.

11. *Adopt a risk-taking attitude.* The fear of failure damp-
ens creativity so be willing to fail on occasion. Also,
it requires many failed ideas to produce one good
one.

12. *Have courage and self-confidence.* Many people surrender just when they are on the brink of a solution.
It is therefore important to persist when you are
seeking a unique solution to a problem.

An underlying theme to these suggestions is that you
need self-discipline to develop more creative behavior. You
have to train yourself to carry out some of the preceding
suggestions. One specific form of self-discipline is the most
important: When faced with a problem that requires a creative solution, conduct a brainstorming session by yourself.

RELATE YOUR EFFORTS
TO CORPORATE GOALS

An effective way to impress a modern manager is to show
how your activities are linked to what the organization wants
to accomplish. When an organization is carefully planned,
top management establishes long-range goals (the company
strategy). All actions in the organizations are then related to
achieving these goals. You will therefore impress your boss
by making a link between your efforts and corporate goals.

Suppose you have called a meeting of your team to
discuss the merits of a customer complaint. Your boss asks

you why you are holding a meeting to resolve the complaint of one customer. You explain that a major corporate goal is total customer satisfaction. Your efforts this afternoon have been directed at achieving that goal, one brick at a time. According to corporate strategy, each customer's problem must receive considerable attention.

Linking your efforts to corporate strategy is impressive because it connotes that you are a well-planned, strategically minded person. One of the highest compliments top management can pay a person is to say that he or she plans carefully. This is true because planning has high status. It is considered to be the essence of good management.

ANTICIPATE YOUR SUPERIOR'S NEEDS

A hard-hitting way of impressing the boss is to anticipate what he or she needs and get the job done without a formal request. Sometimes the anticipated need is a recurring one, such as the boss needing certain figures to prepare a quarterly report. At other times, the needs relate to a one-time problem. Sue Murphy, a legal administrator in a large law firm, has used the tactic in question to advantage. She anticipate her manager's needs by keeping in touch with events taking place in and around the work place. When complaints about inadequate parking space for office personnel mounted, Sue anticipated that her boss would want help with this problem.

Before bringing the problem about the overcrowded parking to her boss's attention, Sue investigated some tentative solutions. One workable alternative was subletting parking space from an office building one block from the law office. Sue then brought the problem and proposed solution to her boss's attention. Sue said her boss was very pleased with her work because her boss had heard rumblings about the problem and wanted to do something about it soon.

Sue's anticipation of her boss's needs, along with outstanding performance in general, has paid off. She began with the firm as a paralegal assistant and now has the highest position in the firm held by anyone other than an attorney.

Anticipating your boss's needs works effectively because it directly feeds into the primary reason your boss wants you on the payroll. A major role for any team member is to take care of tasks the boss cannot, or chooses not to, carry out. Furthermore, it is a pleasant surprise for a boss to obtain information he or she needs without having to remember to make a request.

ANTICIPATE PROBLEMS

Akin to anticipating your boss's needs is anticipating problems in general, even if your boss is not planning to work on them. Anticipating problems is characteristic of a resourceful person who exercises initiative. Instead of working exclusively on problems that have been handed to him or her, the person undertakes other important tasks. Such behavior will impress most bosses because it reflects an entrepreneurial, take-charge attitude.

Frank Harper, a raw material purchaser for a food manufacturing plant, displays the ability to anticipate problems. In one situation he was able to avoid a potential problem with the raw potatoes being used in the production of potato sticks. Frank alerted his boss that the potatoes in the plant storage bins would spoil before they could be used in production. Part of the problem was that the company had accumulated more than enough inventory in potato sticks. He suggested that selling them before they rotted was the best option for the company. Frank was able to sell one million pounds of potatoes to other chippers. With some of that money he was able to purchase fresh potatoes from growers in Florida. The company ended up dumping 400,000 pounds of potatoes, but Frank had prevented a major loss.

Frank's ability to anticipate problems has earned him the respect of his boss and other members of management.

Frank is now thought of so highly by management that he believes he is next in line for a purchasing manager's position.

SHOW A COMMITMENT TO IMPROVEMENT

A slow and steady way of impressing your boss is to be committed to improving work methods and procedures. Being committed to self-improvement is also impressive. One reason a commitment to improvement earns points is that it reflects a philosophy that supports the quality movement. According to the Japanese philosophy of *Kaizen*, people should strive for a continuous gradual improvement in personal and work life. *Kaizen* means roughly, "Every day in every way, I'm getting better and better." The improvement-oriented person looks for things that are not quite right, even if they are not yet full-blown problems. Periodically, point out to your boss the gradual improvements you have made in the way you handle your job.

Wendy Phillips, a restaurant manager, believed in the spirit of *Kaizen*. She also promoted the same spirit among her workers. Several of them decided to begin uncluttering the restaurant by removing some of the less attractive paintings from the wall and some decorations from the bar. Soon, a few customers began to comment favorably on the cleaner decor. Given this encouragement, Wendy and her staff decided to shift to an art-deco motif (characterized by a stark, clean, and modern look). Business increased substantially. Wendy attributed much of this increase to the high-quality appearance of the restaurant.

Wendy's improved business results impressed her boss, the owner of several restaurants. A basic reason that the *Kaizen* approach to improvement impresses management is that you achieve better results without requiring a radical program that involves major new expenditures. As Wendy's boss stated, "You've improved our profits. And we didn't have to shut down the restaurant, redecorate, and open again and hope for a surge in new business."

DOCUMENT YOUR ACCOMPLISHMENTS

An essential career-enhancing tactic is to maintain a dossier of tangible accomplishments. The most impressive type of documentation contains objective evidence rather than subjective opinions. For example, documentation should include such information as the amount of money you saved your firm, how much you increased revenue, or how many customer complaints you resolved successfully. This stands in contrast to a testimonial about your good deeds from another person, such as a project leader or a former boss.

Documenting your accomplishments is also an excellent vehicle for impressing your boss. Submit your dossier at times of performance appraisal, salary review, or when you are requesting a transfer or promotion. Your dossier is also helpful in explaining to the organization why you should be a survivor during a downsizing.

Debra Falkowitz, a telemarketer in an office equipment company, used the documentation technique to attain a promotion into outside sales. She kept a careful record of her monthly sales quotas. At the end of each month Debra documented the amount of sales she actually achieved. After eighteen months on the job, Debra achieved or exceeded her quota fifteen times. She presented these figures to her boss as justification for promotion. Debra's boss then recommended her for promotion to outside sales. Four months later Debra received the promotion she wanted and deserved.

A creative way of documenting your accomplishments is to maintain a "time power book." This technique works best with a boss who keeps close tabs on team members. Instead of just telling your boss what you think you have done for the company recently, keep a time management book that details all your activities and plans. A time power book informs your boss of your progress on a particular project and your creative ideas for future assignments. Your accurate record of accomplishments will reinforce your boss's perception that you are well organized and efficient.

Documenting your accomplishments is an effective impression-making technique because it is based on a principle called the appeal to legitimacy. Pointing to a written record appears more legitimate and authentic than is merely stating orally that you have accomplished something worthwhile. People are also influenced by the fact that human memory cannot be trusted entirely. If you can point to written records, you are not relying exclusively on your memory.

HAVE SATISFIED CUSTOMERS CONTACT YOUR BOSS

The most important objective of most organizations, and the departments within them, is to satisfy the customer. As mentioned previously, customers can be internal or external. If a customer says something nice about you, the comment will receive more attention than one from a co-worker or a subordinate. The reason is that co-workers and subordinates might praise you for political reasons. The motivation of your customer is assumed to be pure because customers are so valued.

Steve Andolina is the manager of the sales administration department at a cosmetics manufacturer. His department supports the fifteen-person sales force in his firm, and Steve interacts daily with these people. Steve makes sure that goods are shipped to external customers on time, and he handles returns and complaints. The sales representatives (who are Steve's internal customers) commented frequently on how he provided them such good service, often beyond expectation. Steve explained to the sales representatives that he was moved deeply by their appreciation. He also suggested tactfully that the appreciation would do him more good if it were passed along to his boss, the director of marketing.

Steve's boss was duly impressed by the positive comments he received from the sales force. The payout for Steve was that his relationship with his boss improved substantially. Steve's suggestions met with a better reception, and his budget was expanded.

ENGAGE IN FAVORABLE INTERACTIONS WITH YOUR BOSS

Favorable interactions lead to favorable impressions. Many people forget this important principle and purposely irritate their boss. Among the many interactions that lead to a favorable impression are giving your boss emotional encouragement, accepting the boss's authority, and laughing at his or her jokes. A study of the interactions between bank employees and their supervisors was published in the *Journal of Applied Psychology*. The researchers concluded that purposely trying to create a positive impression for the boss led to better performance ratings.[2] Although this finding is not surprising, it is reassuring to know that it is backed by statistical evidence.

Presented next is a listing of the behaviors used by employees in the study to create positive exchanges (interactions) with their supervisors. Use these behaviors as a checklist for achieving favorable interactions with your boss. The more of these actions you are engaged in, the higher the probability that you are creating a positive impression.

SUPERVISORY INTERACTION CHECKLIST

1. Agree with your supervisor's major opinions outwardly even when you disagree inwardly. _____

2. Take an immediate interest in your supervisor's personal life. _____

3. Praise your supervisor on his or her accomplishments. _____

4. Do personal favors for your supervisor. _____

5. Do something as a personal favor for your supervisor even though you are not required to do it. _____

6. Volunteer to help your supervisor on a task. _____

7. Compliment your supervisor on his or her dress or appearance. _____

8. Present yourself to your supervisor as being a friendly person. _____

9. Agree with your supervisor's major ideas. _____

10. Present yourself to your supervisor as being a polite person. _____

Nicholas Mattachiera, a bank teller, provides a case history of the importance of engaging in favorable interactions with the boss. Nick tells us: "I never thought laughing at your boss's jokes would be effective until it actually happened to me. When I started working at First Federal Bank, I had no experience in banking. When Mr. Hoffman interviewed me for the positions, he jested, 'That's all we need, another Italian.'

"At first I was very offended, but I decided to keep quiet because I wanted the job. I laughed at his comment and told Hoffman I was a born-again German. Since he was German, he thought my retort was great. After I was hired, I continued to laugh at his jokes even if they were insensitive. After six months, I received two raises and was earning more money than others who had been with the bank two years. When I decided to return to college, Mr. Hoffman offered me a part-time position as a teller in one of the branches. I took the job and discovered I was making more than one of the head tellers."

Nick had a lot more going for him than laughing at his boss's jokes, but these favorable interactions added to the positive impression he created. The principle Nick obeyed is basic but important: favorable interactions lead to favorable impressions, which lead to favorable decisions on your behalf.

KEEP YOUR BOSS INFORMED

Managers need valid information about what is taking place in their organizational units to function effectively. It can be embarrassing not to be informed of an unusual success or problem taking place in one's department. Consequently, another way of creating a favorable impression on the boss is to keep him or her informed about nonroutine events and results. Information about successes and failures is equally important.

Keeping your boss informed can be done informally by a comment such as, "You asked me to investigate why we are so far behind on payments from our biggest customer. I found out that they weren't happy with our delivery dates, so they delayed payments. The problem is fixed, and their payment is in hand."

Another way of keeping your boss informed is to bring work-related information to his or her attention. Such information can help make the boss look good when he or she speaks to high management or colleagues. Margaret Ideman, an internal quality consultant, explains how she uses this technique:

"When I attend a conference or seminar, I take notes on topics of interest to the company. I also look for brochures or handouts that are potentially useful. I think of myself as representing my organization. I therefore collect any information that may be useful even if it does not pertain exactly to my department. For example, when I see new equipment demonstrated that might interest the company, I pick up a product sheet. When I return to the office, I write a report and share my experiences. In that way the whole organization can learn from my experience. My boss gets a copy of any information I disseminate."

Margaret's favorable evaluations by her boss attest to the efficacy of her tactic. She is creating an air of professionalism and at the same time impressing her boss intelligently. She appeals to her boss's need to be recognized by team members as a person with intellectual curiosity and professionalism.

BE THOROUGHLY LOYAL

A surefire way of impressing almost any boss is through loyalty to him or her and the organization. Conversely, disloyalty creates a glaringly negative image. Wayne Calloway, the chairman of Pepsico, points out that vigorous debate is essential to success, but disloyalty hurts an organization: "Criticism behind your back; people who constantly complain, but offer no suggestions for improvement; people who can't be trusted at all because they lack integrity—the one glue that holds everything together."[3]

Loyalty is important because people in charge prefer to have the emotional support of team members. Without displays of loyalty, the boss operates with an empty, scary feeling. When loyalty is not visible, he or she may even worry about being badmouthed by team members. Loyalty can take many forms such as the following:

❖ During a staff meeting you make positive comments about your boss's proposal. You also nod approvingly during the presentation.

❖ The boss is away and the office clown begins his impression of the boss, exaggerating all the boss's weaknesses. You comment that nobody is perfect and that we should also learn to appreciate the boss's considerable strengths.

❖ You talk to people in your network about the wonderful things happening in your department and how well everybody gets along.

❖ Your department is faced with a surge of activity, and your vacation begins in two weeks. You tell your boss you would be willing to reschedule your vacation to help the department through the rough period.

❖ You blow the whistle on an employee within the department who you think is ripping off the company by goofing off much of the time.

AVOID BEING A YES-PERSON

Being a complete yes-person has lost its effectiveness as a method of impressing the boss, particularly when he or she is emotionally secure. The modern manager does not want needless criticism from team members, but does expect some constructive criticism. You can therefore impress the boss by tactfully adding value to his or her ideas and spotting mistakes. Building upon the boss's ideas can be done in staff meetings, but error-correcting is best done in private.

Stan Jordan, a telecommunications manager at a gas and electric company, explains how one of his team members, Ashley, continues to impress him: "Ashley is a computer science graduate with about six years of experience. She is a pleasant and positive person, yet she won't go along with a flawed idea of mine. Ashley attended a presentation I made to upper management about the status of our department. I explained how the company should be linking its computers in the future. I described some of the new equipment we would have to purchase to create these links.

"Immediately following my presentation, Ashley asked if she might have some time to ask me some questions about the points I raised. Flattered, I scheduled a meeting with her for late that afternoon. When we got together, Ashley informed me of some important new technology. It would lower the costs of linking computers for 50 percent less than the system I proposed. I thanked Ashley for her input and asked her to furnish me complete details.

"The package of information Ashley assembled for me was an eye-opener. I wish I had consulted her before I made my presentation. Yet it was not too late. My thinking was only preliminary. When I reintroduced the topic to management, Ashley accompanied me. Management was very pleased that linking the computers would cost 50 percent less than I initially proposed."

If Ashley had been a yes-person, she would have let Stan's thoughts about linking the computers go unchallenged. Instead, Ashley was truly professional, and truly loyal. She helped her boss come closer to achieving his goal of improving the telecommunications system. Ashley has now endeared herself further to her boss.

ESTABLISH REALISTIC GOALS

It is more impressive to establish and attain realistic goals than to make fanciful promises and fail. Keep in mind also that a goal not reached is a negative marker in a system of management by results. A realistic goal in this sense is one that stretches the person but is neither too easy nor too difficult. If you establish realistic goals it impresses others because you demonstrate good judgment and conscientiousness.

John Rogers, a sales manager for a fire safety company, has helped his relationships with his boss through establishing and reaching realistic goals. He provides his boss with weekly sales goals and does his best to exceed the goal. John, however, is not a low-baller who sets up easy goals to surpass them by a wide margin. At a convention John told his regional manager his office would gross $86,000 in sales for the month. Other managers promised the same regional manager sales of $125,000 for the month.

At the end of the month, John was the only manager to meet or exceed his goal. John had demonstrated both good judgment and dependability. He has a better shot at the next promotion than the sales managers who set impressive goals but fail to deliver.

VOLUNTEER FOR EXTRA WORK

A standard technique for getting noticed by your boss and creating a positive impression is to volunteer for assignments. Although this technique is familiar, do not overlook its potency. Aren't you impressed when somebody volunteers to help you? Kathleen Chang was hired as an office temporary in an accounting department of a health-care products company during a year-end closing. Although she had very little experience in accounting, Kathleen offered to help in any way she could. She ran errands, filed, and helped out with anything that needed to be done.

Most of these chores were done voluntarily. Kathleen was hired only to handle the large volume of report copying and distribution. Her attitude and work so impressed the department manager and staff that Kathleen was soon offered a permanent position in the department.

BE HONEST ABOUT YOUR CONFUSION

A low-key tactic for impressing the boss is to be honest when you do not understand directions, assignments, a technical process, or anything else. Pretending to understand something and then wasting time and other resources by mishandling an assignment creates a negative impression. Several years ago I assigned my part-time research assistant the task of photocopying articles on a specific topic: self-defeating behavior. We discussed the assignment for an hour, and she claimed to fully comprehend what I wanted.

My research assistant reported back to me two weeks later with a huge stack of copies and a photocopying bill that exceeded budget. She had proceeded to copy any article or book chapter in sight that contained the word "behavior."

Only one article focused on the topic of self-defeating behavior. My research assistant had underwhelmed me, and I did not request that the graduate office reassign her to me for the next term. Admittedly I showed poor management practice by not asking her to return the next day with a sample of relevant articles. Nevertheless, a worker should express his or her confusion to avoid blowing an assignment.

ACCEPT CONSTRUCTIVE CRITICISM

Many managers dislike criticizing team members. Giving criticism makes them uncomfortable, partly because they know how defensive people become when criticized. If you can accept constructive criticism with an improvement-oriented attitude, you will create a positive impression. The good impression is created in part because the manager is relieved when the criticism is interpreted positively. By accepting the criticism, you have made easier one of the most sensitive part of the manager's job. Steve Roomian, a sales manager in a computer-equipment company, offers this perspective on why a worker should be willing to accept constructive criticism:

"If you really screwed up and are told about it, consider it a favor. Too many people take their jobs too personally. A correction in your work process is not necessarily an attack on your character. If you really did something out of line and are reprimanded, you should apologize and try not to repeat the behavior. The office is no place to argue about proper behavior."

APPEAL TO YOUR BOSS'S NONWORK INTERESTS

A political tactic for impressing the boss is to learn the details of his or her life so you can key into those interests. Knowing your boss's outside-of-work interests helps impress the boss because it facilitates establishing rapport between you. If your boss is a passionate fan of one sports team, you bring in news clippings about that team your boss may not have seen. For example, while traveling, scan out-of-town newspapers to see if your boss's favorite team is mentioned.

Appealing to a boss's interest in golf continues to be an excellent way of building rapport. Women by the thousands have taken up golf to help them build relationships with immediate superiors, upper management, customers, and prospective customers. Judy Falcone, a sales consultant, discovered that golf was a passion for her manager and other managers in the company. Already earning a high income, she was able to join the country club in which many company managers were members. Judy fit right in to the country-club golf crowd because she had played on public links for many years.

The first several times Judy met her boss at the club, she exchanged pleasantries and continued about her game. The two of them shortly developed a better working relationship in the office. Judy was soon invited by the boss to golf occasionally with him and two higher-ranking managers. Judy did not overplay her golf connections, and the tactic worked effectively. Soon she was assigned bigger accounts. Equally important for Judy's peace of mind, she enjoyed the feeling of being part of the corporate in-group.

Judy thus enhanced the impression she was making by developing a significant mutual interest with her boss and others in power. She had to invest considerable time and money to cultivate this mutual interest, but Judy believes the investment was worthwhile.

ORGANIZE FESTIVITIES TO CELEBRATE YOUR BOSS'S ACCOMPLISHMENTS

Craving recognition and flattery is a normal human need. One way to satisfy this need of your boss is to organize festivities to celebrate his or her accomplishments. In the process you will create a good impression despite cries of unfair political game-playing by your co-workers. The reason this technique works so effectively is that managers have fewer opportunities for recognition than do individual contributors. The manager is usually the one dispensing recognition to others.

Claire Hall, a medical records technician, worked at a city hospital. A hospital ritual was to post plaques identifying the employee of the month. A wall near the cafeteria was allocated for these plaques. One month Claire's supervisor, Marjorie Barnes, was experiencing personal problems that dampened her usually congenial mood. Despite these problems Marjorie persevered in being helpful and supportive. To help the boss through her problems, Claire organized the other medical records technicians and support personnel to give Marjorie special recognition.

On the day the employee-of-the-month award was to be made, Marjorie received a plaque from the group entitled, "Boss of the Month." The plaque cited the devotion the supervisor had to the hospital and her employees. Tears of appreciation came to Marjorie's eyes. When she learned who was responsible for this charitable act, Marjorie took an even closer interest in Claire's welfare.

ORGANIZE YOUR DESK IN THE SAME MANNER AS YOUR BOSS'S

Modeling the behavior of your boss can be an effective tactic for creating the right impression. The boss is likely to be impressed because it is part of his or her role to serve as a constructive model for employees. Imitating small aspects of your boss's behavior may create an impression below the level of conscious awareness. The boss may elevate his or her impression of you without realizing the force responsible for the improved image.

Organizing your desk the way your boss does is a simple way of modeling. If your boss maintains a neat and orderly desk with only one paper at a time on the desk, it could provide modeling clues for you. If your boss keeps piles of papers and used beverage cups on his or her desk, you can create a positive impression by doing the same. However, do not follow the model so far that it lowers your productivity.

Sarah Williamson, a loan analyst in a credit union, had to adjust to a new boss when her old one left. The new boss kept a neat and organized desk but adorned it with personal mementoes such as a photograph of her husband, children, and Irish setter. Sarah took the lead and placed photos of her boyfriend and parents on her desk. Sarah's boss mentioned to her one day, "I like the photos on your desk. It shows that you're humanistic. I have the same outlook on life."

USE YOUR COMPANY'S PRODUCTS OR SERVICES

A potent way of impressing a profit-oriented boss is to use the company's products or services. The tactic works for several reasons. By using the company's products or services you show loyalty, appreciation, and a sensitivity to the very nature of free enterprise. If somebody doesn't buy your company's products and services from your company, you will soon be looking for another job.

Using your company's products and services also shows an emotional bond with your company. It will impress most bosses that you have some concern for the welfare of the organization, and indirectly for him or her. Barry Bertram joined a manufacturer of personal computers (Leading Edge) as a production supervisor. Three months into his job he asked his boss, the production manager, where he could find a dealer who sold used Macintosh computers. Taken back, the production manager barked: "What kind of question is that? You're working for Leading Edge? Barry responded, "I know I'm working for Leading Edge. I want to sell my Macintosh system so I can purchase one of our new models. I'm a true believer." Barry's boss shook his hand, put his arm around him, and said, "We like your style around here."

To tie together all this information about impressing your boss, scan the following checklist. It will serve as a convenient reminder of some workable tactics for impressing the boss, so you can thus "gain the edge."

1. Display a strong work ethic.

2. Step outside your job description.

3. Produce creative ideas.

4. Relate your efforts to corporate goals.

5. Anticipate your superior's needs.

6. Anticipate problems.

7. Show a commitment to improvement.

8. Document your accomplishments.

9. Have satisfied customers contact your boss.

10. Engage in favorable interactions with your boss.

11. Keep your boss informed.

12. Be thoroughly loyal.

13. Avoid being a yes-person.

14. Establish realistic goals.

15. Volunteer for extra work.

16. Be honest about your confusion.

17. Accept constructive criticism.

18. Appeal to your boss's nonwork interests.

19. Get to know the details of your boss's life.

20. Organize festivities to celebrate your boss's accomplishments.

21. Use your company's products or services.

❖ 4 ❖

BEING NOTICED
BY TOP MANAGEMENT

To gain a big edge you have to impress higher-ups as well as your immediate boss and a host of others. Important others include co-workers, lower-ranking people, customer prospects, customers, and people in your network. The tactics designed to impress your boss also make a contribution to impressing members of top management. In this chapter, I describe tactics aimed at impressing managers beyond the person to whom you report directly. However, you can also use "higher-up" tactics to impress your immediate superior.

The point emphasized here and throughout this book is to use the tactic that seems to fit the situation best at the time. Nevertheless, the tactics are grouped according to the target person or groups for which they are primarily (but not exclusively) applicable. Next we look at specific ways to impress top management or any other managers to whom your boss reports.

BE VISIBLE IN ANY POSITIVE, SENSIBLE WAY

The most comprehensive strategy for impressing people in high places is to gain visibility for positive reasons. Being visible for negative reasons, such as being charged with embezzlement, will not help you gain the edge. Visibility can lead to being noticed and consequently regarded as a candidate for promotion or a special assignment. Achieving superior job performance may help you gain visibility as word filters up the organization about your exploits. In addition, choose among the tactics described next to attain positive visibility.

Obtain Professional Recognition

Most executives are more concerned about an employee's job results than about his or her professional accomplishments. Nevertheless, achieving professional recognition will impress some higher ups. A good example is Lisa Carson, who passed the appropriate exams to obtain a Certificate of Management Accountant (CMA). The CMA is analogous to a Certified Public Accountant (CPA). The difference is that the CMA certifies a person as a knowledgeable accountant who works as a company employee in contrast to a CPA who works for a public accounting firm.

Lisa was the first person in her company to receive the CMA designation. Her boss mentioned her accomplishment during lunch with a top executive. The executive, who was unfamiliar with the designation "CMA," was impressed. He said to Lisa's boss, "Keep that woman in mind for our management training program. I like people who are willing to plunge into unchartered waters." Lisa gained visibility by distinguishing herself in an uncommon way, thus bringing positive attention to herself.

Participate in the Company Suggestion Program

Employees who actively participate in a company suggestion program achieve good visibility. The vast majority of companies allow people only at the first couple of job levels to receive suggestion awards. Gaining visibility through a suggestion award is not an opportunity for all employees. If you hold a managerial or professional job, you can still submit a suggestion. Simply note that your real concerns are helping the company, not winning a prize. In this way, your altruism could help you gain the edge.

Winning a major suggestion award leads to quick visibility, yet frequent participation also earns recognition points. Helen Boudreau, a graphic designer in a training department, had many creative ideas for improving company productivity. When the company installed a suggestion system, Helen used it as a vehicle for communicating her money-saving ideas. At the department's quarterly meeting, it was announced that Helen had contributed the most suggestions to the program.

Helen's dedication to improvement was mentioned in her performance appraisal. She also received a note of appreciation from the vice president of human resources. Helen's participation in the suggestion program was all the more impressive because she worked in a department (training) outside the mainstream of production. Helen's uniqueness thus helped her gain the edge.

Get Mentioned in the Company Newsletter

Top executives regularly read company newsletters in order to keep informed of company events. A sensible tactic to achieve visibility therefore is to get your name in the newsletter for purposes other than a one-line mention. If you accomplish something you think is newsworthy, contact the editor of the company newsletter. Newsworthy events include work and personal accomplishments and outside professional activities. Have you won a safety award, saved a drowning child, or been elected vice president of your local chapter of the National Association of Accountants?

Being mentioned in the company newsletter is an effective attention-getter because having one's name in print is inherently impressive. So long as the mention is positive, or even neutral, the technique works. An executive at a medical insurance company was assembling a task force to study ways to increase the number of individual subscribers. A middle manager suggested Diane Chou as a possibility for this prestigious assignment. The executive responded, "Diane Chou, of course. A good choice. I just saw something about her in our newsletter." (True enough. Diane was in the newsletter for having placed first in a company bowling tournament.)

Attend Company-Sponsored Social Events

Being present at company-sponsored social events as a way of gaining the edge may appear to be a low-power political play. Yet done effectively, your physical presence at social events can create the name recognition you need to advance your cause. When introduced to a key person, smile, shake his or her hand firmly, and enunciate your name slowly and clearly. Attending company social events is also important because it connotes your identification with the organization. Socializing with co-workers conveys the impression that the company is a meaningful part of your life.

Sven Schiller works for a computer consulting firm in Germany. He believes that the most effective self-promotion tactic for him has been his active involvement in company socials. Sven was pleased with how well he got to know colleagues, higher-ups, and support staff after attending his first two company-sponsored social events. Sven decided to exploit this opportunity further. He volunteered to organize a New Year's Eve bash and a Secretary's Day Party. The president of the firm sent Sven a personal thank you note for his efforts. Sven believes that he has a secure future in his firm and attributes some of his image building to his active involvement in company social functions.

Choose the Most Visible Assignments

A hard-hitting tactic for achieving visibility is to work on assignments the company values highly. If top management has invested emotional energy in a project, a person associated with the success of the project is surrounded with a positive halo. Even being a mediocre performer on a key project can garner visibility. If top management cares little about the outputs of your assignment, even successful accomplishment will not create much visibility.

Lance Bolles was a program manager for a company that refurbished and resold computers. Keeping his political antennae raised, he learned that top management wanted to step up the resale of personal computers. Although reselling personal computers was not a glamorous endeavor, the profit margins on used PCs was high. Furthermore, the demand was strong and consistent.

Lance approached his boss and volunteered to be assigned to the personal computer project. His boss agreed, and Lance was placed in charge of the acquisition and refurbishing of used personal computers. The program continued to be a success, and Lance was required to present status reports to top management. The PC program became a major factor in the promotion of Lance to vice president of operations.

Bring a Festering Problem to the Attention of Top Management

Bringing a potentially serious problem to management's attention before it becomes a crisis usually achieves immediate recognition for the problem-spotter. Your efforts will be appreciated because top management is keenly aware of the importance of preventing a crisis. Ned Garcia worked as a telemarketer in a consumer electronics company. Twice he heard rumblings of discontent about compensation among the outside sales representatives. Four of them were so dissatisfied that they planned to quit en masse to join a main competitor.

Ned gingerly approached his boss, the sales manager, to discuss the rumors he had heard. Acutely interested in Ned's information, the sales manager listened to Ned's findings. He then scheduled a three-way meeting between himself, Ned, and the vice president of marketing. Based on Ned's input, the sales manager and the vice president met with the sales representatives. Ned's observations proved to be true. Shortly thereafter, the company announced a new compensation package for the outside sales representatives. Ned, too, benefited from his heroic act in the form of a larger-than-expected salary increase.

Observe that Ned was not a true snitch. He did not identify the specific representatives who planned to leave. Instead, he brought an important problem to management's attention. In the process, Ned was now known by top management for positive reasons, and was also rewarded financially.

MAKE SUGGESTIONS FOR ACHIEVING CORPORATE GOALS

The major task of top management is to establish corporate goals and develop plans for achieving them. Any activity of people down the organization that helps achieve goal attainment is therefore much appreciated. Conversely, activities that do not appear related to corporate goals will receive scant attention. Corporate goals typically involve earning money, reducing expenses, staying within budget, providing a safe and healthy work place, and doing some social good. To earn your share of visibility, you are therefore advised to make suggestions of the following type:

❖ Our company can increase market share by targeting a few ethnic groups and can modify our products to match their interests.

❖ We can reach our target customers much better by shifting to direct mailings and telemarketing and away from media advertising.

❖ We can increase profits by 350,000 this year by increasing our shipping and handling costs by $1.00

per order. Our shipping and handling costs will still be competitive.

❖ By adjusting the thermostat up four degrees during the warm season, and down four degrees during the cold season, we can save $175,000 per year in energy costs.

❖ We can increase the health of our work force substantially if we replace most of the soft-drink and candy vending machines with those serving fruits juices, fruit, and whole-grain foods.

❖ By donating $350,000 this year to youth centers in the poorest neighborhood in the city, we can reduce crime and drug abuse substantially.

Mary Ketchum, a purchasing manager, submitted a proposal to management that if implemented would contribute to attaining several corporate goals simultaneously. Mary recommended that the company use desktop publishing to replace outside printing services. This act alone would save the company about $70,000 per year. Mary also recommended that the company provide desktop publishing services to other companies located in the same office tower. The combination of money saved and money earned on this suggestion netted the company $106,000 in the first year. Mary received a letter of commendation from top management and within one year was promoted to purchasing manager.

QUANTIFY YOUR UNIT'S CONTRIBUTION TO THE ORGANIZATION

A surefire way of impressing top management is to demonstrate quantitatively how your unit is contributing to organizational welfare. In most instances, the quantification would be expressed in financial terms. For example, if you are a branch manager you might provide top management an informal annual report. Your report would state all the sales generated by your branch and all the expenses charged against those sales. These include salaries, rent, travel and entertainment, and your fair share of corporate overhead. The difference between the sales of your branch and your expenses is a statement of your net contribution to the organization.

Departments that do not receive money from outside customers can also quantify their contribution in financial terms. The manager of a corporate fitness center might calculate how much money the center saved the company in terms of decreased medical claims, absenteeism, and lost productivity. Considerable research and guesswork would be required to produce these figures. The net contribution of the unit to corporate welfare would be the difference between the gross savings and the expenses of the fitness center. Many directors of corporate fitness centers follow the procedures we have just described.

If your unit's work cannot be quantified in terms of dollars, objectify your contribution in terms of important activities. Such indicators of contributions include the number of customer complaints processed, the number of accident victims given first aid, or the number of quality problems repaired.

Gary Matthews, a United Parcel Service manager, found an effective way of quantifying his contribution. Gary decided to construct an income statement of his net value to UPS. His expenses included salary and benefits, truck expenses, office space, and an estimate of his prorated share of corporate overhead. The shipping fees derived from his unit's shipments represented his revenue. The difference between Gary's revenues and expenses equalled his contribution to the corporation. Gary received a substantial raise the first year he submitted his income statement. "One of the reasons I received such a big raise was that my boss's boss was very impressed with my accounting approach to business," said Gary.

Quantifying your contribution can give you the edge because most executives (in both profit and nonprofit) firms place a high value on numbers. Empirical evidence, especially expressed in financial terms, is highly valued. If you frame your contribution in terms of numbers you appeal to a deeply ingrained value. Such a tactic is akin to making an appeal to an evangelist in terms of its religious consequences.

TURN IN COMMAND PERFORMANCES AT MEETINGS

Meetings are a natural showcase for demonstrating your capabilities to others, including higher-ups. Top management typically has to rely on meetings as the only opportunity for forming impressions of lower-ranking people. Keep in mind this checklist of activities for turning in a command performance at meetings. By putting these points into action you are likely to impress others attending the meeting, including any top manager.

1. *Come to the meeting prepared so you can make an intelligent contribution.* Study the agenda and get your facts together to support your position on issues. Bring any necessary documentation with you, including charts, slides, and overheads.

2. *Make the right amount of contribution.* The person who dominates a meeting is perceived just as negatively as the noncontributor.

3. *Ask penetrating questions, particularly of higher-ups.* An intelligent person asks penetrating, perceptive questions. You show that you are listening by asking intelligent questions. Two multipurpose penetrating questions are: "How does what you have proposed fit corporate strategy?" and "What message does this meeting have for employees throughout the organization?"

4. *Be punctual and stay for the entire meeting.* Apologizing for being late or leaving early is unimpressive. It is better to organize your day so you can commit yourself to the full meeting.

5. *Keep your comments brief and pointed.* One of the major problems facing the meeting leader is to keep conversations on track. Staying focused will impress an impatient, time-hungry executive.

6. *Be supportive of people you are trying to impress.* When an executive at the meeting says something you think is valuable, express approval by such means as nodding your head or smiling. He or she will feel reinforced, and you are likely to be remembered.

7. *Listen carefully to the meeting leader and other participants.* Show by your nonverbal behavior that you are concerned about what they are saying. For example, look attentive and enthusiastic—especially when the higher up you are trying to impress is speaking.

8. *Take your turn at being the leader during the meeting.* To accomplish this you might volunteer to make a report during the meeting or head a subcommittee that will report back to the group later.

9. *Formulate creative solutions to problems in full view of others.* If a tough problem is presented for possible solution, think aloud and show people how you can solve tough problems on the spot. Reveal your problem-solving process with a statement such as, "As I visualize the alternatives, one has a glow around it as being clearly the best. It signals a call for action." (This activity is impressive because the essence of a productive person is one who can quickly solve difficult problems.)

10. *Avoid disruptive behavior, such as belittling another participant, frequent laughter, nail clipping, wallet cleaning, newspaper reading, napping, or yawning.*

Many a career has been set back because of poor etiquette displayed in a meeting.

RUN YOUR OPERATION AS IF YOU OWNED THE BUSINESS

Top executives would like employees at every level to act as if they were owners of a small part of the business. In support of this attitude, companies such as Cypress Semiconductor, Inc., divide a large business into as many small units as feasible. Each unit becomes its own profit center. The tactic described here about calculating your unit's net worth to the firm supports the idea of acting as if you owned your chunk of the business.

An important aspect of playing the role of a business owner is controlling costs. The small-business owner recognizes clearly that every dollar spent in running the business comes directly out of potential profit. Furthermore, in most manufacturing firms it requires about $100 in sales to have the same profit impact as $10 saved in expenses. This is true because if $100 worth of goods is sold, only about $10 is gross profit. The other $90 is spent on raw material, salaries, and miscellaneous overhead. If you saved $10 by turning off lights the effect on profits would be the same as selling $100 worth of goods. In retailing, it might take $500 in sales to produce the same profits as $10 in savings.

Another important way of acting as if you were a business owner within a larger organization is to keep abreast of the competition. Assume you manage the credit department within a department store. You are the self-appointed "President of Credit Services, Inc." You study the competition by learning how other retail store credit managers run their operations. Speak to people in your network; apply for a charge account at a competitor; interview people who have done the same.

In the previous chapter you met Jack Newcomb, a vice president of sales at an air freight company. While he was a terminal manager, Jack conducted the business as if he were the owner. By adopting this attitude, Jack would monitor even the most minor details. He worked closely with everyone from the drivers up to his operations manager. Jack conveyed the impression to everyone that he cared deeply about the success of the terminal and the welfare of the people.

Jack took a personal interest in all instances of customer dissatisfaction. He called for immediate action on customer problems. Jack told employees he could be reached 24 hours a day to assist in resolving customer dissatisfaction. Every employee in the terminal was given Jack's home phone and cellular numbers.

Jack's extreme dedication was recognized and appreciated by top management at the freight company, and it facilitated his climb to the executive suite. Executives in most companies are impressed by business-owner attitudes among company managers and employees. Successful business owners are more than conscientious. They take each success and each failure personally, and each customer is a treasured resource. Most top managers realize that these kinds of attitudes facilitate the survival of the organization. You therefore will gain the edge by running your operation as if you were the owner.

PASS ALONG POSITIVE FEEDBACK FROM CUSTOMERS

Favorable comments from customers are cherished by top management. Passing along positive customer feedback can benefit you significantly. A bearer of good news often bathes in the glory of the message. If you can state convincingly to a member of top management that a customer is satisfied, you have engaged in a positive interaction with that executive. A favorable interaction leads to a favorable attitude toward you as well as the customer.

Jake Meyers worked as a sales representative for an investment banking firm. Jake's specialty was selling municipal bonds to business corporations, pensions funds, and endowment portfolios of colleges and universities. When Jake received positive comments from clients who had benefited from their investments, he would pass along the news to his boss, the vice president of tax-exempt investments. Jake noticed that the comments were received very favorably by his boss.

Jake learned that these positive comments from customers were passed along to other principals in the firm. In one instance, Jake was chatting with an administrative assistant to an executive in the mergers and acquisition department. She told him that she had heard about one of his clients who was very pleased with the investments Jake had recommended.

Encouraged by the power of positive feedback, Jake decided to make systematic use of these comments. One of his clients, the endowment-fund manager at a private college, was enthusiastic about the contribution of municipal funds to the college's portfolio. Jake asked her if she might write a memo describing her satisfaction. The endowment fund manager obliged. At the core of her memo was this statement: "The relatively high yield on our selection of municipal bonds has preserved the value of our endowment during a two-year period when the stock market faltered. Without the high yields and preservation of capital provided by our wisely chosen municipal bonds, the value of our endowment would have declined precipitously. This might have created a shortfall in funds for operating the college."

Jake photocopied this glowing commentary from the endowment-fund manager and made it the subject of an FYI memo. Jake's boss in turn made his own batch of photocopies and sent them to principals of the firm. Jake is convinced that his year-end bonus was enhanced because of his legerdemain. Jake had gained the edge because he appealed to the most vital interest of a business-oriented executive group—being liked by clients.

VOLUNTEER FOR LEADERSHIP ASSIGNMENTS

A high-impact tactic for impressing upper management is to volunteer (and be selected for) leadership assignments related to the firm. Such assignments include task forces, special projects, committees, and important community projects. Accepting leadership responsibility helps you gain the edge in two meaningful ways. First, you are perceived as well-motivated and willing to serve the needs of the organization. Second, you have an opportunity to demonstrate leadership. Many managers rightfully believe that leadership skill demonstrated in one assignment is a strong indicator that you can effectively manage another function.

Elaine Spaulding was an office supervisor at a gas and electric utility, an organization with a vested interest in being socially responsible. For several years she had contributed some of her discretionary time to conducting routine functions for the local chapter of the Association for Retarded Persons (ARP). For example, she had helped them with mailings to collect pledged donations and with conducting field trips for the mentally disabled.

Elaine's ARP chapter had grown so big that it needed additional administrative help. Elaine volunteered to serve as the chapter's vice president of administration. She received permission from her employer to spend some work time making phone calls in relation to her community work. After occupying the administrative position for six months, Elaine was given an award from ARP for her several years of meritorious service. A story ran in the local newspaper about Elaine's award, along with a compliment for her company for sponsoring the activity.

Elaine's accomplishments impressed top management at the gas and electric company. They also believed that the newspaper mention of the company as helping the Associated for Retarded Citizens was precisely the public image the utility wanted to project. Shortly thereafter, Elaine's regular job responsibilities were expanded and she was promoted to office manager. Elaine did well by doing good. A similar approach might help you gain the edge.

BECOME A SUBJECT-MATTER EXPERT

As organizations have become increasingly dependent on complex knowledge, new opportunities have been created for impressing top management. The importance of having resident experts on new technology or other subject-matter has led to the new unofficial title of subject-matter expert. Being labeled a subject-matter expert (SME) can bring you favorable attention from top management. It is important to become an SME on a technology or topic that contributes to achieving a high-priority organizational purpose. Company training programs can serve as a vehicle for establishing oneself as a subject-matter expert.

Tom McRae had been working as a design assistant at a manufacturing company for four months. One day at lunchtime he overheard two trainers on the cafeteria line discussing the company's need for instruction in the new electronic mail system. Nearly 350 company employees had the electronic messaging system available to them, but few understood its operation.

The two trainers knew that this computer-based training called for small-group instruction and would therefore be time consuming and labor intensive. Despite the training department's limited resources, they were being pressured by several department heads and one vice president to get the system up and running.

Tom was familiar with the electronic mail system because it was the same one in operation as that at his previous employer. Tom offered to be the subject-matter expert to assist the trainers in course development. He also promised to spend up to 45 minutes per day in the E-mail training courses providing he could be spared by his department. Tom received the clearance from his boss.

With Tom acting as an additional trainer, the class sizes doubled. All company employees were trained in a short time. Tom's key role in training the trainers and in conducting some of the training himself had a career-enhancing outcome. Several managers, including the vice president of operations, talked glowingly about the new design assistant who pitched in so effectively. Tom was recognized for playing a key role in getting an expensive new system running for the company. His first salary increase was above average, reflecting his contribution as a subject-matter expert.

FIND INNOVATIVE SOLUTIONS TO OLD, NAGGING PROBLEMS

The same old, nagging problems plague some organizations year after year. Periodic efforts at fixing the problem are to no avail. After a slight improvement, the problem returns, much like a muscle torn years ago that hurts again when the body experiences stress. Even the Cadillac division of General Motors has not been immune from an unusual nagging problem. A small proportion of young buyers, even among the affluent, purchase a Cadillac. The median age of the owner of a Cadillac Brougham, for example, is sixty-seven. The nagging problem is that Cadillac would like to attract a larger number of youthful buyers in order to expand its market.

One extreme measure taken by Cadillac to cure this problem was to introduce the Cimmaron, a compact car with a Cadillac nameplate. The expectation was that the Cimmaron would appeal to youthful buyers. Young car buyers never cooperated, and old buyers wanted their big Cadillacs, so production was halted on the Cimmaron. Top management at Cadillac was then left with the same old nagging problem.

Larry Olmstead, a warehouse manager for an industrial distributor, found an innovative solution to a nagging problem of lesser magnitude than the Cadillac problem. Nevertheless, it boosted the impression he created on top management. Larry's warehouse receives return material from customers daily. A persistent paperwork problem surrounded the process of dealing with returns. The paperwork necessary to ship the returns back to vendors and to process customer credits was frequently not ready before the return shipments arrived. At other times the paperwork was generated much before the material was returned. Because the paperwork arrived early, it was often mislaid. The result of paperwork arriving both early and late had caused much confusion and customer dissatisfaction.

Larry developed a paperwork system to cure this annoying problem for returns not arriving at the right time. The sales department was instructed to make a folder when the return authorization was given. The folder would contain the customer name, type of goods returned, and appropriate credit information. Should the material arrive before the paperwork arrives, a packing slip would be stored in the folder. Should the credit or vendor-return papers arrive before the returned goods arrive, the papers would be stored in a folder awaiting the merchandise.

Larry's simple folder system ended a lot of confusion, and he was commended by management for his efforts. His innovation was low-tech but eminently useful, and it cured a customer dissatisfaction problem. One might argue that an up-to-date computerized inventory system could have cured the problem. However, this industrial distributor was not ready to invest in such a system.

KEY IN ON HOT PROJECTS

A recurring underlying theme to gaining the edge is to appeal to the needs and interests of people whom you are trying to impress. Yet another variation on this tactic is to key in on hot projects within your organization. Top management becomes impressed with your efforts because you have responded to an urgent need. John Hartwick, an assistant manager in a paint store, employed this tactic in a straightforward and effective manner.

John recognized that the company was concerned about the possible adverse impact household paint could have on the environment. Aside from wanting to be a good corporate citizen, the paint manufacturer knew that environmental groups can create havoc with a company's image. John keyed into this important project in a novel way. Most retail outlets for the company held consumer seminars periodically that gave customer suggestions about painting and wall papering. John added to these seminars information about how to properly dispose of leftover paints, thinners, and tar removers. Ecologically-minded customers were pleased that the company was concerned about the proper disposal of substances that could damage the environment.

Regional management heard favorably about John's environmental seminars. He received a formal letter of appreciation for his efforts. Of more specific impact to John's career, he received the next available promotion to store manager in his city. John gained the edge by initiating work on a project of importance to the corporation.

John took a sharply targeted approach to keying in on a hot project. A variation of this procedure is to bring potentially relevant information to the company's attention. If you bring forth enough information, you might make a proper hit. Rebecca Walters worked as a receptionist at a medium-size medical supply company. She regularly read newspapers and magazines to find articles pertaining to medical supplies. In addition, Rebecca also conducted library research on the topic.

During a company brunch, Rebecca struck up a conversation with her supervisor's manager about current events that could affect the demand for medical supplies. Among the events she mentioned was the accelerating increase of people over the age of eighty in the population. The manager was impressed with Rebecca's interest in the company and with her research. He spoke to Rebecca's supervisor and recommended that she be kept in mind for a promotion.

Several months later an administrative assistant resigned, and Rebecca was asked by her supervisor if she wished to be considered for the vacancy. Rebecca responded affirmatively, and she received the one-step promotion. By displaying an interest in projects of potential concern to the company, Rebecca was discovered. She gained the edge in the sense that her career is on an upward track. Rebecca was also told that with additional schooling, she would be eligible for a supervisory position in the future.

BECOME A CRISIS MANAGER

A high-powered tactic for impressing top management is to effectively handle a crisis or near-crisis. A crisis is a moment of truth that puts the company's welfare or very existence on the line. Helping the company work its way out of chaos requires both inspirational leadership and careful planning. Follow these general steps for crisis resolution:

1. *Calm down and start thinking.* No matter how bad the crisis, take at least an hour or two to think before acting. Impulsive acts might dig a bigger hole.

2. *Clarify the problem.* What is the real problem created by this crisis? Perhaps the crisis has created a credibility problem or a financial problem. Sometimes the crisis has created both, such as a defective product threatening the health of consumers.

3. *Search for creative alternatives.* What options are open? Many managers facing a crisis choose stonewalling the problem over dealing with it openly. In the process they exacerbate the crisis.

4. *Make a choice.* If the crisis is to be resolved, you must make a tough decision at some point.

5. *Develop an action plan and implement.* Now that you have chosen an alternative solution, formulate the specific steps that must be taken to get out of the mess.

6. *Evaluate outcomes.* Did the crisis-management plan work or will you have to try another alternative? A cautionary note: If your first plan fails you may not be invited to try another.

Ted Garland worked as a service engineer for a manufacturer of computer-based medical equipment. He provides an apt example of crisis management. As Ted explains it: "I volunteered for a suicide mission and came back alive. The project required the development of a game plan for the national installation of a major software upgrade. This was a critical project because the upgrade was supposed to solve several serious problems plaguing the equipment. We had lost key accounts, and the other users were screaming. If all the accounts had left, the company would have faced bankruptcy.

"Another gory detail was that the upgrade had to be accomplished with the minimum amount of machine downtime. I would be personally responsible for contacting each district service manager and coordinating with him or her the schedule of service technician training, shipment of the upgrade kit, and the installation schedule. Any problems that occurred would be directly attributed to me. Such was the suicide portion of the project.

"Just when I was about to implement the first upgrade, my manager wanted to see me right away. He told me that the director of marketing and service and the national service manager wanted a presentation of my game plan. Fortunately, I had enough sense to have quickly but carefully developed one.

"The emergency upgrades solved the software problems. Several district service managers called my manager to express gratitude for my support. Volunteering for a project whose failure could have meant my demise worked for me.

Everybody in the executive suite now knew who I was, and I had also created other allies in the company."

Ted successfully managed a crisis and thereby elevated his status in the company. Furthermore, Ted received excellent experience. Crises are inevitable in organizations, and crisis managers will always be in demand. Ted followed the precepts of crisis management in that he had a game plan based on a careful assessment of available alternatives. Like other successful crisis managers, Ted is now known as a troubleshooter—a powerful accolade to receive when one is trying to gain the edge.

IDENTIFY AND TRAIN YOUR REPLACEMENT

A management shibboleth is that effective managers identify and train replacements for themselves. If a ready replacement is not available you might be excluded from consideration for an immediate promotion. Insecure managers are hesitant to identify and train a replacement because they are concerned about being fired once a successor is ready. Because insecurity does not impress most top managers, it pays to proceed with developing your successor.

After you have identified a person with potential as your possible replacement, give him or her the chance to take over your job temporarily. A logical time for such pinch hitting is when you are away from the office for two or more weeks. When you receive the nod for a possible promotion, point to the fact that your potential successor has experience in handling your position.

Laura Walsh, an advertising and sales promotion manager at a food manufacturer, used an unusual approach to identifying and training a successor. Laura worked in the company's Cincinnati office, but was under consideration for a regional managership based in Los Angeles. In addition to being a growth opportunity for Laura, she wanted to move to Los Angeles for personal reasons. Her husband was an electrical engineer who had lost his job in Cincinnati and could not find another one in the area. However, he did find new employment in Los Angeles.

Although Laura was being considered for a promotion, her company was being downsized. Middle managers were especially targeted. A flash of insight hit Laura: "Why not identify a manager on the corporate hit list as a possible replacement for me?" After a few inquiries, Laura was able to find a master list of managers likely to be offered early retirement. Working with her boss and a member of the human resources department, Laura identified a manager with previous advertising and sales promotion experience.

Laura was granted permission to speak to this man about the potential vacancy in her department. However, Laura went one step further. She explained the details of her job to this man who had plenty of time to invest. Most of his time recently had been devoted to conducting an external job search. After several weeks of coaching the manager about her job, Laura scheduled a meeting with her boss. Laura explained that she had now identified and trained an ideal replacement for herself.

The company agreed that the man scheduled for early retirement would be a satisfactory replacement as the advertising and sales promotion manager. Laura consequently received her promotion to regional marketing manager based in Los Angeles. She had also impressed upper management with her good sense to look outside the department to train a replacement.

DISPLAY A POSITIVE ATTITUDE
TOWARD CHANGE

Most executives are aware that the ability to respond positively to change is an essential characteristic in today's work place. The person who develops the reputation of being responsive to constructive change will therefore be at an advantage. Take the accompanying self-quiz to provide a tentative measurement of your responsiveness toward change.

ATTITUDE TOWARD CHANGE

Instructions: Respond to each statement, 1, 2, 3, 4, or 5, using this scale: 5 = strongly agree; 4 = agree; 3 = neutral; 2 = agree; 1 = strongly disagree.

1. Having to relocate geographically is an exciting adventure. _____

2. Changing jobs is an enjoyable challenge. _____

3. Redecorating the home every few years is uplifting, providing it can be afforded. _____

4. I dislike visiting the same place for vacation year after year. _____

5. It would be terrible for me to work for one employer for the rest of my career. _____

6. I welcome using new electronic gadgets in my job. _____

7. Stability and predictability bore me both on and off the job. _____

8. I feel relaxed when I know that changes are soon to come at work. _____

9. I readily volunteer ideas for new work procedures. _____

10. From time to time I have tried new hobbies and recreational interests. _____

Scoring: A total score of 45–50 suggests that you strongly welcome change, and your flexibility should be an asset on the job. A score of 30–44 shows that you have average attitudes toward coping with change. You often welcome change, but sometimes resist it needlessly. A score of 29 or less suggests that you have difficulty coping with change. Try to become more flexible by experimenting with small constructive changes.

FILL AN UNMET NEED IN THE ORGANIZATION

Because most organizations believe in continual improvements, you can gain an edge by filling an unmet need. To begin the process, you must first be perceptive enough to identify a problem. Mike Higgins, an aerospace engineer, supplies us a good example of gaining advantage by filling an unmet need. The professionals in Mike's group complained that the engineering library was too far away from their location to be useful. Mike responded to this concern by informally surveying the group to learn what they needed from a company library and what resources they already had.

Mike's survey indicated that a large part of the needs could be met with resources that were already available. These resources included corporate and personal subscriptions to technical journals and magazines and personal book collections. Mike hit upon the idea of a minilibrary to serve the needs of the group. He approached his group leader and the department manager with his idea. Mike was able to convince them to allocate an office area that would serve as a central storage area for all company reading material held by the group as well as for donated reading material. The response from the group was very positive. Soon the library became a clearinghouse for the resources of the entire department.

Word about Mike's endeavors traveled up to the vice president of engineering, who commended him on facilitating professional updating. Mike's spearheading a minilibrary gave him an edge in the eyes of the vice president because professional updating is an important organizational value.

CLEAR DEVIATIONS FROM POLICY
WITH HIGHER-UPS

Only the most flexible organizations tolerate frequent deviations from company policy. To be recognized for your good judgment, it is therefore important to touch base with your manager on controversial points. Your manager is likely to be perplexed also and will therefore check with the next level of management. As a result, upper management will become aware of your respect for company policy.

Joe Morano worked as an order specialist in a beverage-distribution center. The office supervisor often made on-the-spot changes in policy based on customer needs. These changes were often confused by supervisors and were subsequently implemented inconsistently on different occasions. Whenever Joe recognized that there was substantial controversy, he clarified the situation with the office supervisor. Typically, the supervisor suggested that Joe check with the manager of the distribution center (the supervisor's boss). Joe soon acquired the reputation for high-quality work and attention to detail. Notice that Joe did not run around his boss, but tactfully checked with him first when an area of confusion arose.

DECORATE YOUR OFFICE TO SHOW
LOYALTY AND DEDICATION

A low-key tactic for being noticed by higher ups who visit your work area is through office decorations that reflect loyalty and dedication. The technique can be effective because it reflects identification with the corporate goals. Lisa Vanderstyne, a telecommunications specialist, decorated her cubicle with posters reflecting the company's achievement. One photograph showed President George Bush shaking hands with the company president upon the company's receipt of an Outstanding Quality Award. Her decoration received favorable commentary from a corporate vice president who was visiting company facilities.

One way of using office decorations to show dedication is to display books whose subject fits the corporate mission. If the organization is pushing productivity and quality, conspicuously display books on time management, managing for quality, and customer service. For a finishing touch, keep a book on business ethics in full view. Most employers prefer to think of themselves as ethical even if reality is otherwise.

BE A GOODWILL AMBASSADOR
FOR YOUR FIRM

A high-level tactic for gaining the edge through impressing top management is to become a goodwill ambassador for your firm. Several mechanisms are available for becoming a goodwill ambassador. Knowing these methods may spark your thinking to find others. Some organizations have speaker's bureaus, whereby a select group of people are on call to speak to community groups. The talks can be on any general purpose topic such as "The Stake of Business in Improving Secondary Education," "The Importance of International Trade," or "How Business Is Helping the Environment."

If your employer does not have a speaker's bureau, suggest the idea and volunteer to be one of the speakers. If the speaker's bureau idea is rejected, you can still give talks in the community as a representative of your company. Telephone local clubs, associations, and community groups and volunteer to give a free talk. Let your boss and upper management know of your speaking appearances.

You can also become a goodwill ambassador for your company by volunteering in the community and letting people know that your employer supports your activities. Finally, whenever you are in public make positive mention of your employer. Talk about the good deeds the company is doing to make your community a better place to live. Track down people who have communication links with top management and make your laudatory statements about the company in their presence. A Honda of America supervisor used this approach to goodwill ambassadorship, and he reports: "Let my critics say I have the word Honda tattooed on my chest. Top management admires my loyalty, and that's what counts."

To help focus on all the information contained in this chapter, here is an outline of the major suggestions for impressing top management:

1. Be visible in any positive, sensible way.
2. Make suggestions for achieving corporate goals.
3. Quantify your unit's contribution to the organization.
4. Turn in command performances at meetings.
5. Run your operation as if you owned the business.
6. Pass along positive feedback from customers.
7. Volunteer for leadership assignments.
8. Become a subject-matter expert.
9. Find innovative solutions to old, nagging problems.
10. Key in on hot projects.
11. Become a crisis manager.
12. Identify and train your replacement.
13. Display a positive attitude toward change.
14. Fill an unmet need in the organization.
15. Clear deviations from policy with higher-ups.
16. Decorate your office to show loyalty and dedication.
17. Be a goodwill ambassador for your firm.

❖ 5 ❖

GETTING CO-WORKERS ON YOUR SIDE

To accomplish your work, it is essential to gain the edge with people at your own job level. If you lack the cooperation of co-workers, colleagues, teammates, or team members you will be shutting yourself off from valuable assistance in doing your job. Furthermore, if you lack the support of co-workers you are unlikely to be chosen for promotion. Before someone is approved for promotion, co-workers are often consulted about how well they would accept him or her as a leader.

Here we describe a variety of tactics for impressing co-workers so they will become your allies. With co-workers in your camp you multiply your chances of gaining an edge within your firm and in your career.

BE A TEAM PLAYER

A comprehensive strategy for gaining the edge with fellow workers is to be a good team player. An opinion survey I conducted of managers, professionals, sales, and administrative support workers bears out this observation. Forty-nine percent of men and 42 percent of women surveyed agreed that being a team player is an effective method of getting work accomplished.[1] Next we describe ten sensible and effective tactics for becoming a good team player. Equally important, all the other tactics described in this chapter will enhance your reputation as a team player.

Be a Cooperative Team Member

Cooperation is the essential ingredient for effective teamwork. If you display a willingness to help others and work cooperatively with them, you will be regarded as a team player. Organizations are designed with cooperation in mind. If people do not cooperate with one another the total system breaks down. Not all your co-workers are concerned about the smooth functioning of the total organization, but they do want cooperation from you. By being conspicuously cooperative, you gain the edge in terms of your boss's evaluation of you and the bank of goodwill you create with co-workers.

Kenny Chang, an information systems specialist, discovered a novel way to cooperate with team members that earned him high praise from his peers. Kenny has an extraordinary talent for fixing software problems, including helping combat computer viruses. To cooperate fully with his co-workers, Kenny gave them permission to call him anytime to help fix a software problem. After he unsnarled a few problems over the phone after midnight, his co-workers took him seriously. When a team leader position was created in the group, Kenny was the natural choice. He had gained the edge by being supercooperative.

Make the First Move to Gain Cooperation

Achieving a cooperative team spirit is often a question of making the first move. Instead of grumbling about poor teamwork, take the initiative and launch a cooperative spirit in your department. Pam McKinnon, an office assistant in a department of social services, felt that she was not receiving cooperation from her partner, Angie Bruin, on a particular project. Pam decided to offer to help Angie on one of her work assignments. Pam soon found that Angie became much more team oriented. Pam's first-move tactic communicated that she did not think there was competitive tension on the project.

Pam's initiative worked because Angie soon reciprocated. If Pam had waited for Angie to take the first step, competitive tension between the two might have arisen.

Be a Team Player Even When It Hurts

A teamwork tactic with a long-range perspective is to do what is best for the team even if it causes you immediate displeasure. By being inconvenienced, and even aggravated, in the present you may gain the edge in the intermediate term. Rick Abels was a team leader for a service team that maintained photocopiers in downtown Richmond, Virginia. Rick's boss was replaced by another manager in a company effort to boost productivity. Rick was pressured by the new manager to relinquish his team-leader title and return to being a full-time specialist.

Although hurting from the potential loss in status, Rick told his boss and his co-workers that he wanted to do what was best for the team. Rick worked cooperatively and cheerfully with his new boss and his teammates. Six months later Rick had the opportunity to interview for a supervisory position within the company. The hiring manager was generally impressed by Rick but was concerned that his technical qualifications were light. Rick's boss intervened on his behalf and talked glowingly about Rick's ability to learn technical information. The hiring manager was convinced, and Rick obtained the new position. The cooperative attitude he displayed when he relinquished his team-leader position became an investment in his short-term future.

Share the Glory

A not-to-be-overlooked tactic for emphasizing teamwork is to share credit for your accomplishments with the team. Glory-sharing is not just a manipulative ploy. If you work in a group other members of the team usually have contributed to the success of a project. Jim Krantz, a production supervisor, was recognized at a company meeting for reducing the production time on a critical component by 25 percent. Though Jim originated the productivity-improvement idea, he immediately mentioned several other supervisors and engineers who assisted him. By acknowledging the contribution of other workers at his level, Jim improved his status as a team player. Later that day a production engineer within the group gave Jim a handshake of appreciation.

Help Co-workers Do Their Jobs Better

Your stature as a team player will increase if you take the initiative to help co-workers make needed work improvements. Make the suggestions in a constructive spirit, rather than by displaying an air of superiority. Liz Peters, a software engineer, suggested to the group that they make their overview charts more exciting. She suggested that they add a logo, produce the charts in color, and be more creative. The change dramatically improved the presentations to user groups. People stayed more alert and interested during briefings. Liz received many words of appreciation for her dedication to the group cause.

Engage in Mutually Beneficial Exchanges

An effective team player regularly exchanges favors with co-workers. You explicitly or implicitly promise that the other person will benefit later if he or she complies with your request. A more coercive way to use exchange is to remind the co-worker that he or she "owes you one." A spirit of teamwork develops as group members engage in mutually beneficial exchanges. Here are a few work-place exchanges that can foster teamwork:

1. You agree to take care of an angry customer because one of your co-workers is too stressed today to absorb one more hassle.

2. You cover for a co-worker who needs a few hours off to speak to his or her divorce lawyer.

3. You agree to attend the Little League hockey game of a co-worker's son, providing he or she will attend one of your daughter's soccer games.

4. You help a team member prepare an overdue report, recognizing that you are now owed a favor.

Rarely Turn Down a Request from a Co-worker

Granting requests for help from co-workers is governed by the theory of reinforcement. If you comply with a request from a co-worker, he or she will be rewarded and return soon with another request. If you turn down more than a couple of requests, that co-worker will stop making requests. If you want to be left alone, just turn down a few requests. If you want to be perceived as a team player, however, accept any reasonable request.

Grant Hollingsworth, a hospital administrator, characteristically granted requests from co-workers to do such things as review their reports and budgets. When he didn't have the time, Grant found a way to turn down the request diplomatically. One of his most effective ways of turning down a request gently was, "I wish I could help you right now. Yet with my current workload, I won't be able to get to your project until Sunday afternoon." (Notice how guilty the mention of Sunday afternoon probably made the co-worker feel.) Using this hedge, Grant will be remembered as willing to help. Because Grant used his stalling technique only occasionally, it was effective.

Lend a Hand During Peak Workloads

A natural opportunity for being a good team player arises during peak workloads. If you have any slack time volunteer to help a peer who is overloaded. Even an hour or two of assistance to take some pressure off a co-worker will strengthen your role as a team player. Your psychological costs in using this technique can be reduced if you help out on activities you can easily handle. Nancy Bloom explains how she lends a hand during peak workloads: "Sometimes the owner of the company I work for gives his executive secretary several high-priority tasks to do on short notice. When this happens, I will offer my assistance in doing some of the other paperwork she is responsible for that does not have the same priority as her new assignment.

"I offer to do tasks I am familiar with, such as the Equal Employment Opportunity compliance forms. Of course, I don't help out if it will put me behind in my other work. I definitely think that by my helping out we have a better atmosphere of teamwork."

Be Highly Dependable

An important development in the work place is an emphasis on work teams whereby the group handles a large task. A work team in the office might issue insurance policies and pay insurance claims. Each team member is a generalist who helps with a variety of small tasks. A cooperative team spirit is essential for these groups. An important way to keep this team spirit alive is for each member to be highly dependable. Absenteeism, for example, is frowned upon.

Jerry Katona, a team member at a Xerox manufacturing plant, notes: "We have a spirit of brotherhood and sisterhood working in our Team Xerox unit. Anyone who lets us down is regarded as a poor team player. It would be the same as if a member of a basketball team decided to goof off on the night of an important game."

Keep up the Team Spirit When Things Are Going Poorly

A final method here for being a team player is to take on the role of the motivator when the team hits a snag. Help keep the group focused on possible favorable outcomes even if the situation appears bleak. Jason Williams was a copywriter at an advertising firm that was hard hit by a decrease in client advertising. His message to the group was that advertising always runs in cycles. Jason also noted that the bottom point had already been reached.

Jason encouraged the team by reminding them that management was attempting to increase advertising activity outside the usual channels. Jason proved to be right. The firm soon landed a few big contracts to conduct direct mail advertising. The payout to Jason was that team spirit had not deteriorated, and two colleagues told Jason that they appreciated his support.

UNDERSTAND THE JOBS OF TEAM MEMBERS

A meritorious way of impressing co-workers is to understand their jobs. One reason that the understanding creates a positive impression is because it allows you to communicate more fully with peers. Understanding the jobs of others is also helpful because it places you in a position to appreciate the complexity of your teammates' jobs. Many people feel that other people do not appreciate the complexity and demands of their job. If you show an appreciation for the challenges faced by a co-worker he or she will feel understood and accepted by you. You have therefore created a positive impression that can give you the edge when you need help from that person.

Cindy Baldwin, a registered dietician at a hospital, makes good use of the tactic of understanding the jobs of team members. An important feature of Cindy's work is

patient assessments in which a team of health-care professionals jointly discuss the health status of a hospital patient.
Cindy knows her job quite well, and she also makes it a point
to understand the jobs of other health-care professionals she
works with. Cindy has even conducted interviews with others to understand their orientation toward patient care.

Cindy explains why understanding the jobs of teammates has created a positive impression: "My understanding
the jobs of others helps reduce conflict in our patient assessments. Instead of my pounding my fists and saying that
proper diet will cure everything, I listen patiently. Then I
contribute a few words about how nutrition relates to the
case at hand. I think my ideas are taken more seriously
because I do not suffer from tunnel vision."

Cindy has thus gained a professional edge through
understanding and empathy. Recognize that attempting to
understand what others do can also be a multipurpose tactic.
Most people will be impressed if you understand them.

RECOGNIZE THE ACCOMPLISHMENTS
OF TEAM MEMBERS

A pervasive human need is to achieve recognition. A corner-
stone of the ever-popular Dale Carnegie training programs
is that people want to feel important. If you can learn to
comfortably and genuinely recognize the accomplishments
of co-workers (and anybody else) your impression will be
enhanced. An important guideline is to make the recognition
appropriate to the magnitude of the good deed. A well-in-
tentioned sales representative learned that one of the reps in
the office brought in a difficult-to-attain account. The first rep
bought the second rep a trophy with the inscription, "World
Class Salesman." The second representative responded, "I
appreciate the thought, but I get the feeling that you are
patronizing me."

Here are some examples of giving recognition to co-
workers that are inexpensive and psychologically sound.

They all achieved their purposes of creating favorable impressions.

❖ Jerry Pullyblank, a credit analyst, was out of work ill for two weeks. During his absence, his co-workers pitched in and took over his most important chores. When Jerry returned to work he was not behind. In recognition of their help, Jerry held an "appreciation morning break" in which he brought to the office donuts, bagels, cream cheese, and fruit juice.

❖ Janet Colgate, a college professor, heard that a colleague published a research article in a journal that accepts only 10 percent of all articles submitted. Janet wrote him a note, saying: "Your extraordinary accomplishment creates a luster for our entire department." When it came time for Janet's colleague to vote on her promotion to full professor, he made an enthusiastic presentation about Janet's contribution to the college.

❖ Helmut Ulrich, a contracts administrator in an aerospace company, worked for three years to hammer out a contract that was acceptable to the Pentagon. Another contract administrator in the group used computer graphics to print out a huge sign that said, "Congratulations, Helmut Ulrich, Red Tape Buster." Helmut was touched by the recognition and impressed by the recognition giver.

❖ Margot Pasternak, an accounts-payable specialist, was driving on the highway one Friday night when she noticed a car crash up ahead. Margot pulled over and arrived before the ambulances. She applied a compress to a hemorrhaging six year old. The ambulance medic acknowledged that Margot saved the child's life; a newspaper account of the incident appeared locally. Ralph Barnes, a co-worker of Margot, read the story. He organized a heroine's welcome for Margot when she returned to the office on Monday morning, including a crepe-paper banner and confetti.

SHOW CONCERN ABOUT THE PERSONAL PROBLEMS OF CO-WORKERS

A straightforward human relations tactic for creating a positive impression on co-workers is to show concern for their personal problems and misfortunes. Such concern is justified for humanitarian reasons. Another justification is that an important function served by the work group is to provide emotional support to members. One reason many people dislike telecommuting or working in a very small office is the limited opportunity for emotional support.

Try to find the right balance between morbid curiosity and snooping versus a genuine display of concern. If you show sincere concern for the adversity faced by a peer, you will help strengthen the bond between the two of you. Dolores Matsuko, an engineering technician, was told that her father had lung cancer. The prognosis was that he had a short time to live. Dolores, along with her other family members, took the impending death quite hard.

After telling her boss of the crisis, he expressed concern and allowed Dolores to leave work early on several occasions to take her father for radiation treatments. Nancy Adams, a co-worker, learned about Dolores's problem. She encouraged Dolores to talk about her concerns and then explained how she had gone through the death of her mother, also caused by cancer. Dolores's father died within three months, and the concern that Nancy showed for her contributed to Dolores's overcoming the adversity.

BECOME AN INFORMAL LEADER

Work groups all have a formal leader, one who is appointed by the organization. In addition to the formal leader, many groups have an informal leader, a take-charge person who accepts many leadership responsibilities within the group. For example, an informal leader might express the group opinion on an important issue to management. Emerging as an informal leader usually impresses co-workers because it is more difficult to exercise leadership when you lack the authority granted by the organization.

The informal leader is also the team member whose opinion is taken the most seriously. In many instances the formal leader of a group, such as the manager, will present an idea to the informal leader that he or she wants the group to accept. If the informal leader accepts the idea, he or she will sell that idea to the group. During a problem-solving session, the informal leader is often looked to for a creative alternative solution. When a party is contemplated, the informal leader is often asked to choose the location and theme and make the arrangements.

Being the informal leader is worthwhile because it elevates one's self-esteem and self-confidence. The informal leadership role is also likely to be noticed by management and enhances one's credentials for a formal leadership role. You can work toward becoming the informal leader through such actions as:

- ❖ Carefully developing your ideas and then presenting them to the group during a meeting.

- ❖ Making frequent suggestions to the group about work improvements.

- ❖ Taking the initiative to organize social functions for the group, such as breakfasts, office parties, and house parties.

- ❖ Understanding the group's opinion on important work issues and then presenting that viewpoint to management.

- ❖ Volunteering to act as the scribe during staff meetings and then distributing the minutes of the meetings within the next week.

BE COURTEOUS, PLEASANT, AND POSITIVE

According to employment specialist Robert Half, courteous, pleasant, and positive people are the first to be hired and the last to be fired (assuming they are also technically qualified).[2] The same characteristics and behaviors are very important in creating a positive impression on co-workers. Anybody with work experience or common sense recognizes this basic fact of human behavior. Nevertheless, not everybody puts this simple principle into practice. Many people are not aware of the self-defeating nature of being discourteous, unpleasant, and negative.

Alex Premack was a sales consultant at a branch location of a computer equipment store. The store sold to both private individuals and commercial accounts. Alex was amassing an outstanding sales record. He combined a sophisticated knowledge of computers and peripheral equipment with a high degree of assertiveness and refined interpersonal skills. Alex also impressed the store manager with his professionalism and his suave manner.

Alex's relationships with his co-workers were dramatically different from his interactions with customers and management. Alex was smug, indifferent, and often rude to the other sales representatives. Because Alex had considerable technical knowledge, he was often asked his opinion about a customer-related computer problem. Alex sometimes responded, "Can't you look that up in the manual?"

The sales staff's day of retribution soon came. Rob Lewis, the sales manager, was given the opportunity to become a regional executive. This meant that a new sales manager would have to be appointed. Rob approached the office manager, Eileen Walters, to discuss some of his thinking about appointing a new store manager. Rob casually mentioned, "Alex has been our outstanding producer for three years. He would seem like a natural person to appoint as the new store manager. What do you think?"

"That would be a horrible mistake," said Eileen. "Alex may be a good sales consultant and a good office politician when dealing with his superiors. But the guy is two-faced. He smiles at you and the customers. Yet he treats other people in the office like peons. I've heard that Alex is pretty bad with the other sales people. He's even worse with the office staff. He snaps at us as if we were servants.

"My guess is that if you make Alex the sales manager, we'll have many resignations."

Rob Lewis thanked Eileen for her useful commentary and said that he would weigh carefully what she had to say. Rob spoke to two sales consultants who corroborated in softer terms the points that Eileen made. The sales manager position was awarded to another sales consultant. Alex was perplexed as to why he was not selected for the position and asked to discuss the matter with Rob. He was told, "Alex, you seem to be oriented more toward dealing with customers than with internal people. We want to place players on the team where they can make the biggest contribution."

APPEAL TO YOUR CO-WORKERS' PERSONAL INTERESTS

A basic sales technique is to be familiar with the personal interests of your customers and then appeal to those interests before making a sales presentation. Similarly, managers are advised to relate to the interests of their employees. The same technique works well in cultivating relationships with co-workers. It is especially impressive for a co-worker to appeal to one's personal interests because such behavior is expected more from sales people and managers.

Just as a salesperson does, maintain files on your co-workers, either computerized or manual. Track important and obscure facts about each and mention these interests or ask questions about them at appropriate times. An example:

GERRI STEVENS

Single, usually has new boyfriend each month. Has dog with limp named Charlie. Prefers to talk about vacations rather than work. Mother has severe arthritis; father retired on permanent disability. Vegetarian and animal rights activist. Drinks red wine but won't touch beer or hard liquor. Prefers the Libertarian Party.

Update your cards periodically. Keeping your cards current helps avoid the mistake of asking about the health of a parent who died one year ago or about a relationship that no longer exists. The updated card system also helps you avoid the faux pas of calling a co-worker's spouse by the name of the co-worker's former spouse at a party.

BE PATIENT AND TOLERANT

Patience and tolerance with co-workers creates a positive impression because such treatment makes people feel more secure. The process works in this manner: A co-worker asks you a question about the new vacation schedule because he does not fully understand its implications. If he did understand it, he wouldn't be asking you the question. You begin to explain the implications of the schedule, and he is still confused. You become impatient at his lack of comprehension. Your impatience makes him tense, which further impairs his ability to understand the policy. If you are patient, perhaps he can overcome the block that is preventing him from understanding the policy.

Four professionals were working on the image software for an image-editing product. The four people had been working on the product since its beginning. Donna Albanese, another software engineer, joined the group after about one year. Donna said that each of the four engineers who had been there before her were very helpful. However, she was most impressed by John Barclay. "John just never seemed to tire of my questions even if they were basic. He was always willing to stop what he was doing to help me out.

"In several instances he had to explain things to me numerous times before it finally registered. John never lost his patience. I don't think I could have made it without John's help. He was a real inspiration."

John's patience and understanding benefited him also. Helping develop the professional skills of another person is an inherently pleasant activity and is therefore self-rewarding. Also, John has now created a strong ally whom he can count on in the future as needed.

BE A DIPLOMAT

Another aspect of creating a positive impression on co-workers is to avoid creating a negative impression. Dealing with annoying co-worker behavior is one area that leaves you vulnerable to creating a negative impression. Skillful use of diplomacy may enable you to maintain a positive impression.

Co-workers who irritate you rarely are annoying on purpose. Tactful actions on your part can sometimes take care of these annoyances without your having to confront the problem. Close your door, for example, if noisy co-workers are gathered outside. If a co-worker is consuming too much time in your office or cubicle, stand up. This serves as a nonverbal hint that it is time for your guest to leave, but does not come across as pushy.

Sometimes subtlety does not work, and it may be necessary to diplomatically confront the annoying co-worker. An effective approach is to precede a criticism with a compliment. Here is an example of this approach: "You're one of the most interesting and well-informed people in the office. Yet I just don't have the time during working hours to discuss so many worldly topics. Maybe we could save some of these conversations for after hours."

BE PERSISTENTLY ENTHUSIASTIC

Enthusiasm is a valued quality of a co-worker, as well as of anyone else in the work place. The person who looks at each day's challenges with a positive outlook helps other people see the good in what they are doing. Enthusiasm spreads to other people, so being enthusiastic has a multiplier effect. Another advantage of enthusiasm is that it is much better for mental health than is pessimism. Pessimistic people are stress carriers who bring other people down with them. Here are a few examples of enthusiasm in the workplace:

- ❖ The manager announces some new productivity quotas, and a quiet groan spreads through the department. The enthusiastic person says, "Those figures are a challenge, but I know we can do it."

- ❖ A few co-workers get together for a gripe session and talk about their poor working conditions. The enthusiastic co-worker says, "Okay, we do have a few problems. Yet in comparison to most places I've heard about, I think we are a lot better off than most people."

- ❖ You show a report to a co-worker asking for her honest opinion about how bad it is. She says, "I don't see anything bad. However, I have a few suggestions for using graphics that will add some sparkle to the report."

As illustrated by these instances, enthusiasm is a form of positive feedback. Enthusiasm is therefore a natural motivator, whether it comes from above, at your level, or below your level. Another reason I recommend enthusiasm for impressing co-workers is that it almost never backfires.

USE HUMOR EFFECTIVELY

Much has been written and said in recent years about the importance of managers making effective use of humor to keep workers productive and satisfied. Humor is also seen as a way of defusing conflict and relieving stress. The effective use of humor can also create a positive impression on co-workers. One important characteristic of effective humor is that it is relevant to the setting. The office clown who brings in rehearsed jokes does get a few laughs, but his or her humor is not very impressive. A witty comment about the circumstances creates the most lasting positive impression. Here are a couple of examples of humor that worked because they were tied to the situation.

❖ During a staff meeting, the human resources director was explaining which employees would be eligible to receive suggestion awards. With few exceptions, only people below a certain job level could get cash awards for a suggestion. A group member said, "I get it. If we're already being paid to think, we can't get paid twice for the same idea."

❖ A manager was reviewing some of the bias-free terms employees were now urged to used in place of more biased language. The group was told that the term "African-American" was now favored over black, "gay" and "lesbian" were to replace "homosexual," and "Native American" was to replace "Indian." A team member contributed this thought: "I was watching a television show on the same subject. But I couldn't hear it because my kids were playing 'cowboys and Native Americans.'"

❖ A manager was reviewing the company's emergency plans to get through a crisis created by a few cans of contaminated food. Part of the crisis plan involved extraordinarily long working hours. A group member said spontaneously, "What will the company policy be on conjugal visits for the duration of the crisis?"

Self-effacing humor is standard fare for stand-up comics and is also effective in the work place. You can therefore impress co-workers by occasional self-effacing comments. Avoid overuse of the technique or you will project the image of low self-confidence. Here are a few self-effacing comments used by others that you might be able to adapt to your circumstances:

❖ A store associate quipped to her co-associates, "A customer rushed into the store yesterday and looked somewhat lost. I asked if I could help him. He said I didn't look as if I could, but because he was in a rush he would give it a try."

❖ A senior engineer said to his colleagues, "I've been an engineer so long that I still use a slidestick instead of a calculator or a computer."

❖ An experienced financial analyst said to his co-workers, "I'm sure glad I was hired five years ago into this company. When I compare my qualifications to those of you new people, I know the company would never hire me today."

SHARE GOSSIP

Gossip can hurt reputations and waste time. Yet gossip serves some useful purposes, such as bringing workers closer together. Workers who gossip develop better team spirit. If you are a source of interesting gossip, you will create a positive impression on many co-workers. Nevertheless, if you overdo your role as a source of gossip you will not be trusted. Others will fear that you will soon be passing along rumors about them. You also obviously run the danger of being perceived as a "gossip."

An important consideration in passing along gossip is not to spread negative information about people unless you know it to be true and soon to be public information. Suppose you heard from a reliable source that a company executive was facing charges of sexual harassment. A scandal of this nature almost always becomes public knowledge, so it would not be a discredit for you to pass along such a rumor. (A common misinterpretation is that rumors deal only with false information.)

To impress co-workers with your supply of gossip, you need to cultivate information sources. Usually this means trading information with other people to bring about an equitable exchange between passing along versus receiving gossip. If you only collect information your sources of information will dry up quickly.

In gathering raw material for passing gossip along to co-workers, it is useful to keep in mind what type of gossip is perceived to be the juiciest. Information about job changes, including resignations, firings, demotions, transfers, and special assignment is always in demand. Information about office romances, extramarital affairs, and separations is even more in demand. New areas of high-intensity gossip include rumors about executives coming out of the closet with respect to gayness, charges of sexual harassment, and the contraction of a serious sexually transmitted disease.

Gossip creates the biggest impression when it deals with high-level people and later proves to be true. You can also get a lot of mileage out of gossip by disclosing something racy about a key person's past. This type of gossip seems to have its biggest impact when a person is newly appointed to an executive position.

Linda Reynolds, a receptionist, had impressed her co-workers for a long time with her timely tidbits about key people's pasts. After Linda targets the subject she would like to gossip about, she queries friends if they know anything about the person's past. She operates much like a firm that conducts background investigations. If the target person is single or divorced, Linda can often find somebody who heard somebody say something quirky about the individual. For example, she uncovered the fact that a newly appointed controller was at one time delinquent on his child-support payments and was brought to court.

Admittedly, the gossip is playing for minor stakes. Being a good source of gossip will enhance your acceptance with peers but it is not sufficient to be seen as leadership material by them. Another small way in which gossip will give you an edge is that being a source of interesting gossip marks you as linked to sources of information.

USE SMALL TALK AT THE RIGHT TIME

The successful manager or professional of today is often portrayed as a no-nonsense, fully focused, hard-driving worker with no time for frivolity on the job. Although this image is factual, it is incomplete. The person who makes the best impression in the work place also knows when and how to engage in chitchat. As explained by researcher Teresa Brady, in today's work environment the ability to engage in small talk is essential. It communicates to others your human qualities and enables you to demonstrate your interest in co-workers and subordinates.[3]

Many hard-driving professionals find it difficult to talk about anything but business while on the job. Some get anxious about what they perceive as wasting time, while others lack skills in making small talk. The problem is that avoiding small talk makes you appear uncaring, impersonal, and aloof. You therefore lose out on developing a network of supporters. Follow these guidelines to become a good small talker:[4]

1. *Relax.* Being relaxed and smiling makes your subject matter seem lighter. Your easy approach will make it appear that you are receptive to small talk.

2. *Create the time.* You may have a busy schedule that propels you into working well beyond a standard work week. Still, create at least five minutes a day to engage in small talk with co-workers. Although this five minutes a day will mean that you have to work another 25 minutes per week, the investment is a good one.

3. *Rehearse opening topics.* Develop a weekly routine of small talk topics that involve events most people can respond to. Talk about current events that are

familiar to most people. Ask about family activities, weekend activities, and store openings. Weather talk is almost meaningless unless it is tied to some unusual consequence of the weather such as a water shortage, flooding, or an ice storm. Use the file cards we mentioned earlier to give you ideas for individualizing your small talk to the interests of each co-worker.

4. *Practice.* Try out your small talk on your spouse, close friend, or family. Ask for feedback on the effectiveness of your small talk. Pose these questions: "Am I too boring?" "Would I be too personal? "Am I being too obscure?"

5. *Avoid deep or thought-provoking topics.* Aficionados of small talk don't want to be put on the spot or intellectually challenged. One time I asked a colleague who was celebrating her twenty-fifth wedding anniversary, "How do you think your marriage is going?" She became flushed and walked away from me.

6. *Balance talking with listening.* Create small talk but also be willing to listen to discussions of vacation plans, bouts with the flu, and traffic jams.

7. *Focus on the positive.* Small talk is the time to let people see a soft, positive side of you. Save your critical commentary for gossip and after-hours get-togethers.

In short, the right amount and kind of small talk helps give you the edge by forming better relationships with co-workers. They become impressed with your human qualities.

SHARE YOUR EXPERTISE

An honorable way of impressing co-workers is to share your expertise with them, particularly when it helps them resolve a work problem. You will be admired for having shared your expertise, and you will also have created an ally you can depend on later. A case in point is computer scientist Paul Valone, whose specialty is computer networking (linking computers together). Suzanne Bartrand, a colleague in the same department, was a systems programmer. She was assigned a project that primarily dealt with writing computer programs for a management information systems. The project also involved some networking. Suzanne knew she could handle the programming itself. The networking issues concerned Suzanne, however, because she lacked experience in this type of work.

Paul attended the weekly update meeting and discovered that Suzanne was experiencing technical problems. Immediately after the meeting Paul approached Suzanne. He offered to help her on Sunday with the networking aspects of her project. Suzanne graciously accepted Paul's offer to assist her on his own time. Six months later Suzanne's project was a success. She thanked Paul once again for his vital contribution and promised to do what she could to return the favor.

Paul had thus gained the edge in a meritorious and professional way. He had assisted a colleague by sharing his professional expertise. Paul has created an ally should he need help with a project or the endorsement of a colleague for a promotion or special assignment. He can also keep Suzanne in mind should he need a reference from a co-worker for obtaining a job with a new firm.

VOLUNTEER FOR BURDENSOME ASSIGNMENTS

Every work group has its share of uncomfortable, annoying, tedious, or burdensome assignments. If you volunteer to take care of more than your fair share of these assignments you will create a favorable impression. It is also probable that taking on these tasks will help you assume the role of informal group leader. Burdensome assignments include being the scribe at a meeting, organizing the office picnic, collecting pledges for the United Way drive, or preparing a written report on a group project.

Kent Abrams, a chiropractor, describes how he leveraged taking on a burdensome assignment into creating a favorable impression. Kent was a member of the New York State Board of Chiropractors. The group met about ten times a year to discuss ethical issues related to the practice of chiropracty. At each meeting the group would send out for lunch, filling out forms provided by a nearby delicatessen. When the food and beverages arrived, it was necessary for someone to lay out the cash to pay the delivery person. The charges were usually about $75, including tip.

To pay for the food, the order slips were distributed, each person paid what he or she owed, and the money was passed to the front of the conference table. The process took about thirty minutes while the delivery person fell behind schedule. At the second meeting Kent attended, he came to the rescue. He laid out the money and paid the delivery person on the spot. While the group ate, money was collected and Kent was reimbursed. The board members marveled at Kent's efficiency and admired the fact that he had so much cash on hand. Two years later Kent was elected as Chair of the Board of Chiropractors. He attributes the root of his being perceived as a leader to his willingness to lay out cash to pay for the group lunch.

AVOID BETRAYAL AND BACK STABBING

Part of gaining the edge is not losing the edge. Betraying others, including back stabbing, is a quick route to creating a negative impression. The general approach to back stabbing is to pretend to be nice, but all the while plan somebody's demise. The most common form of back stabbing is for a person to initiate a conversation with you about the weaknesses of the boss. The back stabber encourages your negative commentary and makes a careful mental note of what you say. Later, he or she casually passes these comments along to the boss, making you appear disloyal and foolish.

Sometimes the back stabber is more subtle. After enticing you to make negative comments about the boss, he or she says to the boss: "I hope you can work out your problems with Mary. I know she's a difficult person to supervise." Other forms of betrayal and back stabbing include:

❖ Saying damaging things about the co-worker when he or she is being considered for promotion, such as "Ed can't get along with people."

❖ Contending to the boss that the co-worker is technically competent but a poor team player.

❖ Telling co-workers that the other person has been telling you negative things about them.

❖ Telling your boss that the other person is paranoid and then telling the other person that his or her boss is saying negative things about him or her. When the co-worker confronts the boss about his or her negative comments, the diagnosis of the co-worker's paranoia is confirmed.

Betrayal and back stabbing may sometimes gain you an edge with a naive boss, but it will lose you an edge with co-workers. After you lose your edge with co-workers, your edge with the boss may soon be lost.

GIVE EMOTIONAL SUPPORT TO GROUP MEMBERS

A potent way of impressing co-workers is to give them emotional support during both good and bad times. The same technique enhances your stature as a team player. Emotional support can take various forms such as:

❖ Giving encouragement when a co-worker does something outstanding.

❖ Listening to a co-worker lament about being criticized by the boss.

❖ Cheering up a discouraged teammate.

❖ Helping to bolster a co-worker's self-esteem when the person feels that he or she has failed an assignment.

❖ Listening to a co-worker's personal problems.

You might rightfully argue that the boss is paid to carry out the activities just described so why duplicate his or her function? One reason is that the boss may not have the time to provide all the emotional help needed in the group. Another is that many people would prefer to rely on co-workers rather than on the boss for emotional help. For example, many employees are hesitant to hint of any weakness to the boss for fear of negative evaluation.

Barbara Meadows, a lab technician, is well-respected and well-liked by her lab mates. Among her good qualities are her compassion and the emotional support she provides. One of Barbara's most effective tactics along these lines is to take the initiative in reaching out to team members. When she spots another laboratory worker who appears stressed Barbara will say: "This doesn't look like one of your better days. What can I do to help?"

Barbara's technique, and any other method that gives emotional support to co-workers, is effective for a reason related to why people enjoy work groups. A strong motivator for coming to work for many people is the comfort of belonging to a group—one's family away from home. If you give a person with a strong need to be nurtured by a group emotional support, he or she will form an emotional closeness with you. You gain the edge by satisfying an important need.

SET A GOOD EXAMPLE FOR OTHERS

Finally, one of the best ways of impressing co-workers is to be an exemplar of how to conduct oneself in the work place. Not all teammates may openly express their awe and appreciation but they will be silently impressed. You gain the edge by trying the hardest to be your best. If your boss says, "I wish we had more employees like you," you are probably already setting a good example. A representative example of being the best is Dave Jarvie, a former department manager in a large retail store. A former co-worker said about him: "Dave always set a good example. He came to work and never left before his official quitting time. He treated employees and co-workers with the same respect he did his managers. Dave concentrated on what he was doing and rarely made any mistakes. Always helpful to those in need, Dave was promoted in four years to store manager."

To help you rethink the key points we have made, in order to impress co-workers take the following actions:

1. Be a team player.
2. Understand the jobs of team members.
3. Recognize the accomplishments of team members.
4. Show concern about the personal problems of co-workers.
5. Become an informal leader.
6. Be courteous, pleasant, and positive.
7. Appeal to your co-workers' personal interests.
8. Be patient and tolerant.
9. Be a diplomat.
10. Be persistently enthusiastic.
11. Use humor effectively.
12. Share gossip.
13. Use small talk at the right time.

14. Share your expertise.
15. Volunteer for burdensome assignments.
16. Avoid betrayal and back stabbing.
17. Give emotional support to group members.
18. Set a good example for others.

❖ 6 ❖

CULTIVATING
LOWER-RANKING
PEOPLE

People who work for you are another target group to impress in order to stand out. The category of "people who work for you" includes several groups. One group is subordinates who report directly to a manager on a regular basis. Another group in the "people who work for you" category are project, task force, or committee members. These people report to the leader for the duration of the project, task force, or committee.

People who are not currently assigned to a leadership position also have others who work for them. These are the support personnel, such as administrative assistants, systems analysts, and maintenance workers who help you accomplish your job although they report to somebody else. It is self-defeating to fail to impress, or to alienate, these support people. You can rarely accomplish your mission without the cooperation of support personnel.

What has been said so far about self-confidence, negotiating skill, and impressing those above you would also be useful in impressing organizational members of lower rank. The information presented later about impressing customers and network members also applies indirectly to people who work for you. The focus in this chapter is on tactics and techniques specifically geared toward impressing lower-ranking people. Many of the suggestions are based on the latest developments in the art of effective leadership.

As you read this chapter, remember the major theme of this book: In a given situation search for whichever tactic seems the most appropriate to give you the edge. When you want to impress a person who reports to you, choosing a tactic from this chapter is the logical starting point. However, do not rule out using a tactic described someplace else in the book.

USE THE TEAM MANAGEMENT STYLE

Opinion and research consistently support the idea that a highly effective approach to leadership is team management. The basic idea is that you encourage the people reporting to be fully contributing team members. Instead of merely following orders, team members contribute their ideas and govern much of their own behavior. When team management is working the best, work is accomplished through people committed to helping the company achieve its goals. The people reporting to you depend on each other because they realize they have a common stake in the welfare of the organization.

Because the people depend on one another and believe they are working toward a common purpose, they develop relationships of mutual trust and respect. The team-management style impresses people reporting to you because they feel more self-regulating and powerful. In fact, the team-management style is used to *empower* people. Companies who are known for their high quality, such as Federal Express, Xerox, and the Cadillac division of GM, emphasize the team-management style. They have made the shift because team management leads to pride, which in turn leads to high quality.

The team-management style may at first sound platitudinous and utopian. Nevertheless, there are three concrete steps you can take to adapt a team management style should you be a present or potential manager.

Get the Team Working Together on a Meaningful Task

Self-managing teams first gained popularity with the manufacture of Volvo automobiles. Instead of working in assembly-line fashion, with each worker performing a small task, the workers pitched in and performed different jobs. Teams today do such things as fabricate a large stereo system, design a computer system, or put together loan packages for banking customers. Stretch your imagination (or ask your group) as to how the work you do can be done totally, rather than in small pieces.

Sam Lincoln, who operates a large photo studio, has switched to team management with success. In the past, one person solicited new business, the photographer did the shooting, and another photographer was assigned to the darkroom. Now the group works together as a team and rotates the three different tasks. Turnover is lower, and customer satisfaction is higher, reports Sam.

Encourage Multiskills

As the photography example implies, an important part of being a team manager is to encourage people to develop different skills. Give team members the opportunity to rotate jobs, attend special seminars, and receive on-the-job tutoring. The more ambitious team members will be impressed that you gave them a chance to grow professionally. You gain the edge because you develop a more loyal group of subordinates.

Use Consensus Management

A necessary condition for empowering group members is to allow them to participate fully in making important decisions. Every team member doesn't have to agree with the final decision, yet the input of everybody is given careful consideration. Team members are impressed with the leader because they all feel included. Brian Walworth, the head of a corporate acquisitions unit, is well-regarded for his team-management style. He supports his management style with a consensus-management approach to decision making. The same technique is gaining acceptance in diverse organizations.

Brian's group regularly prepares reports on the advisability of his company's acquiring another company. After each professional in the group has studied the company being considered, the group meets. The deal is carefully evaluated, including a thorough discussion of its strengths and weaknesses. Brian acts as moderator and note taker for this meeting of approximately three hours. Within a few days after the meeting Brian prepares a double-spaced, word-processed report incorporating all the opinions as accurately as he can. Each member receives a copy of the report and is encouraged to edit the report, marking directly on the copy with a pen or pencil.

Next, Brian revamps the report, carefully incorporating each group member's suggestions, additions, and deletions. A second report goes out to the group for each member's approval. Additional editorial comments are welcomed. The process continues until each member is satisfied with the final report.

Brian makes the same observation found by others using this technique. Group members are satisfied because their input is used at every stage of the report, and they are impressed with its remarkable efficiency. The team leader impresses team members because of his or her fast and accurate consensus decision-making technique.

MAKE EMPLOYEES FEEL IMPORTANT

We emphasized previously the importance of appealing to the recognition need of co-workers in order to create a favorable impression. Making lower-ranking people feel important is also essential for creating a positive impression. Sheila Murray Bethela, speaker and author, advises leaders to make use of the Please Make Me Feel Important concept.[1] Visualize that every person performing work for you is wearing a small sign around the neck that says, "Please make me feel important." Your work as a leader is unfinished until you satisfy the need for recognition crying out on those signs. Presented next are several ways you can make people working for you feel appreciated and important.

Hold an Employee Appreciation Day

A simple ceremony to celebrate the contribution of staffers can create a positive impression. Mary Pentworth is the manager of the subscription billing department at a daily newspaper. She was aware that employee morale had dipped during one of the newspaper's busy promotions. The twenty employees reporting to Mary were working six days a week, twelve hours a day. To show appreciation and ease tensions, Mary decided to throw an all-day employee recognition party.

Mary funded the Employee Appreciation Day party with $250 from a miscellaneous expense account. On the Sunday evening preceding the Monday party, Mary decorated the office. She taped a hand-written thank-you note on the bottom of each person's chair and included an instant lottery ticket. Mary bought each employee a small gift related to his or her interests. Donuts, bagels, fruit juices, coffee, and tea were awaiting the employees when they reported to work Monday. Pizza and soft drinks were served for lunch.

Mary reports that the employees took kindly to Employee Appreciation Day. Morale surged, everyone was in a better mood, and the department achieved above-average productivity on that day. Mary's team was impressed with the time and effort she put into creating the appreciation day. They were doubly impressed with Mary's genuineness when they figured out that she bought the gifts with her own money.

Mary had clearly impressed her department members, and her winning edge had a spillover. Mary's boss as well as supervisors from other departments congratulated her for a job well done.

Respect Seniority

In the current era, unprecedented numbers of employees over age forty-five are offered enticements to accept early retirement. Despite tough laws against age discrimination, many job seekers over age fifty believe that their age is a liability. In such a climate, showing appreciation for seniority will be extra impressive. Showing respect for seniority in this context means that you appreciate the employee's long-term contribution.

Appreciating seniority increases in importance when you are a newly appointed, chronologically young supervisor. After five years of work experience beyond his MBA, Marty Fybush conducted a job campaign. He landed a position as the manager of financial analysis at a paper-manufacturing company. Most of the professional members in his department were longtimers with the company. When Marty first arrived he was greeted coolly. Group members were concerned that the act of hiring Marty sent a message that seniority was not valued by the company.

Marty's tactic to circumvent the resistance he felt was to show respect for the lengthy job experience of the group members. He would pose questions such as, "Based on your experience, how should this problem be handled?" and "Can you let me know if what I'm suggesting now has been tried and failed before?" Marty would also make it a point to bring along a resident expert from the group when he made a presentation to management.

Marty's strategy worked. By recognizing and appreciating the seniority-based wisdom of team members, their acceptance of him increased. Marty impressed the group and lowered most of the threat he had posed as a new young manager who might not respect the importance of lengthy job experience.

Give Small Gifts and Send Greeting Cards Throughout the Year

How much appreciation did you feel the last time you received a season's greeting card or major religious holiday gift from your boss? Probably not nearly as much as if you had received a card or small gift at an unpredictable time. Cards and gifts sent or handed to employees at times other than Christmas or Chanukah are likely to be more appreciated because they seem less like a ritual and more thoughtful. Consider sending cards to employees and giving small gifts on President's Day, Martin Luther King, Jr., Day, St. Patrick's Day, Labor Day, Easter, and Passover. Your uniqueness will be impressive, and your card or gift is more likely to be interpreted as expressing appreciation.

To get even more impression-making mileage out of cards and small gifts, send them at unpredictable times related to job performance. Imagine how somebody who works for you would feel if you wrote him or her a newly created poem, celebrating an exceptional work accomplishment? Imagine the impact if it were sent in the middle rather than at the end of the year? The more amateurish the poem the more it will be appreciated, because it will seem original. We don't want to compete with greeting card manufacturers, but you can adapt this one to your circumstance:

There once was a customer rep named Moffit,

who worked so hard to earn us a profit.

Up at dawn, home at dusk, she never leaves until work is done,

> beside that, with her around, the office's more fun.

Keep up the good work, and please never say goodbye,

> workers of your talent and spirit are in short supply.

With much appreciation,

Your supervisor

BE HUMANISTIC

A major concern in the era of downsizings and restructurings is that employers have little regard for the welfare of individual workers. This concern exists despite many corporate programs designed to make work life more tolerable for employees. Among such programs are company-sponsored child care, family leave programs, and flexible working hours. You can capitalize on employee concerns about corporate insensitivity by being purposely humanistic. Show an interest in nonwork facets of the lives of lower-ranking employees without neglecting concern about good performance. Express an interest in the total individual and his or her multiple roles in life.

"Be humanistic" is a catch-all term that can refer to almost any appeal to the emotions and feelings of other people. Here is a list of humanistically oriented attitudes and actions in relation to people who work for you.

1. If you are the manager, initiate a dress-down day that encourages employees to dress in the type of casual clothing they would ordinarily wear doing household chores or while running.

2. Buy a baby gift for a new parent's child.

3. Ask your employees what they might do if they won a big lottery prize. (The answer to this question typically points to a person's ideal lifestyle.)

4. Ask lower-ranking people what you might be able to do to make their jobs easier.

5. Conduct a group meeting to discuss all the programs the company offers that could possibly make life easier for employees. Ask employees if they are taking advantage of programs such as flexible benefits, the employee assistance program (EAP), and the tuition refund program.

6. Grant an employee an afternoon off from work to invest in any activity that will make life easier.

7. Ask employees how well their jobs are fitting into their career plans and what hopes they have for future jobs.

8. Conduct a luncheon discussion about the major sources of stress in the job and what can be done about them.

9. Write personal notes at midyear to high-contributing workers expressing appreciation for their help in keeping the company in business. Also mention how they make life easier for you.

10. Give employees proper credit for any of their ideas that you use. A major employee complaint is that managers use their ideas without giving appropriate credit.

11. Invest at least a couple of hours per month listening to the personal problems and complaints of employees. Let them ventilate about their confusion and anger, but avoid becoming their counselor. If an employee's problem appears to be overwhelming, suggest he or she visit the employee assistance program or seek other outside help.

12. Pay a compliment at least once a month to lower-ranking people with whom you interact. An easy, natural one is "Thanks for the nice job you did for me the other day." To avoid any potential charges of threatening environment sexual harassment, make bland and unisex compliments about appearance. Say "Nice outfit" even if you mean "Your hips look luscious" or "Your new suit shows off your buns nicely."

LEAD BY EXAMPLE

A simple but effective way of impressing and influencing people who work for you is to lead by example. You act as a positive model, just as it was recommended that you set an example to impress co-workers. Example-setting is even more important for subordinates, however, because the boss is expected to set a good example.

The ideal approach to leading by example is to be a "do as I say and do" manager. To accomplish this you are consistent between actions and words. Also, your actions and words confirm, support, and often clarify one another. Suppose, for example, your firm has a dress code. If you explain the dress code and dress accordingly, you provide a role model that is consistent in words and actions. The action of following the dress code provides an example that supports and clarifies the words you used in the dress code.[2]

Aaron Parker, a tax accountant, was impressed the way his boss, Bill Marchand, set a good example. "Bill is truly professional. During our busy season he works as long as it takes to get the job done. He doesn't expect us to work the long hours while he keeps a regular schedule.

"Bill is a good example in another way. He challenges any deduction or underreporting of income submitted by a client that he suspects is dubious. We have lost some clients who think Bill favors the government over them. Bill takes the long-range view that it is better to lose a few clients than to sacrifice the integrity of the firm."

Bill is thus gaining the edge with people who work for him by setting good examples of hard work and professional ethics. R. Bruce McAfee and Betty J. Ricks point out six key areas in which a manager should behave in an exemplary manner.[3] Each of these areas will give you ideas for impressing others through leading by example.

1. *Adherence to policy.* Most organizations have policies covering many aspects of employee behavior, such as absenteeism, tardiness, and dishonesty. Communicate these policies clearly and abide by them.

2. *Work performance.* Lower-ranking people will often look to you to set the work pace in terms of intensity, hours worked, and number of rest breaks. Follow the lead of Bill Marchand, the tax accounting manager who expects no more from staff members than he expects from himself.

3. *Attitudes toward the company and job.* Create a good impression by expressing positive attitudes about the company, your job, customers, and the company's goods and services. If you are pessimistic you will fail to impress most lower-ranking people.

4. *Physical health and appearance.* Organizations have become more health conscious so it is important for you to talk about physical fitness and to appear fit yourself.

5. *Clothing and grooming.* The clothing you wear to work and how you are dressed often influences others. An accolade often given to well-respected managers is that they dress professionally. Impressing others does not require heavy investments in expensive and flamboyant clothing. You just need to dress crisply, cleanly, and professionally.

6. *Interpersonal communication.* You should set the style and tone of interpersonal communication. It impresses others if you can be forceful without screaming frequently and embarrassing or belittling others. An occasional touch of drama will help enhance you ability to influence others. You are more likely to gain the edge, however, if you can be convincing in a calm, restrained manner.

WORK TOWARD BEING CHARISMATIC

An effective way to influence and impress people is to have personal charm, warmth, and magnetism. Being charismatic will help you impress *many* people who work for you and give you the edge. Notice that we italicized the word many. Charisma is subjective. The best a person can hope for is that many people perceive him or her to be charismatic. Even leaders who were well-liked by many people in their prime, such as Ronald Reagan or Jesse Jackson, were also perceived negatively by many others.

Although charisma does stem from many personality traits and characteristics that develop early in life, one can become more charismatic. Such development is possible because the components of charisma have been carefully analyzed by psychologists.[4] The more of these components you can develop, the stronger your charisma.

1. *Vision.* Charismatic leaders offer a vision of where the organization is headed and how to get there. You can often do the same for your organizational unit. A vision is more than a forecast because it describes an ideal version of the future. A vision is also a statement of a dream about the future of an organization of a department. Supermarket owner Randy Callens impressed his employees with his vision of Callen's as becoming the best gourmet supermarket in New Jersey. At least once a month

he preached about how proud he and all the staff would be when Callen's moved toward its goal. His vision became true more quickly than it would have without his inspirational message. Callen's market drew an increasing upscale clientele because of its gourmet selections. Randy Callens kept focused on his vision and did not resort to such gimmicks as double couponing or selling food at a loss.

2. *Masterful communication.* Charismatic leaders spin believable dreams and portray their vision of the future as the only way to go. They use metaphors to inspire people, such as one of Mary Kay Ash's (of Mary Kay Cosmetics) favorites: "Bumble bees are not supposed to be able to fly because they have such heavy bodies and small wings. But they do fly. You too can achieve your goals even if other people say you can't."

3. *Inspire trust.* Charismatic leaders inspire such confidence that employees are willing to risk their careers to pursue their leader's vision. To strengthen the perception that they are leaders, they take the initiative to get recognition for their accomplishments. They toot their own horn without being embarrassed. You too can make your accomplishments known by others around you to appear more charismatic.

4. *Help team members feel capable.* Charismatic leaders help group members feel capable. One technique you can use is to allow people to achieve success on relatively easy projects. Praise these accomplishments and then give out more demanding assignments.

5. *Energy and action-oriented leadership style.* A charismatic leader exudes energy, serving as a model for getting things done well and on time. The team

leader style described earlier is an energy and action-oriented leadership style. Keeping busy and projecting a lot of energy will help you appear more charismatic.

6. *Emotional expressiveness, including warmth.* Expressing feelings openly is an especially important way of being charismatic. Freely express warmth, joy, happiness, and enthusiasm. Kathy McGovern, a bank vice president, claims that much of the charisma people attribute to her can be explained simply: "I'm up front about expressing positive feelings. I praise people, I hug them, and I cheer if necessary. I also express my negative feelings, but to a lesser degree.

BE A NURTURING BOSS

For the right kind of employee, an impression-making tactic is to be a nurturing boss. You nurture along team members, helping them to grow and develop. You invest time in listening to their problems, and you worry about their setbacks and disappointments. The lower-ranking people whom you nurture will become your faithful followers because they want to be nurtured. It will be easy for you to spot the people who don't want to be nurtured. They will back away mentally when you offer them help or try to get too close to them emotionally.

A nurturing approach to leadership is most effective when it expresses itself as a genuine concern for the welfare of the group. Nurturing bosses are found in factories, offices, stores, and mills. Matt Brewster, an assembly supervisor, is an example of a nurturing boss in a production environment. Thirty production workers reported directly to Matt. Four weeks into his position, Matt noticed a bothersome problem. Three people in the stockroom gave his team a hard time when they attempted to sign out any equipment or supplies. Matt's employees complained about their problem but felt inadequate to resolve it.

Matt told his people he would intervene on their behalf. Matt visited the stockroom and assertively demanded that they be more flexible in handing out stock. Matt also told them he wanted to hear directly about any problems the stockroom had in issuing parts to people from his department.

Word of Matt's fighting their battles spread around the department. Matt immediately gained the respect of his employees. Matt continued to get involved in problems facing his employees, such as their not receiving overtime pay promptly and needing replacement tools. Within six months production in Matt's department increased 19 percent and absenteeism decreased 25 percent.

Matt impressed his boss and his employees through his aggressive, nurturing approach. The care he showed in helping employees gave Matt the edge he needed to become an outstanding supervisor. The positive impression he created was based on good deeds, not on manipulation.

PROJECT CONFIDENCE IN TEAM MEMBERS

A subtle way to impress lower-ranking people is to show through your actions and spontaneous comments that you believe in them. Assume, for example, that an assistant says to you, "I'll get all those figures for you by Friday." If you say "That's good" with a skeptical expression your assistant will not think you have much confidence in him or her. If your comment "That's good' is accompanied by a convincing facial expression your assistant will be impressed that you believe in him or her.

Projecting confidence in team members impresses them so much they are likely to live up to your expectations, the phenomenon known as the Pygmalion effect. According to Greek mythology, Pygmalion was a sculptor and king of Cyprus. He carved an ivory statue of a maiden and fell in love with the statue. The statue was brought to life in response to his prayer (expectation). Managers use the Pygmalion effect when they motivate team members by looking and speaking as if they expected the team members to succeed.

Here are a few specific ways of projecting confidence in team members that will usually impress them. You will also gain the edge in another important way: The team members are likely to produce more.

❖ You are the service manager, and quality targets are off by 20 percent. Instead of berating the group for poor quality, you state: "I know we can all do better. Find some ways to reach our quality targets, and let me know how you are progressing." (You have expressed faith in the group's professionalism. The group will choose the methods for enhancing quality.)

❖ As the advertising manager, you bring a sample of the competitive advertising to the office. You point to one of the advertising slogans and say, "Here is the pap the competition created. Show me your competitive response by next Tuesday." (You have motivated the team by implying that they can do much better.)

❖ You are trying to run some new software but you can't even get it to boot on to your computer screen. You invite the department secretary into your office and say to him: "I'm in over my head, and I can't imagine who else could bail me out." (The assurance you project that he is uniquely qualified to assist you technically, boosts his ego, and creates a favorable impression. The lift you give his self-confidence will also help him figure out what went wrong.)

PRACTICE SUPERLEADERSHIP

One of the important new developments in leadership is for managers to help team members become more self-directing. The SuperLeader encourages people to think for themselves and practice self-leadership. This approach to leadership impresses team members because most of them are accustomed to other managers attempting to control them. Oliva Manchester, an aerobics instructor, explains her experience in working for a SuperLeader:

"Derek was appointed the general manager of our health club about two years ago. We had heard about his impressive credentials including an MBA from Duke. Based on what we knew about MBAs, we figured Derek would run everything by the numbers. We thought he would look upon the health club as just another investment to be cultivated for maximum return on investment. We doubted he would have any commitment to making people more physically fit.

"Bit by bit Derek surprised us. Instead of telling us how to run a health club, he asked us questions and was very supportive. When we brought up a problem in a staff meeting, Derek did not have ready answers. Instead, he would make us question our assumptions and look for the right answers.

"I expressed concern that during a recession people would save on health club dues by working out at home. Derek made me analyze why people came to a health club at all if they could readily use work-out videos at home. At first I said it was a fad. Derek made me realize that because aerobics was more than twenty-five years old it had passed the fad stage.

"Finally, I concluded that many people stick with aerobics classes because they want the social support of being in a group. They also like the structure of having an instructor. I was then less worried about the possible impact of a recession on our business. It was incidents like these that really impressed us about Derek. He helped us become more self-reliant."

You can work toward becoming a SuperLeader by following the steps recommended by Charles C. Manz and Henry P. Sims, Jr. Several of these steps will require considerable time and energy.[5]

Step 1—Become a Self-Leader. Before learning how to lead others effectively it is essential to lead ourselves. Self-leadership involves convincing yourself to achieve the self-motivation and self-direction you need to perform. You have to carefully observe your own performance and praise yourself when you are performing well. Zap yourself if your performance is lagging. Visualize yourself as performing the way in which you would like to perform. Engage in positive self-talk, and encourage yourself every day. Another important aspect of self-leadership is to savor the natural rewards in your work, such as helping people or solving challenging problems.

Step 2—Act as a Model of Self-Leadership. In the words of Max DePree, the chairman of Henry Miller, the office furniture maker, "It's not what you preach but how you behave." Show team members that you do a good job of managing yourself. Follow through on commitments without your boss having to breathe down your neck. Look for opportunities to reward self-leadership. If a team member has taken the initiative to improve productivity or quality, publicly recognize that worker.

Step 3—Encourage Self-Set Goals. SuperLeadership can be achieved only if employees set goals for themselves. When employees ask "What should I do next?" respond, "What do you think you should do next that will help the company?" You serve as a model, coach, and teacher, and people who work for you will be more likely to set their own goals. Many important goals will still be set by the organization, but goals set by employees usually support these goals. An ideal example of self-set goals are the Research Fellows at IBM. These high-status scientists and inventors make their own decisions about how to allocate resources.

Step 4—Create Positive Thought Patterns. A SuperLeader transmits positive thought patterns to team members. Get team members started thinking positively about themselves and being self-confident. When the group faces discouragement, talk to them about the good things they have accomplished. The SuperLeader induces positive thought patterns by expressing confidence in the subordinate's ability to become more competent.

Step 5—Develop Self-Leadership Through Reward and Constructive Reprimand. The usual pats on the back and spoken praise are important in motivating people to lead themselves. It is more important, however, to help employees appreciate the joy of good work. Encourage them to find the self-rewarding, exciting elements in their work, such as resolving a difficult customer problem. Self-rewards emerge more frequently when employees choose some of their own work methods. Encourage them to figure out how to get a task accomplished.

Reprimands will sometimes be necessary, even if you are a SuperLeader. The ideal is to look for ways in which a mistake or wrongdoing becomes a learning experience. A new sales representative went through her first month's entertainment expenses halfway through the month. Instead of becoming outraged, the manager reviewed with the sales representative where she went wrong. He asked her how she might use better judgment in upcoming months. With this approach, the sales rep profited from her mistake of lavishly entertaining a minor customer.

Step 6—Promote Self-Leadership Through Teamwork. The approach to developing teamwork described at the outset of this chapter is also an important part of SuperLeadership. When people are working together as a team they usually become more self-directing. Each person develops multiple skills and takes more pride in seeing the finished product. Kevin Brown, an insurance underwriter assigned to a work team in an insurance company, put it this way: "When I go to work, I feel as if I'm headed off to a small insurance agency. I take pride in seeing our business grow. I know my contribution is very important."

Step 7—Facilitate a Self-Leadership Culture. One person cannot change an organization culture alone. You need the cooperation of top managers and as many other managers as possible. What one manager can do, however, is to keep talking about the importance of people managing their own efforts as if they were self-employed. Show enthusiasm whenever someone takes the initiative to work on a problem that he or she uncovered. If you are the manager, encourage self-leadership with words such as, "Manage your own work as you see fit. With all the individual work I have to do, I have only about one third of my time left for supervising people. Besides that, you people know your jobs better than I do."

DELEGATE SOME EXCITING ASSIGNMENTS

Most managers can readily hand over burdensome, unexciting, unglamorous, or hazardous assignments to a group member. An impressive delegator is a manager who turns over an exciting, glamorous, and safe assignment to somebody on the team. The most beloved sales managers are those who turn over good accounts and promising leads to sales representatives on their team.

Delegating exciting assignments enables you to gain the edge because it often creates loyal team members. People usually remember who made their work life better and respond by forming closer emotional ties with that person. Kim Arnold, an acquisitions specialist, recounts her experience along these lines:

"A major frustration in this type of work is that you can work on a deal for 70 hours per week for 5 months and wind up with nothing. Over 95 percent of deals you work on fall through. When a deal does go through to completion, and our company buys another, you are placed on a high that lasts for weeks.

"After being on the job for one year, Patrick, the head of our team, turned over a fabulous lead to me. A small pharmaceutical firm in Louisiana was looking to be taken over by a large, cash-rich company. Patrick told me to investigate and then negotiate the deal if it looked good. Of course, any price I came up with had to be finally approved by the president and boards of both companies. But it was my show, and I was in charge.

"Negotiations proceeded remarkably smoothly, and finally I made the big score. I felt that nothing could stop me now in my quest to become a major league acquisitions specialist. I realize that Patrick could have easily taken this high-probability deal for himself. In its place he could have had me track down a low-probability, messy deal. Instead, he gave me an opportunity to grow professionally, and he has my loyalty."

GIVE AND SOLICIT FEEDBACK

Many employees complain that they work in a no-feedback environment. You can therefore impress lower-ranking people by giving them feedback on the work they perform for you. Positive feedback is generally more impressive than focusing on the negative. Soliciting feedback is also impressive. Inquire about how well you are doing, how well team members are doing, and ask for opinions about improvement. One reason many people are hesitant to volunteer feedback is that they fear repercussions for pointing to problems.

Kenneth Blanchard offers two useful suggestions for developing an atmosphere that welcomes constructive criticism. First, look upon feedback as a gift. After thanking the person who provided the feedback, ask him or her to tell you more. Your goal is to find out as much useful information as possible. Second, learn to separate the feedback from a decision to work on the problem. Worry later about making a decision about the problem uncovered by the feedback.[6]

The sales manager for a line of foreign-language learning tapes hired Gloria Sanchez as a telemarketer. One of Gloria's first assignments was to telephone customers who had purchased elementary versions of the tapes. She would ask how they liked the old tapes and then attempt to persuade them to purchase more advanced ones. Gloria quickly learned that they elementary tapes had many flaws, such as an annoying narrator. Also, too much of the tapes were spoken in English, and not enough in the language being taught.

When Gloria brought this problem to the sales manager's attention, the manager replied: "Thanks. This is a serious problem that's been hinted at in the past. You have brought it squarely to my attention. Can you share with me some more details about the complaints? Maybe we can fix the problem when we revise the tapes."

Gloria was impressed that the negative feedback she gave her boss was not perceived as an excuse for not making sales. The manager had gained the edge by using feedback in such a way that the company's product could be improved.

A useful technique for giving and soliciting feedback is to "manage by wandering around." You visit the work place informally to chat with people about their work and any concerns they might have. Although management by wandering around is often attributed to Japanese management, the technique has been around a long time. A basic principle of naval leadership has always been to make occasional tours of the ship.

As you tour the work area you are responsible for, ask in a friendly manner such questions as, "How are things going?" "What problems should I be aware of?" If a manager wanders around your area, take the initiative to offer feedback. Make such comments as "I appreciate the visit. I have made a lot of observations about things that are going well and not so well. I would be glad to talk about them at your convenience." By offering feedback in this manner you will gain an important edge. You will be seen as interested in organizational improvement.

REINFORCE YOUR WORDS WITH ACTION

One important reason so many managers erect communication barriers is that they fail to follow through on commitments. If you develop the reputation of a person who reinforces words with action, you will impress lower-ranking people. Failing to follow through on promises is unimpressive and casts you in a negative light even though many others behave similarly.

Reinforcing your words with actions is a proactive process. You enhance your impression with others as your reputation develops in a positive manner. John Bartoli, a vice president in charge of mergers and acquisitions, impressed people because he reinforced his words with actions. Shortly after joining the company, John made a presentation to the management group describing what he would do for the company. He told people that his job was to help the company find small businesses to purchase. John claimed that by acquiring companies, new opportunities would be created for middle managers. He also contended that nobody in the parent company would be replaced with a manager from an acquired company.

At the end of two years many people from the company were promoted to attractive positions in the several acquired companies. Furthermore, nobody was replaced by a newly acquired manager. John's reputation as a reliable person was now among the highest in the executive ranks. Whatever message John presented in speaking or writing, people took seriously. John's work and reputation were so highly regarded that he regularly received requests from people wanting to join him on the mergers and acquisition team.

PROMOTE YOUR GROUP
THROUGHOUT THE ORGANIZATION

You will impress your team members if you function as an ardent spokesperson for the group throughout the organization. Collect glory for the group as well as for yourself, and you will gain the edge by developing loyal followers. Lynn McCarthy was a data services manager in a manufacturing company. He developed a presentation for his user groups to illustrate the steps necessary and the time required to develop new software programs for their needs. He identified typical problem areas in doing an exceptional job for a user group and how the data services department dealt with the problems. Lynn's presentations were sprinkled with comments about his "high performing" and "thoroughly professional" group.

When members of the data services team went out to help user groups, they typically met with a good reception. The group was objective enough to realize that Lynn had done considerable pre-selling of their capabilities. As a result, the group worked extra hard to live up to Lynn's expectations. His reputation continued to grow as his group performed so well.

LOVE THE UNLOVABLE

Most large offices or factories have at least one cantankerous person who is dead-ended but not necessarily ineffective. If you take the initiative to befriend an unliked person, you will impress him or her. In addition, your reputation as a humanitarian will spread. Ted Russell, a production engineer in a food-processing company, was given the challenging assignment of updating a basic machine used in canning tuna fish. Although Ted was bright and energetic, he lacked much experience with this type of machinery. Ted knew that a knowledgeable person on this type of machinery was Gabe Jensen, one of the most senior employees in the plant. Ted asked his manager if Gabe could be assigned to work with him on this project. Ted's manager cautioned him because Gabe was considered to be uncooperative and uncommunicative.

Ted told his manager not to worry because he thought he could work well with Gabe. What Ted's manager did not know was that Ted had already established a good working relationship with Gabe. Several times when he saw old Gabe sitting by himself on coffee break, Ted sat down beside him and offered him a friendly greeting. By the third time he approached him, Gabe even volunteered a few words (his way of expressing warmth and affection).

When Gabe was assigned to work with Ted, he shared with him all his relevant experience. Within one month Ted had revamped the tuna-packing machine. Of greater consequence for his career, Ted was now on the recommended list for supervisors because of his ability to get along with people.

LET THE BAD IDEAS DOWN GENTLY

One of the problems with encouraging people to participate in decision making is that you often wind up with unusable suggestions. If you flatly reject all the suggestions you receive from people below you will be perceived as not really interested in empowerment. If you are tactful about turning down the worst ideas, however, at least you will create the impression of being a good listener. Here are a few diplomatic rejection notices of ideas stemming from lower-ranking people:

- ❖ "You say that we could save considerable money by eliminating executive bonuses. The best I can do for now is bring that idea to the next management meeting."

- ❖ "You recommend that we could save a lot of energy costs during the cold months if employees were encouraged to keep their coats and hats on while working. I'll number and date your idea, and keep it on file for review at our next budget meeting."

- ❖ "You say that we should get out of the auto-parts business because the American automobile industry is in trouble. When and if the executive team thinks of another business for us to enter, I will submit your idea."

CONDUCT STAND-UP MEETINGS

Standing rather than sitting is one of the most overlooked secrets for getting more done during working hours, says time-management expert Merrill E. Douglas. People take longer to accomplish activities when they sit down. If forced to stand, they will answer you more quickly rather than become engaged in a long conversation. Because of this fact, many managers schedule stand-up meetings when an agenda is not too long or complicated.[7]

A stand-up meeting will impress many people because they can quickly dispense with the meeting and then get back to other pressing activities. You will be perceived as modern, energetic, and action oriented. However, you will fail to impress people who look forward to long, relaxed meetings in which they have an opportunity to explore ideas leisurely. Because the majority of people dislike long meetings, you will win more positive than negative votes.

PREPARE THOUGHTFUL
PERFORMANCE REVIEWS

An honorable and meritorious way of impressing team members is to prepare thoughtful performance reviews. Conducting careful reviews may also help you gain the critical edge with higher-ups because performance apprais- als are important company documents. Promotions and raises are usually based on the results of performance ap- praisals. In addition, thoughtful performance appraisals help defend a company against charges of discrimination. Performance appraisals will appear much more thoughtful if you follow these suggestions:

> ❖ Say a few kind things about everybody whose per- formance you appraise. If you have nothing positive to say, it will appear that you did not carefully observe the person's work. If nothing else comes to

mind, try this one: "Was able to solve most of the routine problems he faced without needing the help of others."

❖ Base your appraisal on critical incidents rather than on subjective opinions. Instead of using a phrase such as "highly creative" provide a couple of examples of the employee's imaginative problem solving.

❖ Instead of relying on memory, keep a careful record of employee accomplishments and failures. During performance appraisal, use these incidents as raw material for documenting your conclusions. For example, "During a trade show, Doris gathered 25 qualified leads for our computerized telemarketing machine."

❖ Don't depend on hearsay. Base your performance appraisal on results that you and your boss have seen directly. Accept miscellaneous opinions only if they can be carefully documented.

BE COURAGEOUS IN TIMES OF ADVERSITY

A final tactic for impressing people who work for you is to face adversity courageously. Show others that adversity is only a temporary setback that can be reversed with inner toughness and good problem-solving skills. If your budget is being cut, rise to the occasion and learn to get by with fewer resources. If you lose out in a reshuffling and your department now reports at a lower level, don't display bitterness. Instead, inspire your group to perform better than ever. Show that you and your group will earn the right to report at a higher level again.

Alex Carter was the manager of roads and highways for a county government. A new county executive came into power and threatened to privatize as many functions as possible. Many people thought that Alex's group would be one of the first to go. Most members of the roads and highways department became despondent, thinking that their department would be disbanded.

Alex told his group not to give up without a fight. He quickly organized a task force to pull together studies showing what happens after a highways-and-roads department is privatized. With the help of his task force, Alex was able to present a convincing financial argument that his group should remain as public employees. Several studies had shown that costs can skyrocket when private contractors take over entirely the building and repair of highways and roads.

The county executive and his closest advisors decided to keep the highways-and-roads department intact. Alex had scored an impressive victory in the face of heavy adversity. All members of Alex's department were impressed with his courageous efforts. Alex had gained the edge by coping effectively with adversity.

In quick review, there are many attitudes and actions that will create a positive impression on those below you. Choose among the following to gain the edge with lower-ranking people:

1. Use the team management style.

2. Make employees feel important.

3. Be humanistic.

4. Lead by example.

5. Work toward being charismatic.

6. Be a nurturing boss.

7. Project confidence in team members.

8. Practice SuperLeadership.

9. Delegate some exciting assignments.

10. Give and solicit feedback.

11. Reinforce your words with action.

12. Promote your group throughout the organization.

13. Love the unlovable.
14. Let the bad ideas down gently.
15. Conduct stand-up meetings.
16. Prepare thoughtful performance reviews.
17. Be courageous in times of adversity.

❖ 7 ❖

COMMANDING THE ATTENTION OF PROSPECTIVE CUSTOMERS

Impressing a prospective external customer is critically important any time he or she has a choice between you and another supplier. Your prospect also has the alternative of not making a purchase. You must find some way to make the prospect see the merit in you or your product and service. If you are an outside sales representative the importance of creating a positive impression is obvious. It is less obvious, however, that many of your internal customers must also be impressed. A trainer, for example, often has to impress a line manager (the prospective customer). Frequently, the manager has the choice of using the trainer's program or bringing in a trainer from the outside.

The tactics and strategies described in this chapter focus on impressing prospective customers. Many of them also will help you gain the edge with others in the work place. For example, proper use of "stroke your prospect's ego" will impress all but the most callous and self-effacing people you encounter on the job.

QUICKLY LEARN YOUR PROSPECTIVE CUSTOMER'S NAME

Back to human relations 101: Learn and remember the full name of your customer prospect. The challenge is more difficult today because of work-place diversity. Many prospective customers have names of different cultural origins from your own. Furthermore, many women and some men have hyphenated names. It therefore requires extra concentration on your part to learn the person's name. A Jim Smith raised in the midwestern United States may have problems learning immediately the name of his prospect, Afsaneh Nahavandi-Malekzadeh. To assist in learning the prospect's name, Jim should take Afsaneh's business card and say the name silently to himself. Jim should then say, "I'm pleased to meet you, Mr. Nahavandi-Malekzadeh." Jim's prospect may let him off easily by responding, "Just call me 'Navi,' it's easier."

The importance of learning a prospect's name is illustrated by the situation of Bob Delaney, a manager in a photochemical company. Bob had attempted to sell a production manager, Harold Fatima, on a system for improving one of the company's most important photochemicals. The system involved purchasing an expensive computer system. Due to high capital investment, Harold was reluctant to explore the proposal.

Six weeks later, Bob came across Harold while shopping at a mall. Immediately, Bob addressed Harold by name. Harold was impressed that Bob remembered his name and therefore willingly entered into conversation. After a ten-minute chat, Harold asked Bob to call him during the week to discuss how the proposed system would improve quality. Eventually, Bob's group got the assignment, and he now had a major internal customer. Remembering a customer prospect's name created a positive enough impression to facilitate Bob's gaining the edge.

Another critical part of learning your prospect's name is to be hesitant to use a first name unless invited to. Also, avoid nicknames unless the prospect states a preference for the shortened name. Nicknames have decreased in popularity, and many people find it annoying when a stranger uses another form of their name. Even if the prospect prefers a nickname, you may not know the shortened form he or she prefers. For example, nicknames for Richard include, "Rick," "Rich," and "Dick" (mostly for people over fifty).

Many women named Deborah detest being called "Debbie," or "Deb"; some men named James cringe when called "Jim"; many men named Andrew or André recoil when called "Andy"; and many men named Robert preferred to be addressed as "Rob" not "Bob." On the other hand, many people believe that only their parents or spouses should use their full first name. To create a good impression simply ask your prospect, "Which is your preferred first name?" Your good sense of etiquette will help you gain the edge.

After you have learned your prospect's name, use it several times during your conversation. Using your prospect's name helps hold his or her interest in the conversation. Yet avoid overusing the name. You could appear to be an in-person replica of a computerized sweepstakes contest letter that inserts a person's name every other line. ("Yes, JACQUELINE DUMBROWSKI, you are one of 3,000 finalists in our contest. You, JACQUELINE DUMBROWSKI, might be holding the ticket that will make you an instant millionaire. Think of it, JACQUELINE DUMBROWSKI, from CLEVELAND, OHIO, your dreams could come true.")

LISTEN AND ENGAGE IN CUSTOMER PROBLEM SOLVING

There are two basic approaches to person-to-person selling. One is the sales-oriented approach in which the sales representative uses high-pressure selling techniques to persuade the customer. Quite often this approach makes sense because you have one product or service to offer, and the prospective customer has expressed no interest in talking to you. House siding and encyclopedias are often sold in this manner.

Marketing experts more highly recommend the customer-oriented approach to selling. To use the customer-oriented approach, you have to identify customer needs and then propose solutions. This approach often impresses prospective customers because they perceive you to be a professional problem solver rather than a high-pressure sales representative.

The customer-oriented approach to selling begins with careful listening on your part. You have to encourage the person to talk about problems that your service or product could possibly help solve. Rita O'Malley uses a listening approach to enlarge the client base for her collection agency. She observes, "It's largely a waste of time in my business to use the hard sell. What does work for me is to have prospects talk about their cash-flow problems. Most companies have some deadbeats as customers. The trick is to get them to admit it. Then I have a chance for a sale.

"First, I have to get an appointment to see a business owner or the credit manager in a larger firm. We have not found this to be a major problem since most companies are at least curious about our services. Once I'm in the interview, I simply mention that we collect delinquent accounts and charge nothing if we fail. Next, I usually make a low-key request such as, 'Tell me about some of your delinquent accounts.'

"The answer to my first request usually consumes at least five minutes. Then I ask a few specific questions like, 'How quickly would you like to get your money from these customers?' and 'Do you have a large enough staff to track down all people who are hurting your cash flow?'

"After my prospect has opened his books to me, I explain that our firm is designed to help with precisely the problems he or she describes. The prospect is then usually ready for a full description of my services. If I do a good job of listening, I get a new client from at least one third of my client prospect meetings. I am there to show how I can help resolve some important business problems."

Rita makes the right impression partly because she does not think of her meetings with client prospects as sales presentations. Instead, Rita sees them as problem-solving meetings in which she helps companies improve their collections.

At times you may be discouraged because the general picture suggests there is not a good fit between the prospect's needs and what you have to offer. Before giving up and moving on to the next prospect, listen even more carefully for a small potential niche for yourself. Back to Rita. One credit manager she spoke to recently said that he was *almost totally* satisfied with his firm's collection procedures.

Rita's sales instincts bubbled to the surface. "Why not *totally* satisfied?" asked Rita. The credit manager explained that there were a few uncollectible accounts lying around that the company had written off. "Would you be willing to give me a shot at getting back some money from those hopeless accounts? It won't cost you anything unless we bring you back some cash," she asked. Rita did salvage some money for the prospect. Since then she has continued to receive a steady dribble of business from that account. Rita made a good impression by listening enough to help the client prospect realize there was some small room for improvement in his company's collections.

USE AN ATTENTION-GRABBING OPENING LINE

To impress customers, as in many other worthwhile endeavors in life, you need a good opening line. For maximum effectiveness, the opening line should appeal to an important need of your prospect. If your opener is attention grabbing, but is not related to a client need, it will be forgotten quickly and so will you.The attention-grabbing opening line is important for internal as well as external customers. Internal customers will usually grant you more time to make a good impression, however, because you are both on the same payroll.

One reason an attention-grabbing opening line impresses is because it reflects a quick insight into an important customer requirement or need. When the opening line addresses a fear, it can be very impressive. Steve Berkowitz is a sales representative for a firm that sells software to combat computer viruses. One of his opening lines to information systems managers is, "I've got software that will virtually eliminate any fear you have of viruses wiping out valuable company data." Steve's pitch has enabled him to get into many companies to make detailed sales presentations. Once inside the company, he uses a variation of the same line again quite successfully.

Here are some attention-grabbing opening lines for impressing prospective customers. You might be able to adapt the key idea contained in these lines to your circumstances. The general theme is to target in on a problem facing the firm, rather than to focus on your product or service.

❖ "How would you like to convert some of that solid waste you are recycling into low-cost fuel for your company?"

❖ "How would you like to reduce inventory shrinkage in your store to less than one percent?"

❖ "What would be your interest in introducing a program in your company that would increase productivity by 7 percent and decrease turnover by 15 percent?"

❖ "How would your impotent patients like to have a clinically tested device that will enable them to attain an erection whenever they want? Think of how grateful they would be to you, their doctor."

❖ "Do you ever worry about your home being broken into while you are at work or on vacation?"

❖ "How would you like a guarantee that you will have enough money to send your newborn child to an exclusive private college?"

All of these attention-getting lines are designed to satisfy an important customer need. We cannot guarantee that lines of this nature will win over every customer prospect. However, they represent yet another sensible tactic for gaining an edge by creating a favorable impression.

DISPLAY PRODUCT KNOWLEDGE

Establishing good relationships with customers and customer prospects remains an important part of selling. People still prefer to buy from people they like, assuming these people are satisfying an important need. In order to satisfy consumer needs, a sales representative must have intensive knowledge about the product or service he or she offers.

The problem of limited product knowledge is more likely to plague retailers than companies who sell through sales representatives. Retail salespeople often handle so many different products that extensive product knowledge is difficult to develop. The high turnover in the retail field also limits the opportunity to acquire intensive product knowledge. Another problem is motivation. The financial incentives offered sales associates are typically not high enough to motivate them to study carefully the products they sell. Because of these factors, the retail store that makes product knowledge part of its marketing strategy can be at an advantage. A good example is the Stereo Shop.

The Stereo Shop is a small chain of consumer electronics stores with an emphasis on stereo sets. All the sales associates are electronics buffs. Within the last year, I visited my local Stereo Shop to purchase a camcorder. (A very satisfied customer had recommend that I visit the Stereo Shop first.) Not wanting to bother learning a new gadget, I asked the sales associate to show me the simplest camcorder to operate. I insisted that I wanted a model that I could operate much like an old-fashioned movie camera. After recording an event, I wanted to insert the VHS film directly into a VCR for replay.

I found just the model I wanted for $1,200. It even had a light on the top, much like a miner's hat. I said to the sales associate, "Fine, this is just what I want." He challenged my thinking, asking me why I wanted a camcorder and what I hoped to achieve by using one. I mentioned that I would be shooting films of students, training seminars, street scenes, sporting events, and family members. I also explained that I wanted to have copies made of my tapes so I could give them to family members and friends.

The sales associate explained that the model I had in mind would be inadequate for my purposes. If I would be willing to spend an extra ten minutes in learning how to use an 8mm camcorder, I would benefit greatly. The image and sound quality would be much higher than achievable with the VHS (large film size) model. Furthermore, he explained, I could play the output from the camcorder through a television without having to record on a VCR. All I had to do was connect two wires between the VCR and a compatible television set.

The sales associate also pointed out that the best model to fit my purposes was smaller than the one I looked at first, and it cost $400 less. Convinced by his expertise and his ability to understand my true requirements, I bought the camcorder he suggested. The equipment has proved to be ideal, and I have since returned to the same Stereo Shop to purchase a VCR, videotapes, and camcorder tapes.

Twice when I had a problem coordinating my camcorder with the VCR, I called the Stereo Shop. A sales associate solved the problem for me over the telephone. From my standpoint, the intensive and extensive product knowledge of their sales associates has given the Stereo Shop the edge.

SPRINKLE YOUR PRESENTATION
WITH BUZZ WORDS

The choice of the right buzz words will influence many prospects. The setting is especially right for using buzz words when your prospect uses them. Buzz words are effective because they appeal to people's need to conform and belong to a group. If you use the jargon and the popular phrases of the day you will help your prospect feel more comfortable during your presentation.

Buzz words are also useful because they point to problems that affect many organizations. Two buzz words that should remain in vogue for the rest of the century are "cash flow" and "Total Customer Satisfaction." Weave both of them into your presentations to arouse the attention of most prospective customers.

Cash flow refers to the actual cash on hand of any organization or business. A company may have booked $3 million in new business, but until some of that money is collected there is no cash on hand. While waiting for its money, the company still has to pay salaries, real estate taxes, insurance, and scads of other overhead expenses. An effective way of impressing your prospect is therefore to describe how your product or service improves cash flow (his or hers, not yours).

Bart Vanderstyne, a sales representative for a company that distributes vending machines, made cash flow the center of his presentation. He explains why: "I found out that the places I called on weren't too excited about vending machines. The only reason they would let them into the building was to placate employees. Many employers believe that employees spend too much time at the vending machines.

"For a while I emphasized employee satisfaction in my presentation. The people I called on either didn't care about employee satisfaction, or they weren't convinced vending machines made a difference. My placements of vending machines surged when I started explaining how our machines improved cash flow.

"I promised my prospects that they would receive monthly checks from us as a guaranteed commission on sales. We stock the machines, repair them, collect the cash, and pay commissions promptly. Although we couldn't promise large sums of money, it would still be cash in their hands. I found out that even companies you would think are wealthy still want some extra cash each month."

By using the buzz word "cash flow," Bart was thus able to get prospects to listen to him seriously. The term "cash flow" served as a reminder that any legitimate activity that brought in cash would make an important contribution to the company.

Also look for opportunities to incorporate the term Total Customer Satisfaction into your pitch to prospects. Total Customer Satisfaction means that pleasing customers is the primary justification for being in business. It also means that quality is measured in terms of how well the customer is satisfied. Another important consideration is that a company gets very little repeat business, and no referrals, unless customers are satisfied.

During your sales presentation explain how your product or service will enhance your prospect's ability to improve customer satisfaction. For example, a person who operated a delivery service would point out how satisfied a prospect's customers would be to receive their shipments promptly.

Angelo Carpenter runs a tiny subcontracting firm called Quality Components. He was finally able to generate enough cash to make a living after he pitched his presentation in terms of quality delivered to the customer's customer. During his sales presentation Angelo uses the term Total Customer Satisfaction frequently.

Angelo explains to prospects what he would do should anything go wrong with one of his components. He stands ready personally to visit the customer's customer to rectify the problem. Angelo also emphasizes that he works closely with his own customers at every step of the manufacturing process. This close arrangement ensures that his components will satisfy the people who buy equipment from his customers.

A twist on the buzz-word tactic is to use different buzz words to appeal to different prospects. Few salespeople make enough use of this effective technique. Automobile dealer Sam Perkins exemplifies someone who uses buzz words effectively. Sam is one of the leading sales representatives at a large dealership that sells six different makes of autos. After inquiring about a prospect's occupation, Sam skillfully uses a few buzz words related to that occupation.

In talking to engineers, for example, Sam will make this comment: "The reason this car isn't so well known is that the company doesn't invest much in advertising. They would rather put the money into engineering refinements. A lot of people who own this brand are more concerned about engineering standard than trade puffery."

The dealership Sam works for is located near a large hospital. He has therefore also collected a few buzz words appropriate for the health-care profession. When talking to a physician or nurse, he alludes to safety facets of the car. He uses buzz words he picks up in health magazines and in conversation to emphasize the safety features. One of his favorite lines is, "This auto has an air bag designed to reduce head trauma, hematoma, and spinal-cord injuries in case of collision." Sam claims his sales to medical personnel have increased by one third since he began to sprinkle medical buzz words into his sales presentation.

Sam's buzz words are not mere gimmickry. His use of terms of interest to his prospects is a legitimate way of establishing rapport. Using buzz words to better relate to your prospect is yet another variation on the most basic sales principle of all: Appeal to your potential customer's interests.

OVERESTIMATE THE DIFFICULTY
OF THE PROSPECT'S PROBLEM

Assume you are in the enviable position of having found a prospect with a pressing problem. Perhaps you made a cold call and uncovered the problem by encouraging the prospect to talk. Even better, assume that the prospect called you in to help satisfy the problem. A tactic to use to gain the edge in these circumstances is to at first overestimate how difficult—and therefore expensive—it will be to solve the problem. The scenario we describe is akin to the drama that occurs when your car breaks down on the highway and you are towed into an auto-repair center.

After listening to a description of your problem, the estimator says: "It sounds like your motor has seized. If you do need a new one, that would run about $3,500. However, would you like me to begin work and see if I can salvage your engine? If I could do it, the repairs would run about $850." Realizing that you have a cash flow problem, you say with a prayerful tone, "Go ahead. That would be great if you could fix my engine for $850."

By making a worst-case prediction about the extent of your engine damage, the estimator has placed you in a position whereby you grab the opportunity to spend $850 at his or her shop. Here is how overestimating (or exaggerating) the difficulty of the problem can impress an internal customer. Martha Bardot, a training director, was called in by the vice president of manufacturing to discuss a potential training program. The vice president represented an important internal customer prospect for Martha.

The vice president explained to Martha that because the company was shifting the manufacturing of one product line to a plant in Mexico, 250 production workers would be declared surplus. However, the company had about 50 clerical and customer service positions to fill at other places in the company. The vice president wanted to know how large a training program would be required to prepare about 50 production employees for clerical and customer-service work.

Martha was quite enthused but explained that she would have to carefully study personnel records to estimate the scope of the training required. She commented, "Many of our production workers have a literacy problem. They read at a very low level, their grammar is weak, and some of them have never operated a computer. This would indeed be a giant retooling effort."

Martha returned a week later with her analysis of the gravity of the problem. She explained to the vice president that her personnel records indicated that many of the production workers had a higher literacy rate than she had thought. If the right workers volunteered for retraining, the budget for the program would be $150,000 less than she had originally thought. The vice president was impressed, and Martha then prepared a serious proposal to undertake the training program.

Underestimating the difficulty of the problem works because your prospect believes he or she is getting a bargain. This illustrates how the negotiating skills described in Chapter 2 can be applied to diverse situations in which you are trying to gain the edge.

SHOW THAT YOU HAVE THE AUTHORITY TO CUT A DEAL

Small-business owners frequently call on customer prospects. Top corporate executives also invest some time in personal selling. One reason these high-ranking people call on prospects is that they know it is impressive. Prospects enjoy the flattery of being called on by an owner or a top-ranking official. Also, the prospects are impressed by dealing with someone who has the authority to cut a deal. A sales representative who must first check back with the office to approve a price is less impressive.

To impress prospects, it is helpful to make it clear that you have the authority to strike a deal. Sean Anderson, an industrial sales representative, explains how this tactic worked for him: "We were attending a pre-award bid meeting for a major contract. This type of meeting is used to define major points of a contract. The customer let us know that company management had appropriated the funds, that the project was a go.

"Our marketing manager then asked the customer where we stood as far as getting the contract. The customer said that we were approved for the contract. We were among four finalists for the project. Our marketing manager then told the customer prospect that our company would give their company an extra aisle in their system for the same price. However, they had to sign the contract now to get this concession [The "aisle" in the system was worth about $1 million.].

"The customer held an emergency meeting, and we were awarded the contract the next day. We returned home with the contract in hand. The ability to cut a deal impressed the buyer enough to award us the contract and close out the other companies. The fact that the marketing manager was the son of the owner gave him extra clout when it came to making a deal."

Sean's analysis was right on target. The authority of the marketing manager to grant a $1 million concession was impressive and gave Sean's company the competitive edge it needed.

STROKE YOUR PROSPECT'S EGO

A universally effective tactic for influencing people is to flatter them sensibly. The technique is well suited to impressing prospects because the buyer in a buyer-seller relationship feels that he or she deserves special treatment. The only time buyers do not feel they deserve special treatment is when opportunities are limited for receiving the product or service they want. For example, a cosmetic surgeon who has an excellent track record for making his patients look ten years younger does not have to flatter customer prospects. The surgeon has a long line of potential customers clamoring for his or her services.

Use subtlety in stroking the ego of your prospect. Blatant ego strokes may sometimes appear too obsequious. Following are some examples of subtle, refined, and indirect appeals to the ego of customer prospects. Tailor them to your individual requirements.

❖ Careful research shows you that your prospect hit a hole in one on the golf course last year. After a brief introduction you say: "I was looking forward to shaking your hand. I've never shaken hands before with anybody who has hit a hole in one. Despite how much I practice, I doubt I'll ever match your achievement."

❖ "I like the way your office is decorated. The furnishings are impressive yet a visitor like myself feels comfortable here."

❖ "I brought with me a copy of an article you wrote for *Cement Industry News*. I was very impressed. After our business discussion is concluded I would like to ask you a few questions about the article."

❖ "I understand you were the product manager on the new generation of laser printers made by your firm. I want to compliment you. Our firm purchased two of those printers, and they are of the highest quality."

❖ "I've been told you have tremendous technical knowledge. I was therefore looking forward to discussing some of the advanced features of our equipment with you."

Observe that the ego strokes just presented emphasize work accomplishments. The one exception is the comment about the golf score. It is safer to deliver work-related compliments in the first several meetings with prospects or customers. Some people feel that comments about their physical makeup are presumptuous. If a male compliments a woman's appearance she might interpret it as a mild form of sexual harassment. Instead of creating a positive impression, the man has probably disqualified himself as a potential vendor.

LISTEN PATIENTLY TO OBJECTIONS

Objections are almost inevitable in selling face-to-face. Not every external customer will say yes immediately to buying your product or service. Not every internal customer will accept immediately the output or service you have to offer. You will impress your prospect if you listen patiently and carefully to objections. A classic example comes from a marketing handbook published many years ago.

An experienced stockbroker listened to a prospect complain that the security he was offering was flawed because it had been steadily dropping in value. The stockbroker nodded sympathetically. When it became apparent that his prospect had finished expressing his objections, he said: "You are right, Dr. Williams. The price of this stock has dropped 50 percent in the last six months. That is exactly why I am recommending it to you. At this low price, it is now underpriced and is an excellent buy in the opinion of our analysts."[1]

The physician was impressed that his objections received careful attention and were acknowledged. The broker agreed with the physician's observations that the stock had dropped in value. With his observations validated by the sales representative, the prospect was now in a receptive mood to buy. A different approach would have been for the stockbroker to say, "Yes, the stock has declined lately. Yet the decline has been smaller than for many other stocks in the industry." A rebuttal that challenges the prospect's observations may make the prospect defensive and unwilling to buy.

Listening to a prospect's objections is also valuable because it gives you a chance to clarify his or her confusion. Nicholas Barsan, a real estate agent who often earns more than $1 million per year, works hard at dealing with his prospects' confusion. A buyer had agreed to purchase a $250,000 house in Jackson Heights, New York. The buyer later telephoned the home office and finally decided to cancel the deal. The less experienced real estate agent who had set up the deal turned to Barsan for help. Would Nicholas mind talking to the client (who now must be accurately classified as a prospect)?

Nicholas paid a personal visit to the prospect, a meat packer. The man was despondent because his accountant had just informed him that he would be taxed heavily if he sold his current home. Purchasing a new house would therefore be out of the question. The meat packer reaffirmed his intention to call off the deal.

After listening to the prospect's concern and worry, Nicholas explained that the accountant misinterpreted the tax laws. In reality, the tax law favors sellers who buy a more expensive house. The meat packer was still vacillating. Nicholas reminded him that his new home would be bigger and in a nicer neighborhood. Also, it had an apartment that could be rented to help pay the mortgage. After a tense pause the prospect gave a firm nod. Nicholas and the prospect then shook hands on the deal.

Nicholas explained to the younger real estate agent, "He will buy. He was just confused. You have to get to the heart of the problem, what bothers someone."[2] The point here is that Nicholas could never have gotten to the heart of the problem without carefully listening the prospect's confusion. A basic fact about human behavior is that people want their objections heard. Listening to these objections and concerns creates a positive impression.

OVERCOME OBJECTIONS WITH HUMOR

Poking fun gently at your prospect's objections will often create a good enough impression for you to overcome the objection and consummate the sale. The humor has to be good natured and must not hint that the prospect is foolish. Also, the humor should provide insight into the value of your product or service. A story has circulated about a successful sales representative who sold commercial time for a radio station. The rep called on a foodstore-chain executive who had never advertised on radio. According to the executive, radio advertising did not sell because no one paid attention.

The sales representative said, "Would you please give radio advertising a try if I could convince you that people really did pay attention?" The executive responded with a skeptical yes. The sales representative then suggested that the station could run ten spots a day announcing that the stores were all infected with roaches! After the executive stopped laughing, he placed an order.[3]

An impressive form of humor is a comment that agrees with the objection yet exaggerates its veracity. Your humorous comment thus corroborates your prospect's logic but pushes it to its extreme consequences. Two examples will help illustrate this point:

❖ A sales representative at an automobile dealer is attempting to sell an expensive sports car to a middle-age, single man. The prospect places his chin in his left hand and gently strokes his chin with his thumb suggesting interest. He verbalizes an objection: "Isn't this really the type of car for a man who wants to lead a wild life?" "Absolutely right" responds the sales representative. "If you buy this car you'll attract more young women than you can handle."

The car dealer's humorous comment impresses the prospect because it confirms his hunch that the sports car is associated with a wild lifestyle. The comment about the young women also appeals to one of the man's fantasies.

❖ A sales representative from a health-club equipment company is trying to sell an executive on installing a fully equipped athletic room on company premises. The executive muses, "This would be quite an investment, but I guess we would have a lot more healthy employees." "I agree with you wholeheartedly," retorts the representative. "You would have so few employees becoming disabled from heart attacks, you could just about shut down your employee recruitment program."

The sales representative's exaggerated comment helps the executive appreciate more fully the implications of improving employee physical fitness. The executive is impressed because his thinking is corroborated and expanded. As a consequence, the sales representative has moved one step further toward converting the prospect into a customer.

MAKE REFERENCE
TO PRESTIGIOUS CUSTOMERS

A straightforward way to impress prospects is to drop names about prestigious companies who currently use your product or service. The technique is effective because most executives have positive attitudes toward well-known companies. Assume that three of an executive's relatives were laid off by General Motors, and a GM car he bought was a lemon. Despite these problems, the same executive will be highly impressed that a sales representative from an office-cleaning service has GM as an account.

Business consultants routinely attempt to impress client prospects by name dropping. Although ethics often prevents them from mentioning the specifics of what they do for a client, many consultants will freely mention the names of clients.

Jeff Triad was desperately trying to convince a small but high-volume supplier of computer equipment to carry his company's line of peripheral equipment. The supplier was located in New York City. Despite sending marketing literature, technical specifications, and making several phone calls, the supplier's director of marketing was not impressed with Jeff. He would not even agree to an in-person sales presentation.

Jeff then decided to use a little name dropping to give him the edge. He had been working for a long time on a big sale to the United Nations. Jeff telephoned the small supplier's marketing director once more. In the midst of the conversation, Jeff casually mentioned that he would be in town Thursday for a meeting at the United Nations.

At that point the customer became impressed because Jeff was in command of such a large, prestigious account. (Jeff did not actually say that the deal was completed with the UN.) The clincher was Jeff's suggestion of shifting the UN meeting to a later or earlier part of the day to accommodate the marketing director's schedule. The director finally agreed to meet with Jeff. The sales meeting went well. As a result, the computer-equipment supplier now sells peripheral equipment manufactured by Jeff's firm.

The marketing director of the computer supply firm was impressed because the UN appeared to be using the peripheral equipment manufactured by Jeff's firm. The tacit assumption is that the UN, or any other prestigious organization, is staffed by intelligent, discerning people. In reality, a delicatessen two blocks down from the UN might be a more impressive account. A small business often makes more intensive use of equipment than does a large organization that can afford loads of back-up equipment.

MAKE COST-CUTTING SUGGESTIONS

Cost-cutting seems to be permanently in style. Consequently if you show a prospect how to shave costs, you may make a positive impression. Too many sales presentations do just the opposite; they suggest ways for the prospect to increase expenses. Although the expenses may be for laudable purposes, they still decrease cash flow. The standard approach to making cost-cutting suggestions is to show how your product or service will actually decrease costs. Julie Flavin, a human resources manager, used such an approach.

Julie called on her internal customer and boss, the vice president of human resources. Julie explained that she had a new program she thought would benefit the company. Because a lid had been placed on new expenditures, Julie's request for an appointment met with a cool reception. Nevertheless, she was granted the chance to present her proposed program.

Julie explained how she wanted to formalize a program that would reduce expenses by about 25 percent on the hiring of temporary workers. Her plan was to develop a cadre of in-house temporaries who would become a supplementary work force. Instead of the company using the services of temporary worker agencies, Julie's department would keep track of reliable part-time workers. As these workers successfully completed one assignment for the company, they would become part of a pool of office temporaries. Some administrative costs would be involved, but agency fees would be drastically reduced.

Julie's cost-saving—and good-will-building—plan impressed her boss. She was given the authority to proceed with her plan on a limited budget. The program of in-house temporaries proved to be an effective cost saver, and Julie had gained the edge.

A nonstandard approach to impressing customer prospects with cost savings is to point to ways to save money not directly related to your product or service. This tactic must be implemented with considerable tact and sensitivity, however, to avoid appearing presumptuous. Few potential buyers expect a sales representative to tell them how to run their operations. The tactic works best if the cost-saving suggestion is dropped casually into the sales conversation.

Milt Brodsky is a successful office furniture sales representative. He is well liked by his established accounts because of his friendly manner, his sensible recommendations, and his honest deals. Milt also likes to help his established accounts and prospects in any other way he can. One of his helpful methods is to make cost-saving suggestions. Milt was calling on a customer prospect whose business was expanding. He hoped to sell the company the office furniture they would need for expansion.

"Congratulations on your growth," said Milt. "It's nice to know that a local company is doing so well when so many other companies are cutting back. I suspect you may be moving a lot of stuff from one location to another. We moved ourselves a few months ago. We saved thousands of dollars by using a local mover, Byrne Brothers. Have you thought of using a local instead of a national mover?"

In reality, the prospect had not thought of using a local mover and made a mental note of Milt's good suggestion. The prospect was impressed enough to listen more attentively to the balance of Milt's presentation.

Making cost-cutting suggestions helps create a favorable climate because it communicates a genuine interest in the client's welfare. The cost-saving pitch is more impressive when there is no business link between you and the source of your money-saving idea.

KNOW YOUR COMPETITION

A customer prospect is likely to be impressed if you know your competition. A balanced viewpoint of your competitor's strengths and weaknesses is part of knowing the competition. To acquire competitive knowledge, many successful sales professionals keep careful files. Your file should not be so thorough, however, that it appears like snooping. For example, knowing the specific price offered by your competitor might appear to be spying.

Phil Hopkins, the owner of a commercial landscaping service, provides a healthy example of knowing the competition. Phil was attempting to land an account to landscape a newly developed suburban office park. He knew that his firm would be a serious competitor because it had the capacity to handle a project of this magnitude, and its reputation was solid. Phil had kept careful notes on the capabilities of other commercial landscaping firms in his area. He believed that this would be another factor in his favor in obtaining a contract.

Phil met for the third time with the managers responsible for awarding the landscaping contract. Believing that this was his last chance, Phil offered his final rationale for hiring his firm: "I'm glad to know our firm is still being considered to landscape your office park. I think that we can do a beautiful job for you. Our two best competitors also do an artistic job. In fact, Beechmere Landscaping might have one of the best landscaping artists in the business. But we're ahead of the competition in one important respect. If any of our plantings do not take hold, we'll be back right away to redo the job. That's one part of the job that most landscapers hate. Please check our references, and check the references of our competitors."

The principals of the development company did follow up with a reference check of previous customers. Phil's knowledge of the competition proved to be right on target, creating a very good impression. His firm received the contract, and Phil delivered as promised when two pine trees turned brown the first year.

DOWNPLAY COMMERCIALISM

A high-level impression tactic is to appear that making money for your firm is not your major motive. Some firms place sales representatives on salary to downplay commercialism. The rationale is that if the sales representative is not desperate to make a commission, he or she will serve the prospect better. Paul Walworth, the head of an architectural firm, purposely downplays commercialism to impress prospects. After discussing a project with a client prospect, Paul patiently explains that his firm *might* be interested in working with him or her.

A typical sales pitch for Paul is: "We are a very busy, small firm. We are limited in how many clients we can handle. We therefore work only with people who want some exciting architecture performed. We also insist on strong creative control. Our firm simply will not be associated with a design we think has aesthetic pitfalls." A few client prospects reject Paul as being too arrogant, yet most are very impressed. Paul gains the edge by downplaying commercialism. (He is also playing hard to get.)

BE A WALKING ADVERTISEMENT FOR YOUR PRODUCT OR SERVICE

Some prospective customers are impressed if you use yourself for an advertisement. Even if they are not highly impressed, at least you will attract their attention. Ed Falcon, a young sales representative for a home appliance store in Toronto, uses this tactic. He carries with him a red vinyl case with a gold imprint, "Kerwin Home Appliances."

Ed finds his best results with this technique while waiting on line at restaurants and at the bank. Many people react in the same way to his vinyl case: "Oh, you are with Kerwin Home Appliances." Ed smiles graciously and says, "Yes, I am. I suspect you would have not asked me unless you might be interested in a new appliance. Here is my card." Ed and his sales manager both agree that the walking advertisement is a money maker for the store. Ed has gained the edge by self-advertising his products in a novel way.

Being a walking advertisement for yourself is a positive tactic. Similarly, it is important to avoid being a walking advertisement for not using your product or service. Jeff Deckman, a manufacturing engineer, recalls receiving a telephone call from a sales representative for a financial investment firm. The sales rep was pitching corporate bonds that promised a high yield. Jeff inquisitively asked the sales representative how many of these bonds were in his personal portfolio. The representative replied, "I don't buy bonds." Jeff replied, "Neither do I," thus ending the conversation. One of the oldest clichés in sales should not be forgotten when attempting to impress prospects: "Have faith in your own product."

DISPLAY GOOD MANNERS AND ETIQUETTE

Good manners and etiquette have made a strong comeback in recent years as an important tactic for impressing people in business. Conversely, poor manners and etiquette can disqualify you from consideration. Little touches such as addressing people by their last name upon introduction, letting them through a door ahead of you, and sending a follow-up thank-you note can be very impressive.

Michelle Pelouse, a sales representative for an office supply company, provides this affirmative statement about etiquette. "I have found that just by being polite and courteous, I get a lot of new business. I do the basic things I learned at the Bryant and Stratton business program. These include offering prospects my business card and writing them notes of appreciation for having listened to my presentation.

"Before I call on a prospect I make sure I know how to pronounce his or her name correctly. I also ask people when would be the best time to telephone them again.

"Politeness is extra important in my business, because office supplies have become a commodity. Customers simply buy from whomever they like the best, assuming your costs are in line."

One of the reasons good manners and etiquette give Michelle the edge is because too many other people gloss over their importance. Assertiveness may be important in attracting a prospect's attention. Yet combining assertiveness with practicing good etiquette give you a distinct advantage.

DRESS LIKE YOUR PROSPECTIVE CUSTOMER

The stereotyped Dress for Success look is gradually being replaced by Dress Like Your Prospect as a way of impressing potential customers. If you are calling on prospects in Silicon Valley, wear the casual, loose fitting, unisex style of clothing sold at Gap stores. If you are attempting to sell a prospect in an area where protective gear is required, wear a hard hat. If you don't have enough sense to wear the hard hat, you will appear too unfamiliar with the situation to solve a client's problem.

Dressing like your internal customer can also be important. If you are a financial analyst who is analyzing manufacturing costs, take off your jacket when you visit the manufacturing area. If you are a manufacturing representative working with marketing on product design, wear a suit when you visit the marketing department.

Dressing in a manner similar to your customer works because it helps you establish rapport. An important aspect of feeling comfortable with others is the feeling that the other person has similar tastes and preferences.

APPEAL TO THE OLFACTORY SENSE

It's worth a try to impress customer prospects by giving off the right scent. Experiment with different colognes, toilet waters, powders, and perfumes until you find the scent that works best for you. People vary as to which scent is the most impressive for them. Researchers at a Japanese cosmetics company have found that sage and cypress can produce a calming effect, and jasmine can relieve anxiety and cure drowsiness.[4] These scents would therefore put a person in a receptive mood for a sale.

Giving off the right scent can be impressive because the prospect might think it is your presentation, or your presence, that is so relaxing and uplifting. At a minimum, a pleasant scent adds to your impact. Sydney Woods, a seller of Infinity automobiles, claims he would not show up on the salesroom floor without cologne. "It makes me appear distinctive and affluent," he claims.

RELATE WARMLY TO VOICE MAIL

A frustration facing many sales representatives is that they are more likely to hear a voice-mail message than speak to a person when telephoning prospects. The challenge of voice mail is that you have to leave a message so compelling that your prospect will return the call. Ted Garland, a sales representative for a computer components firm, explains how he handles the situation: "My biggest problem these days is that I hardly ever get the chance to talk to a person. Even with established customers, the best I can do is leave a message and hope that he or she returns the call.

"I noticed that the messages I was leaving were beginning to show signs of irritation and frustration. One of my established accounts told me so. I may have been turning off some prospects by leaving messages that sounded angry. So I purposely tried to sound as warm and friendly as possible when I spoke to a voice mail system. The tactic has worked okay. My percentage of return calls has increased, leading to a larger number of sales."

Ted thus gained the edge by having the insight to cope with an important work-place change. You are more likely to speak to a voice-mail system than you are to a person unless you are calling people in the executive suite.

HELP THE CUSTOMER MAKE A PURCHASE

A final tactic here for impressing customer prospects is to help them make a purchase. Customers are often irritated by salespeople who focus on making a sale rather than on helping them make the best choice. Often the pivotal factor is that the customer needs to be hand-held in making up his or her mind. Omar Khan, a successful seller of upscale beds, is especially adept at convincing customers that he is looking out for their needs and interests.

Omar's tactic is to first help prospects define their budget and also to talk about any special requirements, such as back problems. Omar then shows them the bed that best fits their price range, while candidly pointing out the bed's advantages and disadvantages. He also points out the total costs under several different financing plans.

One could readily dismiss Omar's tactic as simply using low-pressure tactics. He goes beyond that, however, because he offers so much helpful advice and presents so many relevant facts. Omar's professionalism impresses customers and gives him the edge.

Quickly tying all the information in this chapter together, following is a checklist of some important tactics for impressing prospective customers. Many of these tactics apply to both external and internal customers.

1. Quickly learn your prospective customer's name.

2. Listen and engage in customer problem solving.

3. Use an attention-grabbing opening line.

4. Display product knowledge.

5. Sprinkle your presentation with buzz words.

6. Overestimate the difficulty of the prospect's problem.

7. Show that you have the authority to cut a deal.

8. Stroke your prospect's ego.

9. Listen patiently to objections.

10. Overcome objections with humor.

11. Make reference to prestigious customers.

12. Make cost-cutting suggestions.

13. Know your competition.

14. Downplay commercialism.

15. Be a walking advertisement for your product or service.

16. Display good manners and etiquette.

17. Dress like your prospective customer.

18. Relate warmly to voice mail.

19. Help the customer make a purchase.

❖ 8 ❖

CAPTIVATING YOUR EXTERNAL AND INTERNAL CUSTOMERS

Impressing your prospective external and internal customers gives you an important, but only temporary, edge. To maintain your edge it is necessary to keep on impressing your customers. The challenge of impressing customers has increased because they are placing higher demands on suppliers. Furthermore, you are competing against a better level of customer service by other firms and employees in your own company. Customer satisfaction has never been a higher priority in both business and nonprofit organizations.

Many of the tactics and strategies described in this chapter will help you stand out against the internal and external competition. Use them in addition to the methods for impressing prospective customers described in the previous chapter. Implementing the tactics and strategies described here will convert lip service into impressive customer service.

CREATE A BOND WITH YOUR CUSTOMER

A high-impact buzz word in selling is to bond, or form emotional relationships with, your customers. The rationale is that if you form warm, constructive relationships with your customers, they will keep buying. Such is the true meaning of "relationship selling." Repeat business is essential for success, so forming a bond with your internal or external customer is a career-enhancing strategy. All the tactics in this chapter will help you work more effectively with your existing customers. However, the seven described in the next several pages are designed for building close personal relationships (bonding) with customers.

Show Care and Concern

During contacts with your customer, show concern for his or her business and personal welfare. How frequently do you ask your internal customers questions such as:

"How's business?"

"What's new in your department?"

"How are you and your boss getting along?"

"How useful has my product (or service) been to your company?"

"What exciting things are happening in your life?"

"How does your granddaughter like the child-care center?"

"How are you enjoying your new task-force assignment?"

After asking the question, project a genuine interest in the response. Many people ask questions similar to those just listed, but far fewer show any real concern about the answer. One technique for displaying interest is to ask a follow-up question to the answer. If your customer says, "Business is wonderful," ask "Glad to hear that. What are the new developments?"

Make the Buyer Feel Good

A fundamental way of keeping a relationship going is to make the buyer feel good about himself or herself. Or make the customer feel good because he or she has bought from you. Offer compliments about the person's healthy glow and appearance, or the report that specified exactly what the vendor wanted. An effective feel-good line is, "I enjoy doing business with you."

Dan Edwards, who sells printing services to book and magazine publishers, reveals positive feelings to his clients. After he gets to know his contact person at the account well, he lets the person know how he feels about their working relationship. Assuming the relationship is positive, Dan often says: "I really enjoy our contacts. It lifts my spirits for the day to conduct business with an optimist. You're on the top of my list of Good News accounts."

Build a Personal Relationships

Building a good working relationship with a customer often leads to a positive personal relationship. A bolder approach is to do the reverse—build a working relationship based on a personal relationship. You gather personal facts about the interests of your customers and then appeal to those interests. Jack Foxboro, a bank president, has gained considerable career leverage by using precisely this tactic.

Several years ago Jack was a commercial loan officer. He acquired a base of existing accounts from the previous officer and gradually increased this base. Jack invested considerable time telephoning existing loan holders. He collected facts about them, such as birthdays, the names of family members, golf handicaps, hobbies, and favorite sport teams. Jack entered all this information into a computer.

Jack would send cards to customers in recognition of their birthdays and special accomplishments. When a customer visited the bank to talk about an existing loan or apply for a new one, Jack would retrieve facts about him or her from the computer. Jack's clients were so impressed that he enlarged existing accounts and received substantial referral business.

When Jack was hired by a competitor bank as the vice president of commercial loans, many of his old customers followed him when they sought new loans. Within several years Jack was promoted to bank president, becoming the youngest bank president in town. According to Jack, building personal relationships with his customers is the single factor that distinguished him from other young bank officers. As president, he still keeps a file on major customers.

Understand Your Customer's Business

Most successful people are emotionally involved with their business. They are therefore more likely to bond with a person who understands their business (or job). The time you invest in understanding your customer's business will often yield a splendid return. Sources of valuable information about your customer include annual reports, newspaper and magazine articles about the customer, and trade magazines. If your customer is a large organization, a book may have been written about the company. For example, several books have been written about Xerox Corporation and IBM. Another way to understand your customer's business is through digging for useful facts.

Sherry Michaels was the manager of a small department that developed videos and slide shows for internal clients. Sherry was required to furnish year-end reports to her boss documenting the extent to which her services were used by other departments. She was thus under pressure to maintain and upgrade her internal-customer base. One of Sherry's most effective techniques for enlarging her services to internal clients was to ask questions about the nature of their operations.

Sherry would typically get started serving a unit within her company by helping them prepare a slide presentation.

As soon as she finished that job, Sherry would ask questions about the activities performed by the department and who used their output. While visiting the department, Sherry would listen carefully to what type of work employees were discussing. One time Sherry helped the health and safety department prepare some slides on accident statistics. Sherry discovered through a series of questions that a major objective of the unit was to prevent health problems and accidents.

Armed with that information, Sherry sold her customer on the idea of her helping them prepare a videotape promoting illness and accident prevention. The knowledge Sherry acquired about her internal customer's operations enabled her to expand her services.

Make Courtesy Calls

After a customer is in tow, your relationship can be enhanced by an occasional courtesy call. The purpose of the telephone call, or personal visit, is to see how well the product or service is performing for your client. Ron Haskins is the owner and operator of a business equipment distributor whose accounts are primarily small businesses. His store is enormously busy and profitable. Ron attributes much of his store's success to a policy he has established for himself and his three sales representatives.

Every customer receives a gentle follow-up call inquiring about how well the equipment is working and what unanswered questions remain. Ron and his sales representatives shy away from making a sales pitch during a courtesy call. However, if the customer inquires about a new machine or supplies, Ron or one of his reps responds affirmatively.

Ron's courtesy calls have created a positive impression on his customers and have helped to increase sales. Nevertheless, a caution is in order. Many firms, including automobile dealerships and health maintenance organizations (HMOs), are overdoing courtesy calls to the point of annoyance. Within several days after buying a car or visiting an

HMO, many customers or patients receive a telephone call. The call proceeds to conduct a brief survey about the quality of service. What could have been a relationship-building courtesy call becomes a bothersome disruption. As a consequence, the potential bond with the customer fails to form.

Smile at Every Customer

Smiling has many benefits, including lowering stress, decreasing wrinkles, and making a person more photogenic and telegenic. Smiling is also a natural relationship builder and can help you bond with your customer. Smile several times at each customer meeting, even if your customer is angry with your product or service. Customer training seminars often coach people on how to smile. In addition, you might practice smiling in front of a camcorder and play back the results. Smiling over the telephone is also recommended because it helps you achieve a warmer voice tone.

Mirror Your Customer's Behavior

Rapport with a customer, or any other person, can often be improved through mirroring. To mirror someone is to subtly imitate that individual. The most successful mirroring technique is to imitate another's breathing pattern. If you adjust your own breathing rate to match your customer's, you will soon establish rapport. You might then imitate a few of your customer's most frequently used expressions. Be careful, however, not to blatantly ape your customer. Your potential bond could quickly break.

Several people who have experimented with mirroring think it has made at least some contribution to getting along better with an ongoing customer. It is best to use mirroring on a supplement to the more orthodox techniques already described.

PROVIDE EXCEPTIONAL SERVICE

The best-accepted axiom about keeping customers is to provide exceptional service. Many successful companies contend that their strategic advantage is good service. Many firms have developed computerized systems to enhance customer service in terms of prompt deliveries and easy returns. Even with those systems supporting you, effective person-to-person tactics are still what count the most in impressing your customers. Six of the most important of these tactics are described next.

Put Their Needs First

Focus on satisfying your customer's needs rather than what is convenient for you or your firm. Assume, for example, the maintenance department in your company chooses to send maintenance workers to make repairs only during the late afternoon. A problem with this policy is that many people want equipment repaired before the afternoon.

The maintenance supervisor justifies his or her policy by noting, "The maintenance technicians are busy with routine upkeep in the mornings." Before long many of the internal customers will be complaining about the rigidity of the maintenance department. Worse, some internal customers will be demanding that the company use outside contractors to handle maintenance. By putting his or her scheduling needs first, the maintenance supervisor has created a negative impression.

Follow Up on Requests

The simple act of following up to see if your service is satisfactory is one of the most powerful principles of good customer service. (The courtesy calls previously described are another application of the follow-up technique.) A simple telephone call to the requestor of your service is usually sufficient follow up. Robin Denny is the word-processing supervisor at a savings and loan association. When large word-processing assignments are needed, they are sent to Robin, who distributes them to one of the word-processing specialists.

After the assignment is completed, Robin checks it for attractive formatting and grammatical and spelling errors before returning it to the originator. Her rule of thumb is to call the internal customer twenty-four hours later to assure that the assignment is satisfactory. Robin gives top priority to rework. Robin's strong service orientation has enhanced her reputation throughout the organization. It has also increased her job security in an industry plagued by job insecurity.

Be Available After the Purchase

We all know that customers are irritated by neglect after the purchase. Nevertheless, this simple principle of customer satisfaction is frequently violated. Many shortsighted salespeople make themselves scarce when their customers have problems. You can therefore create a good impression by cheerfully servicing what you sell.

Steve Altmann, a computer sales representative for Tandy computers, impresses his customers by being available after the purchase. Many of his customers link with other computers the equipment they buy from Steve. Networking (or linking computers together) frequently works poorly, and the customers return to Steve's store for help.

Steve willingly offers assistance even when the problem lies with a computer not made by Tandy. Steve's reputation as a provider of exceptional service has kept his customers coming back for computer supplies and peripheral equipment. Steve has also gained the edge by securing a rapidly expanding base of referrals. Many people enter the store and ask for Steve Altman.

Be Obsessional about Prompt Delivery

A new perfection principle in customer service is to be obsessional about on-time delivery. Prompt delivery impresses customers and therefore gives you the edge in customer retention. Nature's Best, a natural-food distributor, is an exemplar of a company obsessed with prompt delivery. They claim a 99.6 percent success rate in delivering orders accurately and on time. One of Nature's Best customers is Cheryl Hughes, the proprietor of The Whole Wheatery, a natural food store. Cheryl says she can set her watch by the arrival of George, the delivery person from Nature's Best.

From Cheryl's viewpoint, George's promptness motivates her to keep ordering from Nature's Best. For eight years she has relied on the company for everything from vitamins to the food she sells in a restaurant located in her store.[1] Other distributors may sell food similar to that offered by Nature's Best, at competitive prices. However, promptness on deliveries gives George's employer the edge. George's personal commitment to the company policy has fortified his job security.

Go Beyond the Call of Service

Because of the heavy competition to provide good service, innovation may be necessary to give you the edge. Create a way to distinguish yourself by providing unusually helpful service. Grant Micklei, the proprietor of a fur and leather store, achieved such a feat. Customers who purchase such upscale items want to concentrate on making the right selection. Grant observed that when parents brought young children to the store, the children often distracted the parents by running around, knocking down coats, and leaving the store. Grant seethed with anger when a child would knock down a $6,000 sable coat, but he felt helpless in controlling a customer's child.

Grant's daughter and clerical worker, Sara, came to his rescue. She began to care for the children while Grant worked with customer prospects and repeat customers. (Although few people returned to the store again soon to buy another fur coat, many did return for lesser purchases.) Sara brought the children back to the office, talked to them, and allowed them to draw on photocopying paper.

When parents with young children entered the store, then, the serenity necessary for purchasing furs and leathers was achieved. Sales increased because customers could concentrate better. Another problem was also alleviated. In the past, many parents who brought along children said they would return soon without their children. These prospects got away because most of them failed to return. Impulse buying is important even for luxury items.

The child-care plan innovated by Sara takes only several hours a week away from her regular duties because only a small proportion of shoppers for furs and leathers bring along children. Exceptional customer service has helped Grant's store achieve a competitive edge.

Be Flexible About Time Availability

Another hallmark of good service is to meet your customer's time schedule even if it is inconvenient. (The maintenance department described earlier violated this principle.) The greater the deviation from a normal work schedule, the more your service will be appreciated. Gil McPherson, a field service technician, helped his company retain accounts by his willingness to meet customer schedules.

One of Gil's duties was to run acceptance tests on machinery. An acceptance test is a method of determining if a machine is running properly in the field. These tests are usually run over a thirty-day period during regular working hours. Traditionally, a representative from the customer and Gil's company had to be present to log and correct any errors that occurred during the tests.

A scheduling problem developed during a test in a bakery whose normal working hours for the first shift were

5:00 A.M. to 1:00 P.M. The bakery management wanted the test run during the first shift because the machinery was placed under heavier pressure during that time period. Gil's company wanted to run the test between the first and second shift during normal working hours to avoid overtime costs.

Gil volunteered to work the first shift to run the test and be on call for the rest of the normal working day without overtime pay. The acceptance test went smoothly, and many problems were resolved on the spot. After the test was completed the customer wrote a complimentary letter to management thanking them for making Gil available when they needed him most. Shortly thereafter, the customer signed a new service agreement with the company. Gil's flexibility was noted by management. His flexibility helped retain an important customer and elevated his standing with his employer.

MAINTAIN DIRECT LINES OF COMMUNICATION WITH THE CUSTOMER

An effective way of holding on to and impressing customers is to maintain direct lines of communication with them, particularly with respect to service problems. Few customers are overly impressed if the primary purpose of open communication lines is to solicit more business. The major purpose of the open communication should be to satisfy customer needs.

A standard approach to maintaining open lines of communication is to conduct periodic satisfaction surveys, either over the telephone or through the mails. These surveys have an important contribution to make and if not burdensome to answer will be well received by external and internal customers. However, a missing ingredient in these surveys from the standpoint of the customer is that he or she may not have a problem at the time. The most effective open communication with customers allows you to know promptly when they are facing a problem that could lead to a loss in repeat business.

The courtesy calls described previously help keep open lines of communication. A more timely device is to encourage customers to telephone, or send you a fax, whenever a problem arises. If you cannot respond immediately to rectify the problem, at least let the customer know that help is on the way. Tim Jackson, the vice president of customer service for an industrial pump company, used the help-is-on-the-way technique to provide improved service.

Industrial pumps must be kept running smoothly because manufacturing can come to a halt if the pump stops operating. Although most companies have a maintenance staff of their own, pumps are so complex that factory-trained experts are often needed for repairs. Because some of the pumps sold by Tim's firm cost over $500,000, the customers want prompt help. However, Tim's department cannot afford a large enough staff of service technicians to take care of peak loads when several customers are experiencing equipment failure simultaneously.

After Tim's customer service supervisor receives a customer request for service, he estimates a tentative arrival time for the technician. As soon as an accurate time can be forecast, the service supervisor sends a fax confirming the estimated time of arrival. According to Tim, "We have found that pinning down a time when help will arrive usually calms down a very upset customer. Even if the help is a half day later than the customer wanted, just knowing that help is on the way seems to work."

The policy of maintaining direct lines of communication with customers has helped Tim's employer retain a substantial customer base. Customers are impressed that the service supervisor gives accurate estimated times of arrival for the service technicians. Although few customers will ever throw out a piece of capital equipment in anger, they can look to a competitor for the next pump.

CONVERT CONSTRUCTIVE CRITICISM TO ACTION

Complaints and criticisms from customers are almost inevitable. Virtually no product or service is perceived to be flawless by every customer. Many of these customers with reservations about what you are doing have no compunction about voicing their complaints. Customers have become increasingly assertive about expressing dissatisfaction as buzz words like Total Customer Satisfaction have become popular.

Customers whose criticisms are listened to carefully, and acted upon, often become loyal customers. In contrast, customers whose criticisms are dismissed as trivial often badmouth your product or service. Although the natural response to criticism is defensiveness and the urge to retaliate, look for the opportunities for improved service contained in the criticism.

Nick Kalfos, a restaurant owner, used to think that his customers were launching personal attacks on him when they expressed complaints. Nick would often stand near the restaurant door and ask customers how they enjoyed their meal. Once a couple commented that their moussaka was tasty, but the portions were too small. Nick responded in a defensive, accusatory tone, "Are you still hungry? Didn't you get enough to eat?"

The cashier who overheard the interchange commented to Nick that perhaps he came on too strong in response to the diners' criticisms. Nick has worked hard at improving his ability to listen to customer criticisms and suggestions. For example, he now serves larger portions of moussaka even though he still thinks people should be satisfied with smaller portions. Nick thinks that his openness to suggestions has impressed some of his customers enough to keep them coming back.

Before constructive action can be taken on complaints they have to be listened to carefully and compassionately. The most important part of compassionate listening is to allow your external or internal customer to express his or her feelings. Nick did a poor job at first of letting the customer express his feelings about what he perceived to be a small portion of moussaka. By quickly responding, "Didn't you get enough to eat?" Nick was attempting to deny the validity of his customer's feelings. Here are a few suggestions for doing a good job of allowing customers to express their true feelings regarding a complaint:

❖ Ask the customer, "How do you feel about the problem you describe?" Encourage a full expression of feelings by nodding affirmatively while your customer is ventilating. Only after the anger has simmered down will you be able to deal with the problem.

❖ Learn to accept feelings as feelings. Do not argue with a person about the correctness of his or her feelings. Statements such as "You shouldn't feel this way" bring back memories of an angry parent telling a person how he or she should feel. Facts can be right or wrong, but rightness and wrongness does not apply to feelings.

❖ Show that you accept the customer's right to feel the way he or she does. For example, you might say, "I accept the fact that you are upset with the shipping error. I hope, however, you will reconsider canceling the order. Please accept our offer to ship you the correct merchandise this afternoon, by express delivery.

INVOLVE YOUR CUSTOMER IN WORKING OUT THE PROBLEM

Mistakes and problems in serving customers are inevitable, however hard you and your co-workers strive for perfection. To minimize the sting surrounding these errors, involve your customer in deciding what should be done about the problem. By involving the customer in the solution to the problem, he or she is more likely to accept a deviation from the service promised originally.

Seth Bradbury is a sales promotion specialist at an advertising agency. A furniture store hired the agency to prepare and mail 3,000 postal cards advertising a new line of furniture. One side of the postal card contained a photograph of the furniture, and other side contained product details and space for addressing and stamping the card. After the cards were mailed, Seth received an urgent call from the client. "The photograph of the furniture is printed vertically. It looks horrible. We agreed on a horizontal shot. This means 3,000 cards have been mailed out with a mistake."

After allowing the client to finish his complaint, Seth responded, "You are right it is a vertical shot. Perhaps we misinterpreted your directions. However, I think your furniture still looks beautiful. The extra white space the vertical shot provides creates an interesting effect.

"It's unfortunate that the cards have already been mailed. What would you like us to do? It's important that you are satisfied."

The client responded, "I guess there is nothing we can do to change the photograph. Would you be willing to give us a discount off the original price we agreed on?"

Seth checked with his boss, and the agency agreed to a 15 percent discount on the job. The client accepted these terms and was doubly pleased because the mailer proved to achieve the targeted response rate. Seth had impressed his client because he listened fully to the complaint and involved the client in achieving a workable compromise to settle the problem.

FIND WAYS TO BUY FROM YOUR CUSTOMERS

One of the biggest challenges in opening some new accounts is that they are already involved in cozy, reciprocal arrangements with their own customers. Assume, for example, you are trying to sell office supplies to a bank. Despite whatever good service and high-quality goods you can offer at a fair price, another supplier is already a major depositor at the bank. The only way you can acquire the bank as a big customer is for your firm to become a big customer of that bank. At that point you would still be able to get only a piece of the bank's business.

The lesson here is that to impress your existing customers, look for ways to buy as many products as possible from that firm. Ask your customers for a full listing of the products and services offered by their firm. If you are the business owner, look for ways to buy any of these products. If you work for a larger organization, contact your purchasing department to see if the company has need for any of your customer's products. No purchase is too trivial, including key rings, coffee mugs, or grass seed. Making major purchases, however, is more impressive.

Max Prentis is a successful manufacturer's representative. Among the lines he sells are material-handling systems to the automotive industry. Max earns a higher income than the president of some of the companies he represents. His outstanding accomplishment as a manufacturer's rep is that he sells to General Motors, Ford, and Chrysler.

Part of Max's selling tactics is to buy three brand-new cars every third year, a top-of-the-line model from each of the three manufacturers. Owning a Cadillac, Lincoln, and New Yorker simultaneously may appear cost-prohibitive. Max's cars last longer because he owns three, thus offsetting some of the costs. As a manufacturer's representative, Max drives about 90,000 miles per year on business. He will call on an automotive company only if he is driving one of their models.

Max believes that his show of good faith in his customers' products has created a very favorable impression with each of the auto giants. Max's high income suggests that buying his customers' products has given him an edge.

BE A CUSTOMER CHAMPION

A customer champion is someone who acts as the eyes, ears, and voice of the customer. If you are a customer champion, you represent the customer in your organization.[2] Championing your customer impresses him or her for a logical reason. Customers rightfully believe that satisfying their needs is more important than dealing with internal bureaucracy. If you keep fighting for your customer you gain the edge because you develop customer loyalty.

Alice Peters worked as an industrial sales representative for an electronics equipment manufacturer. She received a phone call from Ken Oriskany, the chief engineer at an account Alice's president thought was difficult to please. Ken somehow had forgotten to order spare parts for the equipment Alice recently sold him. He was anxious to get the parts as soon as possible. Alice told Ken that the manufacturing department was shut down for two days for an inventory audit. Yet she promised to do anything possible to get the spare parts shipped.

Alice visited the factory, pulled the parts off the shelf herself, and instructed the sales secretary to prepare an invoice. She then shipped the equipment overnight to the local representative, who hand-delivered them the next day. Alice caught flack from the manufacturing, engineering, and shipping departments for crashing the system. Yet Alice heard through the local representative that Ken kissed the box when it arrived. He also expressed his unswerving gratitude for the company bailing him out of a potential jam.

Alice felt vindicated because Ken's company evolved into one of her own company's top ten customers. Furthermore, the president thanked Alice for satisfying the demands of what he thought was a very difficult customer.

Admittedly, Alice chose a risky course of action. She circumvented company procedures to satisfy the concerns of a customer. In many companies this would be politically unwise. However, Alice's devotion to her customer paid off in terms of customer retention and development. Alice had gained the edge by being a customer champion.

EDUCATE THE CUSTOMER

At times it is necessary to educate your customer about the proper use of your product or service. Without this education, misuse is possible, leading to dissatisfaction and a negative impression. Mike Dalton, an industrial sales representative, received an irate phone call from a customer. He had mistakenly used a carboy (a large containment vessel) for an ill-suited application, and the product failed.

Mike calmed down the customer and explained what went wrong. He then offered to send the customer an appropriate replacement part even though Mike's company was not at fault. The customer accepted the generous offer and became an excellent source of repeat business. In addition, the customer wrote a letter to the president of Mike's company expressing appreciation for the way Mike handled the situation. The combination of educating the customer and paying for his mistake was impressive.

A notable aspect of educating an internal customer is to explain why you classify him or her as a customer. Many people within an organization are still surprised when informed that they are customers. As the company limousine driver said to the visiting executive, "Congratulations, you are my first customer of the day. What can I do to make your journey pleasant?"

HELP YOUR CUSTOMER VISUALIZE GROWTH

Growth is a magic word in business. Most of your customers hope their department, division, company, or store will grow. Computer Associates, a software company based in San Jose, California, runs an advertisement that captures the growth fantasy. The headline reads, "Accounting Software So Sophisticated It Even Lets You Multiply." Under the headline is a series of three photographs. The first shot depicts a roadside stand with a few rabbit cages outside. The sign on the stand reads, "Andy's Bunnies." The caption says "Small business will get off to a jackrabbit start with ACCPAC® Bedford®.

The second photo is of an enclosed store, with a sign that says, "Andrew's Rabbits." The copy reads, "As your business grows by leaps and bounds, move up to ACCPAC BPI®. The third photo depicts an attractive modern office building with a sign on the lawn, "Hare Inc." The ad copy reads, "Even the most sophisticated breed of business is handled by ACCPAC®.

Few of your customers will be looking for accounting software to run a rabbit breedery, yet you can capitalize on this growth fantasy. An important first step is to anticipate what type of growth is possible for your client or customer. Will your customer be able to expand into international markets? Will your client most likely be able to experience profit growth by cutting back on expenses? A second step is to construct an exciting graphic showing how your customer is likely to experience productivity growth if he or she uses more of your product or service.

Lorraine Winters runs a temporary employment agency. After working with a client for about six months, she asks for the opportunity to make a presentation to top management. The heart of her presentation is a graphic showing how an increased use of temporary office workers will boost profits by reducing costs. Her argument is that when permanent workers retire or leave voluntarily, their activities can be handled by temporary workers. Lorraine believes that the profit growth she depicts has led many clients to expand their use of her services.

STAY INFORMED ABOUT THE COMPETITION

Knowing the strengths and weaknesses of your competition is an important tactic for impressing a customer prospect. After your prospect becomes your customer, to keep the edge you still need to stay informed about the competition. Rick Magnum sells heavy equipment to the construction industry. He happened upon an unusual way of implementing this important tactic. One of Rick's customers was a contractor. He asked Rick if he could recommend anyone who might be interested in earning extra money by plowing snow at night and on weekends.

Rick surprised the contractor by responding that he would recommend himself to do the plowing. Rick knew that he would be operating a competitive loader. As a result, this would be an excellent opportunity to obtain hands-on experience with a competitive product and also earn a few dollars. (Sometimes it is a long time between commissions when you sell heavy equipment.)

Rick capitalized on his part-time experience. When speaking to present and prospective customers, Rick was able to make accurate comparisons between his loader and the primary competitive brand. Several customers, including his boss, were quite impressed that Rick had gone that far to obtain product knowledge. Rick thinks his first-hand knowledge about the competition helped him close two important sales.

MAINTAIN A CUSTOMER PROFILE

Earlier we talked about creating a bond with your customer. To create such a bond requires substantial knowledge about your customer or client. Knowing relevant details about your customer is also important for impressing him or her in general. Many successful sales representatives maintain a formal customer profile that they update periodically. To maintain such a profile, record personal facts as well as business facts. It is difficult to predict which tidbit will be the most effective at a given time, so the more facts the better. Here is a sampling of the kinds of information found in a customer profile that might prove useful in impressing external or internal customers:

❖ Who are the main competitors?

❖ What are my client's personal interests?

❖ What is my client's family and personal status?

❖ What is my customer's budget cycle? When is the best time of the year to close a sale?

❖ What is the best time of the week and day to talk to him or her?

❖ To what extent does he or she like to be entertained?

❖ Which type of entertainment does he or she like? (We pick up on this theme again later in the chapter.)

❖ Why is my customer doing business with me?

❖ What does my customer dislike about me?

❖ How much decision-making power does my customer have?

❖ How long does it usually take my customer to reach a decision?

❖ At what frequency does my customer seem to like courtesy calls?

❖ How much help with technical matters does my customer need?

It would be difficult for you to obtain complete answers for all these questions. However, collect as much valid information as you think might be cost effective. If your customer appears destined to always be a small customer, spend less time on your profile than you would for a major player.

GIVE A POSITIVE "NO"

A major marketing philosophy is that the customer is always right. Nevertheless, when a customer makes an unreasonable demand you may have to say no diplomatically. For example, an external customer may want such a large price concession that your profit vanishes. Or an internal customer may want so much of your time that you cannot serve your other customers. Merrill Douglass advocates that you give a positive no to a demand that you cannot meet. He recommends three techniques for declining offers that are unreasonable or that cannot be met for some other legitimate reason.[3]

1.   *Let others help you.* Call in a third party, such as your boss, to help you decline an offer without hurting the feelings of your customer. You might say, "I tried to get you a 35 percent discount, but my boss says 18 percent is as far as we can go." Your customer might be impressed because you at least tried.

2.   *Offer alternatives.* If you are unable or unwilling to meet your customer's requests, refer him or her to someone else who can. Assume you are a tax accountant and your client asks your advice about investing in collectibles. You are aware that giving such advice is unethical because you are not an investment counselor. Your response could be, "I am licensed to give you advice on the tax consequences of your investment. However, I am not licensed to give investment advice. I can recommend, however, that you speak to an investment counselor." Your sense of ethics and professionalism will create a good impression.

3.   *Be gracious but firm.* When saying no becomes necessary, make it a firm no. Any response but no (such as "maybe") is usually interpreted as yes. Gwen Evans, who sold interior-decorating services, was

asked by one of her established customers if he would receive a kickback for placing a large order with her firm. Gwen didn't want to lose the potential order but her firm forbade kickbacks, and she felt they were unethical. Gwen replied, "I realize such buyer incentives do exist. Yet our firm just does not offer those kinds of payments. But we can offer you high-quality service at a competitive price." As difficult as it is to impress a sleazoid, Gwen's statement made the buyer respect her integrity.

MINIMIZE SMALL TALK

The right amount of small talk can help strengthen your relationship with customers and attract you to some prospects. When you are dealing with professional-level customers, however, minimize small talk and maximize talk about the product or service. A study based on the actual observations of sales representatives found that successful sellers invested very little time in small talk.

The industrial psychologist who conducted the study observed, "The more time spent in small talk, the lower the customer's regard for the seller." In contrast, in a sales-focused call conversation was focused on the products the seller had to offer.[4]

Although many potential buyers initiate small talk, the seller who focuses on the product gets the most respect. To gain the edge, use just enough sports talk and chitchat to establish rapport, and then dive into big talk.

PAY IN ADVANCE FOR BUSINESS ENTERTAINMENT

Small touches sometimes create a strong, positive impression. Some customers feel awkward when their sales representatives pay the entertainment bill in front of them. At times, a moment of discomfort may arise when the decision has to be made about who is paying. Furthermore, signaling to the server and then taking out cash or signing a credit card can detract from the business discussion. For this reason, it is impressive to pay in advance for business entertainment. It also adds to your power image to have an open account at a restaurant.

Lisa Conti, who sells employee benefits programs, points to an additional reason why prepaid customer entertainment is impressive: "It is no longer unusual for a woman to pay for a man during business entertainment. Yet a lot of men still feel uncomfortable when I pick up the tab. To take care of this problem, I have an account at Resti's, a first-rate restaurant for the business trade. After our meal is completed I simply say, "No need to wait for the check. My company has taken care of our meal in advance." Very smooth, very impressive.

TAILOR-MAKE CUSTOMER ENTERTAINMENT

Our discussion about prepaid business entertainment was oriented toward the reasoning that much of business entertaining involves eating in restaurants. The vast majority of business entertainment does center around lunch or dinner, with attending sporting events a distant second. But why be stereotyped in your thinking? To be truly impressive, find out what type of business entertainment your customer prefers and proceed accordingly. If your ongoing customer would prefer to play miniature golf after work, take him or her miniature golfing. How about visiting an exercise club with your customer?

Jason Ludwig, a commercial insurance broker, has a novel and effective approach to tailor-made, customer entertainment. Many of his clients are unattached people looking to improve their social lives. To meet their entertainment preferences, Jason organizes singles outings, such as picnics or bowling parties. He has found that at least one third of those he invites attend these social functions. Several of his customers have developed long-term relationships stemming from contacts made at these gatherings. Can you think of any bigger favor a sales representative might do for a customer?

DISPLAY STRONG ETHICS

Good business ethics are more widely preached than practiced. Another tactic you can therefore use to impress customers is to be conspicuously ethical. Look for ways to show that you are so ethical that you would not mind making your sales tactics public knowledge. Also, treat customers the same way you would like yourself or your loved ones to be treated. Just going about your business in an ethical and responsible manner is not enough. Take positive steps to let your customer know that you are ethical. Here are three examples:

❖ Your customer inquires about a late order. Instead of claiming that the order will be shipped immediately, you respond: "We've made some mistakes in production scheduling. Your shipment will take another three weeks. Would you like an immediate refund? I can give you the name of a supplier who might have what you need already in stock." Your customer's anger will be defused, and you will be admired for your honesty.

❖ Your company implements a Zero Defects program, and you are supposed to supply parts without any defects to another department. You tell the other department head (your customer), "My employees are already overworked and overstressed. I can't expect them to push any harder to produce components with zero defects." Your customer is impressed because he or she never thought of the ethical consequences of Zero Defects.

❖ Your customer thanks you for having installed a billing system that is saving the company thousands of dollars per month. You respond, "I appreciate the thanks. Our billing system has improved your collections as much as we said it would. However, the real thanks belong to your new collections specialist. She's the best I've seen in the business." Your client is overwhelmed by your ethics to the extent that you have solidified your hold on selling him the next financial system he needs. You have gained the edge through superethics.

Impressing your external or internal customers requires the use of multiple tactics and strategies. Use the following checklist as a reminder of tactics that may help you break through to a new level of customer satisfaction and retention:

1. Create a bond with your customer.

2. Provide exceptional service.

3. Maintain direct lines of communication with the customer.

4. Convert constructive criticism to action.

5. Involve your customer in working out the problem.

6. Find ways to buy from your customers.

7. Be a customer champion.

8. Educate the customer.

9. Help your customer visualize growth.

10. Stay informed about the competition.

11. Maintain a customer profile.

12. Give a positive "no."

13. Minimize small talk.

14. Pay in advance for business entertainment.

15. Tailor-make customer entertainment.

16. Display strong ethics.

❖ 9 ❖

OBTAINING
THE SUPPORT
OF PEOPLE
IN YOUR NETWORK

People in your network are another important target group for you to impress to break through in your career. Your network includes all your contacts inside and outside the company who can assist you to achieve work-related goals. People with whom you work directly, such as co-workers and superiors, are important contacts but are usually not classified as members of your network.

Your network, in the context used here, includes diverse people. Among them might be the president's secretary, the loan officer in your bank, a human resources worker from another organization whom you met on vacation, a fellow member in your professional society, or a person in your car pool who has technical knowledge that you need. A network contracts and expands, much like friends and acquaintances in general.

Impressing network members is important because these people are more likely to offer their assistance if they have faith in your capabilities. One reason is that many people prefer to help those in the work place who are the most likely to make good use of the assistance. If the world were completely fair, the least impressive people would be offered the most help by network members. The world is not always fair, however. For example, the wealthiest people receive the biggest salary increases and the most expensive gifts.

The tactics and strategies described in this chapter are aimed at impressing people outside your day-to-day work contacts. However, many of them can be applied to any people you are trying to impress in order to gain the edge.

DISPLAY A POSITIVE ATTITUDE

As in most aspects of life, being positive impresses people. A positive attitude is especially important for impressing network members because their help is voluntary. People you work with directly may feel an obligation to offer you assistance. But network members must be motivated to go beyond their job description to provide you the help you need.

Gregg Joseph, a marketing manager in a consumer products company, was laid off because his position became redundant after a merger. After putting together a plan for finding new employment, Gregg began his job search by speaking to network members. Instead of bemoaning his fate and making negative statements about his former company, Gregg spoke in positives. He told network members that he was now faced with his important career challenge, finding a new job at age forty-five. Gregg talked with confidence about finding the right match between his skills and experience and an opening that must exist somewhere.

One of the many people in his network Gregg told his story to was Austin Bailey, an occasional squash partner. Austin commiserated with Gregg's plight, but had no suggestions to offer. Three weeks later, however, he heard from his sister that the marketing manager in her company had quit suddenly. Austin's sister casually mentioned that the company president did not want to go through the hassle of formally recruiting a replacement. Instead, the company wanted to quietly and quickly fill the position with a competent person. Austin told his sister that he knew a very enthusiastic guy who might be interested in applying for the job.

Austin ran into Gregg at the squash club two days later and informed Gregg of the opening for a marketing manager. Gregg telephoned Austin's sister, obtained the necessary information, and then called the company president the following day. After the president received a copy of Gregg's resume, Gregg was invited for a series of interviews. As a result of these interviews, Gregg received the nod to fill the marketing manager position. Although Gregg had to take a $6,000 pay cut, he was very appreciative. The roots of Gregg's successful networking began with the positive attitude he displayed toward his contacts.

An extremely professional way of expressing a positive attitude is to communicate to network members that you take joy in accomplishment. Let your contacts know that you take pride in your work and that you thrill at meeting your daily challenges. Your network members will be impressed and will be more likely to extend help than if earning money were your only motivation for working.

Eloise Barzan owned and operated a successful wine and spirits store in Boston. She spoke with whomever would listen about the excitement of purchasing interesting wines and making them available to her customers. The love Eloise had for her work helped attract wine connoisseurs to her store.

Eloise's love for her work helped her in another important way. One of her customers recommended Eloise to teach a wine-selection class offered in a local adult-education course. The joy in accomplishment Eloise displayed lead to an exciting professional opportunity. Eloise's class also helped her expand the store's customer base because about one third of her students became customers.

PROVE YOUR WORTH

Because network members are more likely to offer assistance to a winner, it is important to prove your worth to your contacts. Proving your worth is often difficult because most of your network members, as defined here, are not people who work with you regularly. Casually mentioning awards and recognitions you have received, such as Employee of the Month, is helpful.

Larry Betlem, a telecommunications technician, found a high-tech way to impress network members. Larry is responsible for repair and maintenance on the telephone switches for an insurance company. Larry implemented a monthly preventive-maintenance program to decrease telephone downtime and increase the reliability of the system. Larry uses a monthly problem log to show all the downtimes of the telephone system. Larry enters this information into a personal computer to prepare an attractive graph showing management how well the technicians are doing in comparison to the industry standard.

When Larry observed how impressed his superiors were with the graphics on telephone-system performance, he decided to leverage his accomplishments. He sent copies of two of his most dramatic graphics to six people in his network. A network member who ran a telephone equipment business saw considerable merit in Larry's analysis of uptime and downtime. He offered Larry part-time, off-hours employment as a telephone-system troubleshooter.

Larry thus gained the edge by proving his worth (and documenting his accomplishments).

INGRATIATE YOURSELF
TO NETWORK MEMBERS

A major strategy for impressing network members is to get them to like you. Before asking for a favor, put your contact in a good mood or make him or her think favorably of you.

Ingratiating tactics are more effective when they have been used repeatedly, rather than when they are used exclusively when you need a favor. At the point of asking for a favor, however, use an extra jolt of ingratiation. Following are a sampling of sensible ingratiating tactics that have worked for others. However, the general principle is to remember to go out of your way to get network members to like you.

Acknowledge Favors

Whenever a network member does a favor for you of any size, acknowledge the good deed. A telephone call, a thank-you note, or a token gift should do the job. Elaine Rafferty, a real estate broker, has memo pads printed with her name, company, and a headline, "You really helped me out. . . ." Elaine then prepares a handwritten note acknowledging the specific type of help received and an expression of appreciation. Thank-you notes are important for Elaine because she is so dependent upon network members telling her about people who are potential buyers or sellers of houses. If you are not in a business where leads are so critical, an acknowledgment note would be even more impressive.

Take the Initiative in Exchanging Favors

Knowing that you may need a favor from a network member in the future, take the initiative to exchange favors. Offer to do a favor, or just do it, without stating that you will expect future repayment. Ram Gupta, an international student, wrote a note to his finance professor (with a copy to the dean of the college) explaining how much he enjoyed the course in corporate finance. His note read in part, "You are the most enthusiastic professor I have met in the United States. Our College should have more professors like you."

One month later Ram requested a favor from the professor. He wanted him to write six letters of recommendation for graduate school. The professor remembered so fondly this fine student with the excellent judgment about quality teaching. He prepared a glowing recommendation, with a special comment about Ram's love of knowledge.

Treat Suppliers with Respect and Kindness

Your suppliers can be key players in your network. They can help you out of a jam when a quick delivery is needed, and they can offer you special prices that will make you look good. It is therefore productive to get suppliers to like you. The easiest approach is to thank your suppliers for their fine service (when deserved) and even *pay for a supplier's lunch* at least once a year. Be prepared, however; he or she may have a brief cardiac arrest.

Befriend Key Administrative Assistants

Very important network members include administrative assistants to powerful people inside and outside your firm. Administrative assistants can help you obtain an appointment with a powerful person. They can also be instrumental in blocking you from getting the appointment by not putting you on the executive's calendar. It is therefore important to look for sincere yet impressive ways of befriending administrative assistants.

Thanking administrative assistants when they do get you an appointment is a good relationship builder. Another act of friendship is to remember the names of your target administrative assistants. Greet them warmly and enthusiastically and address them by name. Ben Okata, a management consultant, uses a sensible and effective way of ingratiating himself to administrative assistants.

According to Ben, "If I have more than a few contacts with an important executive secretary, I bring her a small gift. It's usually something like an attractive ball-point pen or bookends. I include a note saying how much I enjoy doing business with her. I can't trace specifically what leverage I have obtained from these gifts, but I do seem to get better treatment when I try to get through to the boss."

Ask for Advice

A multipurpose way of ingratiating yourself to people is to ask their advice. Most people are flattered when you ask their advice, providing the advice is not interpreted as brain picking. Another reason that asking advice may ingratiate you to network members is that giving advice is part of a network member's role. By asking advice, you are therefore giving your network member an opportunity to feel useful.

Ask advice about job-related issues. It is more effective than seeking advice about personal matters if you are trying to gain the edge in a work context. Here are a few representative advice-seeking questions to ask network members.

   ❖ How would getting an MBA help me in my career?

   ❖ Should I wait for the economy to improve before beginning my job search?

   ❖ Will letting my co-workers know I am gay have a negative impact on my career?

Be a Do-Gooder

Reach out and provide assistance to network members who are experiencing adversity. Your kindness will be remembered when you have any favor to ask. Rachel Pinsky, a surgical nurse, learned that the daughter of one of the surgeons she worked with was having a Little League fund drive. Rachel delivered two large trash barrels of bottles and cans to the surgeon's house as a contribution to the fund drive. The large donation helped the surgeon's daughter go over quota. From that time forward, the surgeon paid more careful attention to the nurse's advice when they teamed together.

Send Birthday Greetings

Sending birthday cards to network members is an effective ingratiating tactic because it has a surprise element. Birthday cards from employers and co-workers are much more likely to be perceived as a routine gesture, even if they are appreciated, than are cards from a more casual acquaintance. Kerry Baskin, an employment-agency owner, systematically collects information about the month and day, but not the year, of the birth dates of people in her network. She enters these into her computerized file. When the computer sends a message about a birthday, Kerry sends a card accompanied by a personal note to the network member. Kerry believes strongly that her birthday cards create a positive climate that leads to many referrals for her agency.

BEFRIEND COMPETENT
AND SUCCESSFUL PEOPLE

Befriending competent and successful people benefits your career in two important ways. Above all, winners can do more for you so they are your most valuable network members. The same strategy can be used to impress people in your network. Other people will be more eager to enter your network if they think they will be joining a select club.

Many people want to associate with people who themselves associate with winners. Notice how quickly people flock to meet and greet a person who has achieved a major promotion. A primary motive of theirs is to associate with the newly successful person. However, many of these well-wishers also want to move in on the successful person's circle of contacts.

Maureen Braden became the first woman bank president in Duluth, Minnesota. "I received calls from people whose names I didn't even know," said Maureen. "If I wanted to, I could have had a luncheon appointment every working day. The owners of small companies wanted me to join their boards of directors—with no fee, of course. Several corporate women wanted me to share with them my secrets of success. Others wanted me to preapprove loans before they went through normal bank procedures.

"Several people wanted to arrange get-acquainted meetings with me and other officers of the bank. I guess they just wanted to be exposed to as many important people as possible."

One of the points illustrated by Maureen's experiences is that potential and actual network members will be impressed by the caliber of others in your network. One-by-one as you bring competent and successful people into your network, you will gain a stronger edge.

DIVERSIFY YOUR LUNCHEON COMPANIONS

Luncheons have always been a primary setting for effective networking. Many important contacts are initiated and nurtured during business lunches. At times these network lunches consist of groups of three, four, or five people. Avoid the comfortable trap of nurturing the same old contacts during lunch. It is more effective from a career standpoint to diversify your luncheon companions. A network multiplies in value rapidly as you add more members. Each new network member may make your name known to a few more people, thus multiplying your number of direct and indirect contacts.

Diversifying your luncheon companions is especially impressive for group lunches. You impress regular members of the luncheon group when you invite a new, interesting (and influential) member into the luncheon group. Rich Manley, an executive for a paper company with offices in the Pan Am building in New York City, puts considerable effort into diversifying his luncheon group.

When Rich hears or reads about an interesting and influential person, he jots down the name. He often extends that person an invitation to join him and several companions at the restaurant atop the Pan Am building. Rich's pitch is that he and his friends would like to get to know such an accomplished person. Rich's invitees have included newly appointed corporate officers, inventors, sports figures, and political figures.

Rich's network members are impressed by his ability to attract such interesting luncheon companions, which entices them to stay in his network. Rich, of course, is rejected by many of the people to whom he extends cold-call luncheon invitations. Nevertheless, he receives many acceptances because of the novelty of being invited by an executive to dine at a prestigious restaurant.

STAND OUT AT TRADE SHOWS, SEMINARS, AND PROFESSIONAL MEETINGS

Trade shows, seminars, and professional meetings are a natural setting for building your network. Business cards are exchanged at a dizzying pace during such meetings. Because so many participants at these events are actively networking, you have to compete with others to gain attention. Keep these suggestions in mind for creating a good impression at large, work-related gatherings:

❖ Carry distinctive business cards. Some people now distribute business cards with a notch on the bottom that fit directly on small, desk-top files on a wheel. (Rollodex is but one brand of these files.)

❖ Look fresh, crisp, well-rested, and sober. Pack clothing that does not wrinkle readily, or bring along a travel iron so you can press your clothing daily.

❖ Take the initiative to talk to interesting and important-looking people. If you wander around aimlessly you won't look important.

❖ If you choose to enhance your social life during the gathering, do not use the same opening line on everyone, and do not hit on too many people. The reputation of a "lech" spreads as rapidly through a convention as Legionnaire's disease.

❖ Take a leadership role of any kind. Take your turn at a booth, be a panelist or a discussant, or arrange to make even a brief presentation. Being on stage gives you an allure that will impress potential and present network members.

❖ If your organization will pay for it, schedule a happy hour event in your room. Cocktail and fruit juice parties are a major attraction at seminars, trade shows, and professional meetings. Network members will be impressed with your generosity, thus giving you the edge.

BECOME A RESOURCE PERSON

A valuable role for a network member is to be a resource person for technical know-how and imaginative ideas. Let it be known that you are capable and willing to share technical expertise and help others solve problems. Your contacts will be so impressed that they will mention you to other people and nominate you for good assignments.

Wayne Randall was a young electrical engineer working with several other engineers, most of whom had completed college several years before. He was also a member of his local electrical engineering society. Wayne's group was working on a product controlled by microprocessors and operated by software written in the C-programming language.

While all members of Wayne's group were computer literate, several had difficulty adapting to writing software in "C language." Most of the members in Wayne's engineering society had similar difficulty with this new programming language. Wayne, who was very knowledgeable of the language, volunteered to help co-workers and society members with any problems they encountered.

Over the course of three months, several colleagues in his work group and engineering society came to Wayne for technical advice on the C-programming language. Because he was such a valuable resource, Wayne was invited to be the president-elect of his local engineering society. Wayne believes that this accomplishment will help him gain more job visibility. Being a resource person has helped Wayne achieve a mini breakthrough in his career.

CULTIVATE POTENTIAL SUPPLIERS

Suppliers are an important part of your network. They can provide you with the resources needed to accomplish your job quickly and at a good price. Quick access to out-of-the ordinary suppliers also makes another contribution. You will impress others in your network if you have ready access to key resources. Assume that a network member from another organization telephones you mentioning that she is facing a problem: "My firm is taking some heat from the Equal Employment Opportunity Commission. We are underrepresented with Latino accountants. Do you know of any experienced Latino accountants who might be looking for a new opportunity?"

You mentally flip through your files and respond: "I think I can get you in touch with the person who can help you. He runs an employment agency that specializes in recruiting professionals who are minorities. Let me give you his number, and tell him I referred you." Whether or not the employment agency can help your friend hire several Latino accountants immediately, you have created a positive impression. Being such a good resource person will make you a more powerful network member.

SEEK OPPORTUNITIES FOR MENTORSHIP

Being a mentor to younger, less experienced workers, whether they are subordinates or co-workers, is an important activity. Your superiors will be impressed because you have taken the time to teach the ropes to and generally develop other people. Mentoring can also help you impress others in your external network if you act as a mentor, or coach, to others who do not work for the same employer. If you volunteer to help a less experienced person develop professionally, he or she is likely to become a loyal supporter.

An example of a possible direct payout from mentoring took place in the consulting field. Self-employed consultants typically do not extend help to other consultants in their field because of the competitive nature of landing clients. Harvey Strand, a human resources consultant, had a different attitude. While attending a human resources convention, he met Teresa Adornato, a young consultant in the same field. Teresa was building a clientele of smaller firms that lacked a separate human resources department. Harvey invested some time in discussing client development with Teresa, with an emphasis on how to pin down consulting contracts.

Harvey's advice and coaching proved useful to Teresa. A small-company general manager mentioned that the parent company was searching for an experienced person to become the director of human resources. Teresa did not think that she had the experience necessary for the position. Nor was she particularly interested in leaving the consulting practice she had worked so hard to develop.

Teresa gave Harvey's name to the manager as a possible candidate for the position. The company contacted Harvey, and he wound up taking the position because he was looking to get back into corporate work. The good impression Harvey had created by mentoring Teresa lead to a breakthrough in his career.

GIVE GIFTS OF AFFECTION AND WARMTH

We have mentioned several times the positive impact of unexpected gifts in solidifying relationships in the workplace. Gifts are especially well suited to impressing members of your network because they are unanticipated. As with co-workers and lower-ranking people, give small surprise gifts that suit your network members' interests. Bring back from a vacation a gift showing warmth and affection for the network member you would like to impress. Sandra Hewlett, an interior designer, knew that one of the people in her network, Roger Askew, had a passion for spring-driven watches. Roger's problem was that these watches were no longer manufactured, and so few could be found in working order.

While on a business trip in Boston, Sandra went for a walk in an older neighborhood. Browsing in a jewelry store, Sandra spotted an older make of a Bulova wind-up watch. When Sandra picked up the watch to examine it, the jeweler said: "You know that's a spring watch. Are you sure that's what you are looking for?" "Precisely," answered Sandra. "This would make the perfect gift for a friend of mine."

Sandra brought back her find and presented it to Roger as a gift. Roger was both appreciative and impressed. He kept Sandra's name clearly in mind as an interior decorator to recommend to one of his clients should the issue arise.

DISTRIBUTE PERTINENT ARTICLES

If you want to impress network members at a more professional level than dispensing gifts, send them useful articles from newspapers and magazines. To accomplish this activity you need an updated file on the professional interests of your network members. Bruce Hayward, a financial analyst who uses this method, offers constructive advice for receiving appropriate credit when you send articles: "Make sure you write a brief note on the article to prevent someone from taking credit for your discovery."

Clipping and sending articles is doubly impressive. First, it shows that you are alert to developments in your field outside your specific job. Second, it reflects a genuine interest in the recipient's welfare. Either of these reasons, or a combination of the two, could be enough to give you the edge in a competitive situation.

USE YOUR BEST TELEPHONE AND VOICE-MAIL ETIQUETTE

Much networking takes place over the telephone because most network members work outside a person's work place. Using your best telephone etiquette therefore can help create a positive impression with network members. Many aspects of telephone etiquette are well known. As a quick review, however, I list examples of poor telephone and voice-mail etiquette. Avoiding as many of these actions as possible will create a good impression:

- ❖ Not returning messages for over one week, even though you are in town.

- ❖ Interrupting your conversation with a network member to talk to somebody else who is passing through the office.

- ❖ Putting your caller on hold while you switch over to a second caller who is on call-waiting.

- ❖ Eating or drinking while on the phone.

- ❖ Reading mail while on the phone, and murmuring "mmmh," "mmmh," to pretend you are paying full attention to your caller.

- ❖ Yawning while talking over the phone.

- ❖ Leaving a message on an answering machine or voice mail such as, "If I don't hear from you, I will assume that you can meet me at 12:30 on January 9, at the Pine Oaks for lunch." (You had made no previous mention of this luncheon date.)

- ❖ Leaving inane, annoying messages on your machine, such as an impression of the President of the

United States saying that you are attending a cabinet meeting and will return later.

On the positive side, by listening attentively and having brief, focused telephone conversations, you will impress your network members with your professionalism. Call back after hours those network members who want to talk over personal problems at length and who need your emotional support.

TURN DOWN REQUESTS VERY GENTLY

The major purpose of belonging to a network is to receive and give support. You help out a network member in some way, and he or she returns the favor later. If you turn down requests for favors you will quickly become an unimpressive network member. However, there are times when the favor requested of you is more than you are willing or able to handle. At that point you may have to politely reject the request.

At other times, a request may not be overwhelming, but you have received so many similar requests that you feel exploited. Elizabeth Pryor, a vice president of human resources, made such a complaint: "I must receive two calls a week from people in my network, all making the same request. They want to get together with me to discuss job opportunities, or future job openings. They have all learned not to ask outright that they want me to help them find a job in my company.

"If I granted all these interviews, I could never get my own work done. For more than 90 percent of these callers, I have had to explain that my regular job responsibilities involve extensive interviewing of potential applicants. I therefore have no more time for in-person interviews about job exploration. However, I do offer to spend a few minutes over the phone answering questions they might have about conducting a job search."

Elizabeth turns down requests gently and gives network members a modicum of help. She may not be creating the most positive impression, yet she is offering enough help to avoid creating a negative impression.

DECORATE YOUR OFFICE TASTEFULLY AND CREATIVELY

An effective way of impressing network members who visit you at work is to decorate your office creatively. Unless you are a top executive or a business owner, you have little say about the size of your office. However, you can often negotiate to have certain unattractive pieces of furniture removed and replaced. In some circumstances you can bring in some furniture of your own to make your office unique.

To impress visitors from your network, find a way to make your office stand out because of its tasteful and creative flair. If your office is small and cramped, remove as much clutter and wall decorations as possible. Very few powerful people in business or government work in cluttered offices. Highlight one or two pieces of original art. Attractive art can often be obtained at low prices at flea markets. Only a minuscule number of people can tell the difference between the work of well-established artists and that of talented, but unknown artists. The art department at a local high school or college might have excellent original works of student and faculty art for sale at nominal prices.

Many network members who visit the office of university official Tom Plough are impressed by his stand-up desk. In addition to being a tasteful piece of Swedish furniture, the stand-up desk impresses because of its novelty. Many first-time visitors to Tom's office ask questions about this unusual piece.

When decorating your office creatively, guard against putting decorative items in your office not warranted by your rank. For example, do not duplicate the fine china used to serve coffee in the executive suite. To do so is a career demerit.[1] In the past at IBM, for example, the amount of overhang on your office desk was tightly controlled by rank. ("Overhang" is the distance the top of the dish extends beyond the back of the desk.) A supervisor was allowed no overhang, while a top executive could overhang by as much as two feet. IBM has loosened these restrictions in recent years.

DISPLAY CULTURAL SENSITIVITY

Many organizations today are celebrating cultural diversity. These firms go beyond the legal requirements for practicing equal employment opportunity. They take the initiative to welcome the fact that their work force is composed of people from different racial, ethnic, and religious backgrounds. Toward this end, some firms have established a cultural diversity week. Activities include posting art from different cultures and serving a variety of ethnic foods in the cafeteria. The same companies aggressively recruit a culturally diverse work force.

Capitalizing on this trend, you may be able to impress many people in your internal and external network by displaying cultural sensitivity. Demonstrate to others that you go beyond lip service in talking about a diverse work force. Take the initiative to show an awareness of how to respond to cultural differences. Abundant opportunities are not found for showing that you welcome cultural diversity. When the occasion arises, however, seize the opportunity. Use the following examples of being sensitive to cultural diversity to jog your thinking about additional possibilities.

❖ Send African-American members of your network Martin Luther King, Jr., Day greeting cards and messages. Also send them Kwanzaa to recognize African history.

❖ Avoid saying "Merry Christmas" to Jews, Muslims, and Hindus. If you wish to extend greetings for a religious holiday, choose the one, such as "Happy Chanukah."

❖ When negotiating with Asians or Latin-Americans, be slow and deliberate. Most people from these countries feel awkward when relationship building does not precede getting down to business.

❖ Practice pronouncing names from different cultures so you can say correctly the name of a person from another country on first meeting. You will take pride in the person's smile when you pronounce his or her name correctly. Your network member will also be very impressed. As an investment analyst from China, Hanchio Zhou, told an American manager, "You are first person in America who pronounce my name right, first time."

BE ARROGANT SELECTIVELY

Many powerful people use arrogance to their advantage. Occasional arrogance helps project a high degree of self-confidence. Your touch of arrogance lets others know that you think you fare well in comparison to the competition and that your ideas are sound. Be careful not to push arrogance to the extreme whereby you appear unwilling to listen to criticism and suggestions.

You may lose some popularity among network members by arrogance, but the loss will be offset. You will attract people who want to be associated with winners. When Steve Jobs, one of the co-founders of Apple Computer, founded another computer company, Next Computer, many industry analysts were skeptical. Jobs was told that the competition was too tough, the market was flooded, and his machines would be overpriced. Jobs persisted in telling others that his new computers were the best and that they would revolutionize the workplace. Investors and prospective employees ignored the critics and streamed toward Jobs.

When the first computers produced by Next Computer met with moderate reception from the media, Jobs persisted in his arrogance. He told others that his company had established the new standard of excellence in the industry. Potential customers in Jobs' network eventually sided with him, not with the critics. Steve Jobs' arrogance paid off as his company reached $1 billion in sales within several years, a feat accomplished during a downturn in the computer industry.

In summary, choose among the following tactics to help give you the edge with network members. By gaining the edge, you may be able to break through the pact and achieve your goals.

1. Display a positive attitude.
2. Prove your worth.
3. Ingratiate yourself to network members.
4. Befriend competent and successful people.
5. Diversify your luncheon companions.
6. Stand out at trade shows, seminars, and professional meetings.
7. Become a resource person.
8. Cultivate potential suppliers.
9. Seek opportunities for mentorship.
10. Give gifts of affection and warmth.
11. Distribute pertinent articles.
12. Use your best telephone and voice mail etiquette.
13. Turn down requests very gently.
14. Decorate your office tastefully and creatively.
15. Display cultural sensitivity.
16. Be arrogant selectively.

❖ **10** ❖

CONVINCING
PROSPECTIVE
EMPLOYERS

Vacancies among good managerial and professional jobs are scarce. Impressing prospective employers has therefore become more important than ever. Whether you are conducting a job campaign because you are unemployed or to find a better job, you will have to stand out from other job seekers.

We assume you have already studied a book about conducting a job search and have mastered the basics. Here we touch lightly on the familiar and concentrate on the current challenges faced by job seekers. Among these challenges are rampant age discrimination and the issue of being overqualified. We also emphasize the subtle psychological approaches that have a big impact on who gets hired for a good job.

WRITE AN ATTENTION-GETTING
COVER LETTER

After you have found a job lead through whatever source, it is imperative to send a cover letter to the prospective employer. Usually the cover letter accompanies a job resume, but it can stand alone. The cover letter is the first document the hiring official sees when he or she opens your envelope. The purpose of the cover letter is to grab the prospective employer's attention within ten seconds. The cover letter explains in two or three paragraphs how you can help the prospective employer and what are your most significant biographical facts.

A cover letter must accompany the resume because the cover letter links you to the particular prospective employer. A resume is more general, even if it is tailored to meet the requirements of a specific position opening. Most cover letters are far too bland. To circumvent this problem, prepare a hard-hitting, almost brash, opening line specifying the contribution you intend to make. Here are two examples:

1. Person seeking employment in credit department of garment maker: "Everybody has debt-collection problems these days. Let me help you gather in some of the past-due cash that you rightfully deserve."

2. Person seeking employment as customer service manager for an electronic equipment company: "Who needs disgruntled customers who turn to competitors and bad-mouth you to their business associates? With my track record of improving customer service, I know I can reduce customer defections."

Many people who have used an attention-grabbing opening line say the method works. However, there is a small downside risk. You may create the impression of being too arrogant. The risk of using a more conservative opening line is that your cover letter will go unnoticed among a flood of others.

USE A MODERN RESUME

A modern, compelling resume is needed for almost all job searches at the managerial, professional, and technical levels. Even in situations where an organization takes the initiative in asking to interview you, you will be still asked for your resume. The mechanics of good resume writing are well-known. Less well known is the importance of highlighting skills and accomplishments in your resume and of using action words.

Skills and Accomplishments

Important facts such as your work experience, education, and position objective are still part of the modern resume. To pick up on the theme of what you can do for your employer (rather than the reverse), however, you must highlight skills and accomplishments related to the position under consideration. The greater the number of job applicants available, the more employers insist on valuable skills and accomplishments. Here are some skill areas to help you think through which skills you currently possess:

Communication: writing, speaking, knowledge of foreign language, telephone skills, persuasiveness, listening.

Computer: ability to run specific software programs such as Wordperfect, Lotus, DBase, and Harvard Graphics; ability to learn new programs; skill in using computers to improve decision making.

Creative: originate ideas, think of novel solutions, develop several options for a problem.

Customer service: serve customers, handle complaints, deal with difficult people.

Interpersonal relations: ability to get along with others, be a team player, diplomacy, conflict resolution, understand others.

Management: ability to lead, organize, plan, motivate others, manage time, coordinate activities.

Mathematics: math skills, analyze data, budget, statistical analysis, chart preparation.

Sales: persuade others, identify customer needs, negotiate, close a sale.

Your resume should emphasize the skills that best fit the job you are seeking. Listing all of the preceding skills would appear too generic. The more focused your skills are as they apply to the position under consideration, the better the chances of your being invited for an interview. In today's job market, even top-level managers (who are supposed to be generalists) are hired in part because of their specific skills. For example, some presidents are hired because they have special skills in turning around a financially troubled company.

Accomplishments

A concise listing of accomplishments is essential for today's competitive job market. Your accomplishments can be described in a separate section or listed with each job. Even if you did not accomplish anything unusual in a given position, stating the results you did achieve may sound impressive. For example, a tax accountant might write: "Prepared income tax reports for 1,550 individual and small-business owners. No client was investigated for tax fraud by the Internal Revenue Service." Following are several examples of concise statements of accomplishments found on the resumes of successful job seekers:

"Recruited, selected, and trained sales force of 10 people to open the Southeastern region for our company. During the first year, our team sold $6,000,000 worth of building materials. Exceeded forecast by $2,000,000." (The sales manager who noted this accomplishment pointed to two vital accomplishments: building a sales force and exceeding sales quota.)

"Successfully introduced an automated bookkeeping system, using IBM line of personal computers. Kept all financial records for company with annual sales of $4,000,000. Saved more than $10,000 in uncollected accounts receivable by offering cash discounts. Trained five bookkeepers, all of whom stayed at least two years."

(The head bookkeeper who listed these accomplishments focused on major contributions for any bookkeeper: automating a bookkeeping system and finding ways to save money.)

Action Words

Another important feature of an effective resume is the presence of action words. Typically these action words are verbs but can be an adjective such as "lengthy experience." The purpose of these words is to communicate the message, almost subliminally, that you are energetic, purposeful, and action-oriented. Each sentence on your resume should begin with an action verb, such as "Rejuvenated a failing product," or "Cannibalized obsolete machinery to repair working equipment." Here is a sampling of action words for use in your resume.

Achieved	Established	Maximized
Activated	Expanded	Modernized
Analyzed	Forged	Negotiated
Balanced	Formulated	Planned
Broadened	Generated	Spearheaded
Completed	Headed	Streamlined
Conquered	Implemented	Targeted
Delivered	Innovated	Updated
Designed	Juggled	Visualized
Developed	Launched	Zapped
Eliminated	Liberated	

Using these action words has another advantage for resume construction. It circumvents the problem of using "I" frequently. Begin a sentence, "Juggled," instead of "I juggled."

PERFORM AT YOUR BEST EVERY MOMENT

As noted by career counselor Julie Griffin Levitt, "time out" does not exist during the interview. The quality of your interaction with the receptionist and administrative assistant is often reported back to the interviewer. Your first impression and your parting words all count in forming an opinion about your job qualifications. Following are some of the most important interview behaviors for performing at your best and impressing the interviewer.[1]

Shake hands firmly

Everybody knows that a firm, dry handshake is important, but few people practice to develop a convincing handshake. Remember to lean toward the interviewer while shaking hands.

Project an air of self-confidence and pride

Walk confidently into the interview situation as if you deserve the position. Maintain good posture while standing, walking, and sitting. Consciously minimize nervous mannerisms such as hand wringing, cuticle tearing, hair twirling, and face scratching. As a manager from the Hilton Hotel chain said, "If an applicant for a hotel manager position acts like a winner, we're interested. If the applicant looks like a loser, he or she has no chance of receiving a job offer."

Display optimism, energy, and enthusiasm

Akin to projecting self-confidence is the display of optimism, energy, and enthusiasm. Sprinkle your conversation with positive phrases such as, "I'm sure I could make a positive impact if given a chance," and "I can deliver high-quality customer service." Project energy by talking at an above-average pace but guard against slurring words and appearing nervous. Talk about personal interests and hobbies that require physical energy such as chopping wood, racquet ball, and volley ball. Show you are mentally energetic through mention of reading related to your specialty and to business in general.

Display organized thinking

To an experienced interviewer, the quality of your thinking reveals as much about you as the specific facts you describe. Use noticeable beginnings, middle, and ends to your answers. Strive for concise, thoughtful answers. Above all, avoid rambling. An interviewing tactic used by some industrial psychologists is to ask the job applicant an open-ended question such as, "What are you good at?" The psychologist then says nothing and times how long the person keeps talking without any response from him or her. (The record holder is a man I interviewed who kept talking for sixteen minutes. A background check revealed that the applicant was indeed a compulsive talker whose rambling frustrated co-workers.)

Concentrate on being likeable

Just or unjust, likeable people get hired more readily and are the last to be laid off (assuming they are good performers). Ingratiate yourself to the interviewer by smiling, giving compliments, and expressing appreciation for being interviewed. At the right moment, mention how you help others both inside and outside your organization. Be a tad self-effacing if the opportunity arises. For example, if the interviewer says, "I notice that you were the tenth highest sales producer in your company." You respond with a smile, "True enough. But we had a very small sales staff."

Remain professional and slightly reserved

Despite the importance of being likeable, do not attempt to become the interviewer's chum. You could run the risk of being perceived as presumptuous or aggressive.[2] Don't ask questions about the interviewer's family or talk about possible future social activities together. As in many impression-making tactics, finding the right balance between two opposite sets of behaviors is important. Find the appropriate midpoint between friendliness and likability versus professional reserve and aloofness.

FOCUS ON HOW YOU CAN HELP THEM

At every stage of the job search, emphasize how you can help the prospective employer. Be much more concerned about your potential contribution than about presenting a litany of your experiences and current interests. Assume the mental set of a consultant who is being considered for solving an important problem facing the organization. Explain how a skill you have mastered could be put to use in helping the company. Whenever appropriate, explain how you might be able to bring in more revenue for the company or might be able to cut costs.

Dave Rodgers, a production engineer, impressed a prospective employer by taking the initiative to explain how he could improve one of their systems. Although the example is technical, it is worth noting because it illustrates the key tactic of focusing on how you can help the prospective employer. The engineering manager interviewing Dave asked him to review a layout of a conveyor system. Dave commented briefly on how the system would have inherent gridlock.

The interviewer asked Dave to back up his assertion. Dave explained that the configuration required that all loads must pass by two locations twice on each transaction. One pass was on the input trip and another was on the output trip. According to an important principle of conveyor design, all loads must pass each location only once on each trip. Dave explained that because of the throughput requirements the system would not work.

The interviewer excused himself from the interview and said he would return in fifteen minutes. After speaking to his boss, the interviewer returned and invited Dave back for a second interview the next day. Dave's analysis impressed several people at the company, and he received a job offer at the end of his second interview. Dave had gained an edge by giving the prospective employer a sample of how he could help them.

Prospective employers, in increasing numbers, are demanding that job applicants show how they can be helpful. The demand often takes the form of asking the applicant for a skill demonstration. An applicant for an administrative assistant position was handed a ringing phone, and told, "Here, you answer this call the best you can." Nonplussed, the applicant impressed the interviewer by saying, "Good afternoon, Blackstone Associates. Although this is my first five minutes on the job, I will do the best I can to help you." She was hired.

MAKE THE INTERVIEWER FEEL IMPORTANT

Back again to one of the most universally effective way of creating a good impression: Make the interviewer feel important. Avoid being a sycophant, but look for openings to acknowledge the interviewer's status and to give compliments. If the interviewer makes an original statement, compliment his or her innovative thinking. An example:

INTERVIEWER: The tie business has boomed during the last recession. Apparently many men who couldn't afford to buy new suits were sprucing up their wardrobes by buying a couple of ties.

YOU: Your analysis is a real eye-opener to me. I never thought the tie business was resistant to a recession.

An impressive way of making the interviewer feel important is to conduct research about him or her. You might uncover information you can use to appeal to his or her status needs. Laura Bechtel applied for a position as a chemical lab supervisor. After receiving a letter from her interviewer, she searched *Chemical Abstracts* for any research articles published by the interviewer. Laura found abstracts of two such articles about how resins perform at extreme temperatures. During the warm-up part of the interview, Laura said sincerely, "I notice that you are an expert on how resins respond to extreme temperatures." Laura and the interviewer developed an immediate rapport, and the rest of the interview proceeded beautifully.

SHOW KNOWLEDGE OF THE COMPANY AND ITS OPERATIONS

All job-finding primers state adamantly that the applicant must be familiar with basic facts about the prospective employer. You are urged to read annual reports, company brochures, and possible newspaper and magazine articles about the company with whom you have an interview. Because every sensible applicant recognizes the importance of obtaining basic knowledge about the company, you must proceed one step further to gain the edge.

The impression-making additional step is to use the company's product or service beforehand, or interview someone else who has. The same principle applies to seeking employment in a nonprofit organization. For example, if you apply to work at a hospital, interview a couple of former patients. During the interview, speak knowledgeably about the product or service. Done with tact, it may be impressive to discuss problems associated with the product or service.

Susan Okata, a marketing major, applied for a position with Waterman Pens. When asked if she had any questions about the company, Susan responded affirmatively: "I have a concern more than a question. I worry that Waterman pens are too durable. My father has had his Waterman for twenty years. It works perfectly. Repeat business must be a real problem when your pens are of such high quality."

The interviewer, who was very impressed, smiled and responded: "You are quite perceptive, Susan. Our pens do last almost a lifetime. However, people such as your father often buy our pens and pencils for others as gifts." Susan had gained an edge by using her knowledge about the company's products to offer a constructive criticism.

DESCRIBE INTERMEDIATE-RANGE CAREER GOALS

An inevitable interview question is to be asked to describe one's career goals. The job seeker faces an immediate dilemma. If lofty future goals are expressed, the interviewer might conclude that the applicant regards the position under consideration as merely a stepping stone. If the applicant does not project goals beyond the present position, he or she might be interpreted as lacking ambition.

A recommended way around this dilemma is to concentrate on the intermediate range when discussing goals. Be honest but avoid appearing gluttonous. If career growth interests you, talk about your hopes of advancing after you have established yourself as a solid contributor in the assignment under consideration. Emphasize that you are interested in future promotions, but you also believe in growth within the job. Explain that in your opinion too many people overlook the chance to add to their skills in their current job.

The higher the position you apply for, the more contentment you should express with that level of responsibility. Jim Petri, an unemployed executive, applied for a position as a division general manager at a midwestern appliance maker. During a series of interviews Jim talked about his hopes of becoming the CEO of a major corporation, including that appliance company. Jim was one of two final candidates for the division general manager position. Stunned that he did not receive an offer, Jim asked for an explanation of why he was rejected. The president responded, "Jim, we felt that you weren't really interested in this job. It looks as if you would be content only as the CEO. We want somebody in this position who would be truly happy."

Jim had failed to achieve the important breakthrough he desperately needed in his career because he talked too glowingly about a job beyond the division general manager-ship. Jim might have received the offer had he talked more about the challenges he saw in the position for which he was applying. Instead, Jim projected the impression that taking a position as a division general manager was an interim step toward his real goal.

HAVE REASONS TO JUSTIFY YOUR PLANS

Sometimes you must defend your reasons for seeking a specific position or trying to gain entrance into a new field. More justification is required when a position is far removed from your current or most recent position. Develop a truthful and plausible explanation why the position under consideration represents a sensible career move.

Louise Talty was a product manager in a food products company undergoing consolidation. Although her position was not yet scheduled for elimination, Louise thought her future with the company was unstable. For Louise's tastes, her company was too riddled with uncertainty. Louise also found the political game playing insufferable as people competed to hold on to their jobs. She was bothered particularly by how readily staff members blamed one another for mistakes. To escape this hostile environment, Louise launched a job search.

Several months into her job search, Louise interviewed for a position as a store manager for a unit of a national firm that sold imported gifts. Although the regional manager who interviewed Louise was impressed by her credentials, he was skeptical. He asked Louise why she was willing to take a pay cut and move out of the industry into retailing. Louise launched into her carefully prepared explanation: "First of all, money is not my only reason for working. Besides, if I perform well for you I suspect my income will rise back to where it was. My most important reason for wanting to manage your Fountain View store is that I want to be in control of my fate. I also want tangible evidence of my accomplishments.

"The future of my position in my company is uncertain. Because of the consolidation, people are scrambling around and are not sure who is responsible for what. I want a job with a clear focus, so my results can be measured. Managing a store with a reputation such as yours would feel like being the owner of a successful business.

"As a product manager, it's much harder to measure my results. So many people are involved, and there is so much politics. I want to go home each week and be able to point to what I've contributed to the corporate welfare."

The regional manager was impressed by Louise's logical and honest explanation of why she wanted a career shift. This presentation along with her good overall credentials helped swing the employment decision in favor of Louise. She gained the edge by having excellent reasons to justify her plans.

DESCRIBE HEALTHY WEAKNESSES AND WHAT YOU ARE DOING ABOUT THEM

A standard job interview question asks about the candidate's weaknesses. A self-defeating response to such questioning is that you have the right to avoid self-incrimination. Unfortunately, the rules for court appearances do not apply to a job interview. Besides, if you deny having weaknesses you will appear defensive, uninsightful, or both. Another complication is that an experienced interviewer may spot your weaknesses anyway, or they might be revealed through reference checking.

Questioning about weaknesses or limitations is best handled in two ways. First, describe weaknesses that could be interpreted as strengths. In other words, the weakness you describe also has a beneficial aspect. Second, explain what you are doing to overcome the problem. A few examples of healthy weaknesses and remedial action plans follow.

- ❖ "I've been told that I'm too impatient. When people don't follow through with their commitments, I get upset. It also upsets me when people do sloppy work. I'm trying to calm down more so I don't intimidate people."

- ❖ "I admit to being a perfectionist at times. Before I sign off on a project, I want to make sure that everything is as perfect as it can be. I would rather a piece of work be late than lousy. What I'm doing about this problem is to recognize the law of diminishing returns. Some minor projects aren't worth polishing to perfection."

- ❖ "A former boss of mine accused me of being too customer oriented. I will fight the company to do what is best for my customer. To me, the real boss is the customer. I have been trying to develop more of a company perspective. I guess there are times when a customer's demand cannot be fully met without causing the company problems."

A person presenting the type of weaknesses just described would have fulfilled the interviewer's requirements of finding something negative to say about the candidate. All three weaknesses, however, would be admired by many. Being humble enough to work on these weaknesses would also contribute to gaining the edge for the candidate.

ASK INSIGHTFUL QUESTIONS

Asking the right questions during the selection interview can create a positive impression. A guideline is that higher-level, higher-paying positions require more insightful and penetrating questions. Asking about cost-of-living increases would be more appropriate for a telemarketing specialist than for a sales manager. However, even if you are applying for an entry-level position, remember to ask several impressive questions.

The most impressive questions are those that reflect a sincere interest in the work itself, the welfare of the company, and in the joy of accomplishment. Unimpressive questions relate to such matters as employee benefits, parking facilities, and how the potential employer can satisfy your needs. Instead of asking about basic employment information, request a copy of an employee handbook.

Here is a sampling of questions that reflect an interest in higher-level aspects of the position under consideration and of work in general. Rehearse them before an interview so they appear natural.

1. If hired, what kind of work would I actually be doing?

2. How much contact would I have with decision makers?

3. What would I have to accomplish on this job to be considered an outstanding performer?

4. What did you like best about the previous incumbent in this job?

5. What mistakes did the previous incumbent in this job make?

6. How do you measure accomplishment in this job?

7. What kind of advancement opportunities would be available to me if I performed outstandingly in this job *for a long period of time?*

8. What personal characteristics are most important for success in this job?

9. To what extent do you want the person who holds this job to be imaginative and creative?

10. Where does this position fit on the organization chart?

11. If hired, what would be the ideal contribution I could make to your organization?

Observe carefully how all the above questions focus on either the potential contribution of the applicant or on other important features of the job. The thrust of these questions is away from self-gain and toward helping the prospective employer accomplish his or her mission. Such a line of questioning is impressive.

MAKE EXTENSIVE USE OF ACTION AND POWER WORDS

In Chapter 1 we described the importance of speech in projecting a dynamic, self-confident image. A job interview is yet another situation in which effective speech is important in creating a good impression. Using correct grammar and minimizing junk words and vocalized pauses are important. Many people who use poor grammar and vocalized pauses themselves will be impressed by another person who speaks well. The reason is that many people are not aware of the weaknesses in their own speech.

Also to impress during an interview, extensively use action and power words, much like those in your resume. Action and power words help create a mental image of you as a person who will accomplish results for the employer. During your job interview, look for the opportunities to use action-filled, and powerful words and phrases such as these:

❖ "I would jump in with both feet to turn around the poor customer service record you describe."

❖ "I would do an end run around the competition."

❖ "I want to be paid for the results I achieve."

- ❖ "You can expect me to hammer out win-win solutions to the problems you describe."

- ❖ "I would bring a situation like that to a climax."

- ❖ "I might have to rattle a few cages, but I would get the job done."

- ❖ "I would pound the boards until something good broke loose."

- ❖ "I hope we can strike a deal because I know I can achieve the results you want."

- ❖ "Believe me. I have a good sense of what tough decisions have to be made to turn a profit."

In addition to these being action-oriented sentences, they reflect the jargon of business that will add to your credibility. Notice also the lack of equivocation and suppositional thinking. If not overdone to the point of sounding comical, action and power words can have an almost hypnotic effect on the hiring official.

WEAR IMPRESSIVE CLOTHING

Every sensible job applicant dresses well for a job interview, so merely dressing well is a defensive strategy. If you dress poorly you will disqualify yourself, while dressing appropriately will keep you only competitive. My advice is to dress fashionably in a style that meshes with the prospective employer. It is also important to avoid wearing brand-new clothing because it may look unnatural, or bought just for the occasion.

Scrutinize the fine points, such as well-polished shoes with heels and soles in good condition. In addition, add a flare such as a jacket-pocket handkerchief for a man or a silk scarf for a woman. Rings worn on more than one finger can project an image of confidence and power. A cleanly polished attaché case can also enhance your image. A good scent from cologne or perfume makes good sense.

Try out several different combinations of clothing to find a mix that helps you feel confident and comfortable. Ask the opinion of several friends as to which outfit does the most for you. After you have chosen what you think is an impressive outfit, give little further thought to clothing. Your appearance is but one of many other factors that will give you an edge in impressing the prospective employer.

CHOOSE A LATE-AFTERNOON INTERVIEW

Given a choice, accept a late-afternoon interview because it increases your chances of being selected among many applicants. According to employment counselor J. I. Biegeleisen, during the mornings and early afternoons the interviewer is inclined to be extra choosy. The last person interviewed has the best chance of being remembered. He or she is impressive just because of being remembered better than the other applicants.

A study revealed that the last in a string of applicants interviewed in one day is three times more likely to be hired than are preceding applicants. The first person interviewed may not receive much attention and usually does not get the job offer.[3] This study applies mostly to a situation in which the applicants have comparable qualifications.

If your interview is early in the day, take the results of this study as a call to action. Work extra hard at impressing the interviewer in the many other ways described in this chapter.

TAKE THE INITIATIVE IN DISCUSSING OVERQUALIFICATIONS

Many unemployed people enter the job market realizing that they may not be able to find another job at the same level as the one they left. Being realistic, these people seek new employment at a lower level and are willing to accept a salary well below what they were making. Unfortunately being willing to take a cut in pay and responsibility usually fails to convince the job interviewer. Many of these job seekers are rejected by prospective employers as overqualified. They are told repeatedly that the company is reluctant to hire them into a lesser job because they will leave once they find a better position.

Although the problem of being overqualified is a major dilemma, the situation is not hopeless. You can impress the prospective employer by convincing the company official that you are adjusting to the new reality of the work place. Emphasize strongly that in today's economy it is necessary for many people to drop down the occupational ladder to earn a living. Point out that a vacancy for a position such as your most recent one can hardly be found. Explain that your family is behind you and that you are learning how to live acceptably on a lower income.

Mona Baker had worked her way up to vice president of consumer loans at her bank. After the bank was consolidated with a larger one, Mona was one of many employees to be laid off. Two months into her job search, Mona realized that finding a comparable position in another bank seemed improbable. All the banks in her area were trimming down rather than hiring, except for a few teller positions. Mona then directed her efforts toward finding any position within or outside banking. Several times when Mona applied for a much lesser position than she had held previously, she heard intimations of being overqualified. Mona then revamped her tactics. She took the offense on the issue of over-qualifications. Here is how she approached one employment situation:

"I applied for the position as the credit union manager at a hospital, at about a $10,000 pay cut. Before I even heard cries of overqualification, I explained that I was fully aware that this job pays less than the one I had. I also explained that the job I had no longer exists and that my $242 per week in unemployment benefits would soon run out.

"I emphasized to the hospital administrator that my fifteen years in private banking would be very beneficial to the hospital employees. The hospital would be getting a banking professional to manage its credit union. I also emphasized how appreciative I would be to use my past experience to benefit me in a career shift. I said that I looked forward to the stability of working at a hospital, after the turbulence I experienced in banking."

Mona got the job. Had she not taken the initiative to confront the issue of overqualifications she would have failed to get the job she needed. By getting the job, Mona gained an important edge.

CONFRONT THE AGE FACTOR

A major concern of unemployed job seekers over age forty-five is that they are victims of job discrimination. Thousands of middle-age job seekers lament, "If you are over forty-five, forget it. Nobody will hire you." Despite the gross illegality of age discrimination in hiring, it is widely practiced. One exception is for people at the very top of their fields. Presidents of giant corporations who lose their jobs find many job opportunities. Another exception is that many retail stores and franchise restaurants have been hiring some people in their fifties and sixties for entry-level positions.

In short, the vast majority of middle-aged job seekers face job discrimination based on age. Older people are simply overlooked when it comes to making a final selection of candidates. A person's age might be inferred from school graduation dates, years of experience, or appearance. Confronting the issue can sometimes work because all employers have an official policy of "no job discrimination." Say upfront to the prospective employer, "As you can surmise, I offer a wealth of experience that comes from many years of productive work. I am proud of my age and experience. I am not hesitant to mention my age because I realize it is not a disqualifying factor."

After hinting that you are aware that age can sometimes be a negative employment factor, the hiring manager may worry about appearing to practice age discrimination. No sensible employer would overtly deny a job candidate fair consideration because of his or her age. The legal repercussions are too great. His or her response to your hints about age is likely to be: "We are an equal opportunity employer. Age itself is never the basis for making an employment decision." You might gain the edge by alerting the company to the importance of not denying you a fair chance because of age.

BE OPEN AND POSITIVE
ABOUT HAVING BEEN TERMINATED

Lying about having been terminated usually backfires because the truth will surface during a background investigation. Recognize also that if you have lost your job involuntarily, you have plenty of company. Laying off competent workers at all levels has been widespread in recent years. An impressive approach is to state the facts surrounding your termination and admit to some wrongdoing if appropriate. Emphasize the more acceptable and palatable reasons for your job loss. Make sure to emphasize that you are not angry, embittered, or revengeful. Here are some healthy reasons for being terminated that could possibly explain your situation.

> ❖ "I was the victim of a political squeeze play. I fell into disfavor with my boss's boss because he wanted a close friend of his to take over my position. My boss was helpless to prevent me from getting axed. I'm appreciative of the good years I had with my company."

❖ "When the new management took over, it became arbitrary as to which people would be included in the 20 percent downsizing. Unfortunately for me I was one of the 20 percent who was asked to leave. I'm disappointed but not angry. I was doing some important things that I wanted to complete for the company."

❖ "The company president decided to replace me after I had received ten consecutive above-average performance appraisals. I wish it hadn't happened, but I wasn't surprised. She had fired twelve managers in four years. The job was a wonderful experience, but I'm not unhappy about having left the company. I would like to work in an atmosphere of better human relations."

❖ "I was let go because I let my professionalism interfere with being a good politician. I knew I had the best program for improving quality, but the vice president of manufacturing thought otherwise. I pushed too hard for what I believed in. If I had to do it over again, I would have been more patient in advancing my program."

In each of the preceding explanations for being fired, the job seeker gives a plausible reason. He or she also appears able to keep the termination in perspective—an impressive quality.

STAY COOL
DURING THE STRESS INTERVIEW

The stress interview is designed to test under pressure your actions, logic, and emotional control. Using this technique, the interviewer deliberately makes you uncomfortable through such means as direct insults, false accusations, and by questioning your integrity. Other stress-inducing techniques include the interviewer creating a long period of silence or asking you a series of rapid-fire questions. It is easy to become defensive, distraught, or angry when the interviewer does such things as:

❖ Sits across from you and says nothing, waiting for you to begin talking about yourself.

❖ Comments, "Most people with your type of experience have been a big disappointment to our firm. What's so special about you?"

❖ Asks, "Why did you attend the college you did? Weren't you able to get accepted to a first-rate school?"

❖ Yawns when you describe your strengths.

❖ Asks you a long series of questions in five-second intervals.

❖ Asks you why you have so many nervous mannerisms.

If you encounter a stress interview or stress questions, be cool. Take a deep, relaxing breath, show you are in control, and be courteous. To relieve some tension, smile politely at the interviewer. Another approach is to handle the pressure by expressing your feelings assertively. State how you feel but avoid being abrasive or hostile—even if such a response is deserved. Two possible comments are:

"I feel as if I'm being placed under pressure. I don't mind because I work well under pressure."

"Is this what is called a stress interview? It makes me tense, but I'm willing to cooperate."

Expressing your feelings helps relieve tension and enables you to think more clearly. If you remain calm under the heat of a stress interview you have gained the edge because you have demonstrated your ability to handle pressure.

TALK ABOUT COMPETITIVE JOB OFFERS

Under the best of circumstances, your job search will yield several offers. Having one or more job offers in writing can work to your advantage if they both arrive within about thirty days. We specify a time bracket because many job offers are withdrawn if not accepted within a month. Having a job offer from another firm in hand adds to your allure, following the principle of playing hard to get. Prospective employers, as well as most people you might be trying to impress, attach a higher value to someone who is in demand by others. The prospective employer may trust his or her own opinion of your potential value as an employee. Nevertheless, the fact that another employer wants you is reassuring.

An employer will assume that another firm has also screened you carefully, including checking your references and conducting a background investigation. The latter usually includes a thorough credit check. Employers consider a good credit record to be an important part of the screening process. Employees in financial trouble are considered poor security risks.

The competitive-offer technique must be executed with finesse and sensitivity. Bluntness about your offer may be interpreted as a strong-arm tactic to pressure the prospective employer into making a quick employment decision. Marvin Stith was searching for a position as a telecommunications manager in the San Francisco Bay area. Marvin wanted to remain in the Bay area for family reasons, yet his employer was relocating to lower-priced quarters in Salt Lake City.

Marvin's job search brought quicker and better results than he anticipated. Within two months Marvin had received an offer as the telecommunications manager at a large financial services firm. Before deciding on the offer, Marvin followed through on one more job interview. It was scheduled for one week later, which was soon enough to avoid a long delay on reporting back to the investment firm. The second interview was with an insurance company and appeared to be even more promising than the first. If hired, Marvin would be in charge of a telecommunications group twice as large as the one at the investment firm.

As Marvin reached the end of a day of interviews at the insurance company, he was told that his credentials had been received favorably by the series of interviewers. He was also told that the company would be interviewing other candidates for the same position. Marvin was then asked how much interest he had in exploring the position further. Marvin replied, "I like what I see, and I'm happy that you people are interested in me. Yet I do have a timing problem facing me. Apparently the demand is high for a person in my field. I have a solid offer that I must either accept or decline in three weeks. I am not pushing for a quick decision on your part, yet timing is a factor."

Marvin's moderate-pressure tactic worked. He was invited back for a half day of additional interviews and was made an attractive offer one week later. Marvin had gained the edge by using his first job offer to strengthen his appeal to the second employer. By stating politely that he had received a competitive job offer, Marvin had made himself a valued resource.

SEND AN ENTHUSIASTIC THANK-YOU OR FOLLOW-UP LETTER

Your responsibilities in job hunting do not end with the employment interview. The vital next step is to mail a courteous thank-you letter several days after the interview. Even if you decide not to take the job, a brief thank-you letter is advisable. You may conceivably have contact with that firm in the future.

If you want the position, state your attitudes toward the position and the company, using action words and specifying your potential contribution. Summarize any conclusions reached about your discussion. A thank-you letter is a tip-off that you are interested in the position. Sending such a letter may therefore give you the edge over other applicants.

A follow-up letter is slightly different from a thank-you letter. If you have not heard from the prospective employer within one month after the interview, send another letter indicating that you are still interested. If there is still no response write one or two more follow-up letters. Point out that although this position is your first choice, you may now be forced to give serious thought to a competitive job offer. (After two months have passed without a response, the applicant is usually slipping away from consideration.)

Fax technology has added a new dimension to thank-you and follow-up letters. A fax correspondence adds a touch of drama and urgency to your interest in the job. The disadvantage of a fax is that it may appear too commercial and lacking in warmth. Because a thank-you or follow-up letter is intended to reflect courtesy and good etiquette, send the letter through the mail.

Following is a copy of a thank-you letter written by a woman who interviewed for an assistant service manager position at an automobile dealership. She received a job offer two weeks after her letter was received.

Dear Mr. Monroe:

Thank you for my recent chance to discuss the assistant service manager position with you and Mr. Ralph Alexander. It was illuminating to see what a busy, successful operation you have.

I was impressed with the amount of responsibility the assistant service manager would have at your dealership. The job sounds exciting, and I would like to be part of the growth of the dealership. I realize the work would be hard and the hours would be long. However, that's the kind of challenge I want and can handle.

My understanding is that my background is generally favorable for the position, but you would prefer more direct experience in managing a service operation. Because the car repair and service business is in my blood, I know I will be a fast learner.

You said that about two weeks would be needed to interview additional candidates. Count on me to start work July 1, should you extend me a job offer.

Sincerely,

Rita Mae Houston

Impressing the prospective employer encompasses many different actions and attitudes. In addition to being well qualified for the position, choose from among these tactics:

1. Write an attention-getting cover letter.
2. Use a modern resume.
3. Perform at your best every moment.
4. Focus on how you can help them.
5. Make the interviewer feel important.
6. Show knowledge of the company and its operations.
7. Describe intermediate-range career goals.
8. Have reasons to justify your plans.
9. Describe healthy weaknesses and what you are doing about them.
10. Ask insightful questions.
11. Make extensive use of action and power words.
12. Wear impressive clothing.
13. Choose a late-afternoon interview.
14. Take the initiative in discussing overqualifications.
15. Confront the age factor.

16. Be open and positive about having been terminated.

17. Stay cool during the stress interview.

18. Talk about competitive job offers.

19. Send an enthusiastic thank-you or follow-up letter.

❖ 11 ❖

A MASTER PLAN FOR STANDING OUT

So far we have presented about 330 tactics and strategies for standing out and gaining the edge in a given situation. Gaining the edge will often enable you to break through to a desired outcome in a given situation or in your career. Pick among all the tactics presented to fit your particular circumstance and personal style. Remember, however, that gaining the edge and breaking through requires hard work and patience. At times you will achieve a quick success with one tactic, but long-term success requires diligent application of many of the tactics and strategies already described.

In addition to the suggestions you may have already begun to implement, or have contemplated implementing, study the master plan in this chapter. It incorporates and integrates some of the suggestions already offered, but also presents new ideas. The master plan is an overall strategy, based on sensible principles of human behavior and business strategy, designed to help people succeed. The plan has twenty widely applicable components. Not all of them will be relevant to your circumstances. Only you will know what will work best for you, so choose accordingly:

1. Be self-confident, positive, and enthusiastic.
2. Develop a useful specialty.
3. Develop a synergy between both halves of your brain.
4. Perform beyond expectations.
5. Develop charisma.
6. Be an effective negotiator.
7. Be proactive more than reactive.
8. Maintain a dossier of your track record.
9. Be an effective listener.
10. Flatter people sensibly.
11. Get talented and influential people on your side.
12. Think of everything.
13. Advocate total customer satisfaction.
14. Be composed under pressure.
15. Make a deliberate show of ethics.
16. Work hard and play hard.
17. Look upon adversity as a challenge.
18. Combat self-defeating behavior.
19. Visualize yourself standing out.
20. Choose an edge-gaining tactic to fit the situation.

BE SELF-CONFIDENT, POSITIVE, AND ENTHUSIASTIC

The basis of self-improvement is that you control *most* of your thoughts. We use the term "most" because, at least for the short range, some thoughts are not completely under our control. For example, most people cannot avoid feeling angry and depressed if they lose their job. Yet you can prevent those negative thoughts from dragging you down for months. You can learn to develop a generally positive outlook, both about yourself and other people, and about outside events.

Being confident, positive, and enthusiastic gives you the edge in several important ways. Because you believe in yourself, you are less likely to do things that defeat your own purposes, such as thinking that you will fail on an important assignment. Being positive is beneficial in your interactions with others because most people would prefer to interact with an optimist rather than a pessimist. Without realizing it, people will withdraw from the pessimistic, dour person. If you are a positive person, others are more likely to want to hire you, promote you, buy from you, and sell to you, and to be a member of your network.

Todd Daniels, a vice president in international marketing, presents an oft-repeated rationale for being confident, positive, and enthusiastic: "In my experience, managers seek out enthusiastic employees for promotions and exciting new assignments. My favorite employees are always willing to try something new and approach their work with energy and optimism. It is sometimes acceptable to voice frustrations with a difficult situation, yet not in a complaining manner.

"The worst impression you can create is apathy. If a manager approaches with a suggestion or idea, never respond with a shrug or act as if it doesn't interest you."

DEVELOP A USEFUL SPECIALTY

An endless controversy is whether being a specialist or a generalist improves one's chances for success. Early in a career, being a specialist has a clear advantage. Most of the higher-paying jobs are offered to people with definable occupational skills. To become a high-level manager, one must gradually become a generalist—a person who has some skills in several activities important to the organization.

Although a high-level manager is indeed a generalist, the most in-demand executives are generalists who also have developed a useful specialty. Executives who are selected for breakthrough jobs are chosen because of their leadership ability combined with a unique expertise. Among the areas of expertise in demand are turning around a troubled company, opening new markets, and making deals.

Vittorio Cassoni, the executive vice president of operations at Xerox Corporation, exemplifies an executive whose specialty enabled him to achieve a breakthrough in his career. Prior to being recruited to Xerox, Cassoni held key posts with Olivetti (in Italy), AT&T, and IBM. Vittorio was known for his leadership and management abilities, but his esoteric specialty was in forming strategic alliances with other companies.

A strategic alliance is basically a joint venture between two companies in which they share expertise. Cassoni was hired in 1992, an era when forming strategic alliances was regarded as an important talent. This was true because evolving technology promises to obscure the differences among office machines that copy, print, and create documents.

Just as having a specialty is important for an executive, have a subspecialty is important for a specialist. Find a niche that you can fill better than others with the same occupational title. At any job level, develop a talent that distinguishes you from others doing comparable work. Donna Larson, an administrative assistant at a mail-order company, became the resident expert in installing computer programs that combated several strains of computer virus. The attention she received for this important accomplishment helped to propel her to the position of office supervisor.

DEVELOP A SYNERGY BETWEEN BOTH HALVES OF YOUR BRAIN

Highly effective people have the capacity to be logical *and* analytical, and creative *and* intuitive. They know how to achieve a synergy between both halves of the brain. The left side of the brain is the source of the most analytical, logical, and rational thought. It performs the tasks necessary for well-reasoned arguments. The right side of the brain grasps the work in a more intuitive, overall manner. It is the source of impressionistic, creative thought.

To gain the edge in most situations, you decide whether it is time for logical and analytical, or creative and intuitive thought. For example, at one phase of a project you might be generating dozens of possible solutions to a problem. At another phase of the same project it may be necessary to scrutinize the advantages and disadvantages of each alternative.

The creative person achieves a synergy between both halves of the brain. Robert Gundlack, a physicist who has amassed more than 150 patents during his 35-year career, explains it this way: "Being creative means developing a synergy between the left half of the brain—the analytical half—and the right half of the brain—the creative half. I learned that at home during my childhood. My mother was an artist, a painter of landscapes. My father was a chemist, an inventor of Wildroot hair oil. Both my parents influenced me equally well."

With practice you can hone both halves of your brain, thus achieving a synergy between the two. Devote time to both analytical and logical and to creative pursuits. If you are mostly the analytical type, spend more time doing creativity-enhancing exercises such as writing poems and brainstorming. If you are mostly the creative type, spend more time with activities such as playing chess, running computer software, or developing a budget.

PERFORM BEYOND EXPECTATIONS

The single most important principle for gaining the edge, breaking through, and being successful in general is to perform beyond expectations. Be focused and concentrate intently on what you are doing; strive for peak performance. Find out what ordinary people are supposed to accomplish in your job, then do your best to be extraordinary. This same principle can be used to impress everybody with whom you interact in the work place.

A useful perspective for performing beyond expectations is to regard your job description as a document describing minimum performance. The person who does only what is routinely expected by the organization is destined to mediocrity. Step outside your job description if it means that you can make a bigger contribution to the organization. (And don't forget to toot your own horn softly.)

Bill Schuyler, a former production supervisor in a scrap-metal company, illustrates what is meant by stepping outside one's job description. In the scrap-metal business the biggest challenge often is finding scrap metal to melt down and separate into salable components. At Bill's company there is a backlog of customers waiting for reprocessed metal. Although not paid to purchase scrap metal, Bill stays alert to sources of supply for his company. While on a fishing vacation, Bill overheard a man say that his employer would soon be tearing down an old factory because it was obsolete. Bill sprang into action and asked, "And what will you be doing with all the rubble? I'm sure my company would be interested in taking away all your old metal."

Bill's quick-thinking inquiry led to an enormous supply of very salable scrap metal for the company. His willingness to step outside his job description in this and on so many other occasions helped Bill be promoted to plant superintendent. And he continues in his informal role as a good will ambassador for his company.

DEVELOP CHARISMA

An effective way to impress people is to have personal charm, warmth, and magnetism. Although some aspects of charisma are tied in with basic personality traits, you can take steps to be more charismatic. In Chapter 6 we described six suggestions for becoming more charismatic as a leader. Two of the points are also applicable in all aspects of the work place. Learn to be a colorful communicator and how to express your feelings in a positive way. You can also add to your charisma by developing a unique quality such as a penetrating sense of humor or the capacity to remember names.

Lorie Probst, a retailing executive, rose rapidly in her career partly because of her merchandising savvy. However, her distinguishing ability to individualize her approach to dealing with store personnel enhanced her acceptance as a leader. When Lorie had business to conduct with a department head or a store associate, she did not jump into her agenda immediately. Instead, she began by asking about a project or concern of the person with whom she spoke. She kept these important facts both in her head and in a notebook. A typical conversation opener was this, "Terry, I recall that your department had reduced the return rate on goods sold. How is that figure holding up?"

The simple expedient of showing knowledge about and interest in all her team members enhanced Lorie's leadership image. Her individualized approach to people contributed as much to her charisma as the warmth she projected. The series of promotions Lorie received were a tribute to her charismatic handling of people. The promotions were also the breakthrough she wanted in her career.

BE AN EFFECTIVE NEGOTIATOR

As described at length earlier, negotiating is an essential skill for gaining the edge. Without effective negotiating skills you are unlikely to gather your fair share in a variety of work situations. Among them are reaching a decision on a starting salary, termination agreement, the size of your budget, travel allowances, furnishings for your office. Add to this list buying and selling and working out provisions to a contract.

In addition to mastering the negotiating tactics described in Chapter 2, keep in mind two crucial points about negotiation. First, recognize that many more agreements and decisions in the work place are negotiable than are ordinarily thought. You can often get more than first offered simply by asking. Instead of taking what is handed you, ask for something more or better if you think your request is legitimate.

Anna Atkins, a claims processor, provides a case example of asking for what you want. She signed on as a part-time employee on a work-at-home assignment for an insurance company. The company supplied Anna with a personal computer to send her completed documents directly to the company. Anna also saw that she would need a fax machine. Just before purchasing a machine with her own money, Anna asked if the company would be willing to make the purchase. To Anna's delight, the company did provide her a fax machine.

A second major principle of negotiating to remember is that an important goal is to arrive at win-win solutions. If both parties walk away from the negotiation with important needs being met, they will be able to preserve a good working relationship. When both sides are satisfied, there is much less chance that the deal will have to be renegotiated. Your challenge as a negotiator then is to develop options for mutual gain. Ed Barnes, a small-business owner, provides us a useful example of arriving at win-win solutions to a negotiated agreement. Ed owns and operates a store that provides floor coverings to businesses and individuals. A party house was negotiating a carpeting contract with Ed's firm. After all the selections were made, the estimate came to $15,000. The customer prospect then decided to delay installing carpeting because of the expense.

To save the deal, Ed offered to hold all his office parties at the party house for the next five years. In addition, he would be willing to refer any business he could to the party house. The owner of the party house agreed to the deal because it meant extra business for her. She did not lose out on the carpeting because Ed offered a fair price. Ed gained the edge because he intended to schedule parties anyway, and he was able to supply the carpet from inventory.

BE PROACTIVE MORE THAN REACTIVE

A basic principle for gaining the edge is to take constructive action before a problem surfaces that requires urgent attention. Besides, being proactive rather than reactive is another buzz word in vogue. Being regarded as proactive is more beneficial than carrying the label "reactive." By definition, a proactive person is a careful planner. In contrast, a reactive person is a fire fighter. One can never eliminate the need for some fire fighting, yet balancing between planning and responding to emergencies is important.

To become more proactive, a person has to develop a keen sense of anticipating problems and opportunities. If you wait too long to respond to an opportunity or to solve a problem, it may be too late to gain the edge. Carla Sanchez, the director of nondegree programs at a small college, used proaction to help save her program and her job. The nondegree program at Carla's college was shrinking rapidly. Carla predicted that if enrollment in her program did not stabilize or improve the program would lose its status as a separate entity.

Rather than wait for the college to collapse her program, Carla surveyed current trends to see what new demands might exist for her program. One day she read an article about the many businesses in her community engaged in overseas trade. Carla saw this as an opportunity to offer foreign-language training for business people. Carla made a pitch to several firms, and her ideas met with immediate acceptance. Her unit of the college offered special classes in Japanese, Spanish, and German for businesspeople. The program has been a continuing success and a joy of accomplishment for Carla.

MAINTAIN A DOSSIER OF YOUR TRACK RECORD

Maintaining an updated dossier of your tangible accomplishments is another bedrock principle for gaining the edge. A current resume is necessary but not sufficient. Also include work samples and quantitative assessments of your contribution to making or saving money. Work samples include such items as a copy of a customer service training program you helped develop, or a strategic plan for developing a new product.

Graphics can add drama to your dossier. Sam Ebersole, a health and safety director, developed a graph depicting his accomplishments. The amount of employee time lost due to accidents and sickness was plotted on the vertical axis. Time was plotted on the horizontal axis, covering a twenty-year period. At year ten an arrow was drawn, with the notation, "Sam Ebersole appointed." The graph showed a steady decline in employee lost-time since Sam joined the company.

BE AN EFFECTIVE LISTENER

A multipurpose tactic for gaining the edge is to listen intently. In review, the central skill in listening is to concentrate intently on what the other person is saying and not saying. If you listen carefully, you will often gather solid clues as to the other person's interests and motives. You can then modify your tactics to gain advantage. Sales trainers, for example, often tell their clients, "selling is listening."

An example of the power of listening took place at a firm that provides maintenance services to office buildings and free-standing companies. The president of the company had returned from a Total Quality Management training program. Enamored by the teamwork ideas in TQM, he spoke to his top staff about the importance of teamwork. Jerry Landau, the sales manager, listened intently. He observed that although the president waxed ecstatic about teamwork, he still kept referring to impressive individual performances. Other staff members did not listen carefully enough (or lacked the insight) to observe this discrepancy.

In the ensuing weeks, several members approached the president with proposals for more teamwork in the company. The president nodded in agreement but made no commitments. Jerry, in contrast, proposed a new contest for the "maintenance technician of the month." The president bought the idea and complimented Jerry on his ability to find a sensible way to motivate workers. Ironically, Jerry's acceptable proposal focused on individual rather than on team effort. Jerry had gained the edge by listening to what the president was *really* saying.

FLATTER PEOPLE SENSIBLY

One of the least expensive, and most effective, tactics for gaining the edge is to flatter people sensibly and credibly. Despite the risk of being called obsequious, a cheap office politician, or a sycophant, the flatterer wins. An intelligent, perceptive person like yourself can probably see my point. Just the fact that you are reading this book is a credit to your professionalism and your quest for valid information. As reported in a management newsletter, "There is virtually no limit to the amount of praise that most people can swallow, provided that a spoonful of credibility is added."[1]

An effective, general-purpose piece of flattery is to tell another person that you are impressed by something he or she accomplished. A management trainee at a General Electric business unit told the purchasing manager that she was impressed with his modern operation. "It's very similar to the ideal materials management system described in my productions and operations management course," said the trainee. Her flattery appeared to be instrumental in her being asked to become a permanent member of the purchasing department after her training period ended.

GET TALENTED AND INFLUENTIAL PEOPLE ON YOUR SIDE

Many successful people freely admit that much of their success is attributed to their valuable contacts. The greater the number of talented and influential people in your internal and external network, the better the opportunity to break through in your career. The tactics described for impressing superiors and people in your network all apply to getting talented and influential people on your side. Talented people are the most useful when you will be needing business or technical advice. Gaining visibility is especially important for capturing the attention of influential people.

A germane example is Milt Richards, a securities representative and certified financial planner. A person who sells investments can hardly earn a living without good contacts. Sensing the competitiveness of his field, Milt volunteered to be the treasurer of the tennis club to which he belonged. Members of the board of governors of the club came to know Milt well as he carried out the duties of the treasurer. Most board members were people of substantial income and were influential within the community. Within six months, at least 50 percent of Milt's clients stemmed from contacts made directly and indirectly at the tennis club. By incorporating influential people into his network, Milt gained the edge.

THINK OF EVERYTHING

Many potentially successful people fall off the success track because they believe themselves to be beyond taking care of details. "I'm only interested in the big picture; the details are for somebody else," boast many people headed for trouble. It is true that some top-level executives let others worry about many details. Yet they are still aware of which details should be taken care of and by whom. To gain the edge, it is helpful to think of all the little things that could possibly go wrong and take care of them in advance.

Running a successful business or a unit of the organization is much like planning a vacation or a big party. Both will work much better if you think of which details need taking care of beforehand. For example, the overseas traveler must remember to bring along a copy of his or her personal identification number (PIN) that accompanies a bank credit card. Many people forget this number, but it is often needed to obtain a cash advance from an automatic teller machine.

Ned Katona worked as a middle manager at a video supply house. His dedication to details was well respected because he so thoroughly took care of his assignments. Ned's proclivity to think of everything ultimately triggered a promotion he deserved. His company operations were completely computerized, which concerned Ned because of the possibility of computer failure. When Ned learned about the burgeoning of computer viruses, he took it upon himself to make floppy disk copies of all important company files. He stored these in the company warehouse. When the virus Michelangelo struck the company computers, the president was horrified.

Ned calmly informed the president that he had taken the initiative to keep a separate set of computer records. Because the information was stored on disks away from the company computers, they were safe. Ned was applauded and promoted. He had gained the edge by thinking of everything.

ADVOCATE TOTAL CUSTOMER SATISFACTION

Successful businesses have always been built on the idea of pleasing the customer. The current emphasis on total customer satisfaction differs in two significant ways from the traditional emphasis. One change is that all departments today—not just marketing, sales, and customer service—focus on customer satisfaction. Another change is that "total customer satisfaction" has become a buzz word throughout the organization. The politically astute worker makes frequent mention about pleasing internal and external customers. To do otherwise is to imply that you are not a member of the customer satisfaction movement.

Linking your efforts to total customer satisfaction can help you gain the edge. Incorporate pleasing external and internal customers into any goals you set for yourself. At staff meetings, pepper your conversation with anecdotes about superior customer satisfaction. Present gory details about customer dissatisfaction and what you did to rectify the problem. When another staff member makes a suggestion, or enters into a discourse, ask, "How does what you are proposing help our customers?"

Cheryl Hurley, an administrator in a health maintenance organization (HMO), was conducting an analysis of patient enrollment trends. She concluded that the HMO was losing 15 percent of its patients each year. Based on an idea she found in the *Harvard Business Review,* Cheryl proposed that the HMO begin a "No Patient Defection" drive. Brief seminars would be held that pinpointed reasons why patients dropped their membership. All employees at the HMO would be encouraged to wear "NPD" buttons. The hospital administrators approved Cheryl's program.

Even before the effectiveness of the No Patient Defection program was assessed, Cheryl was given a one-step promotion to senior administrator. She had gained the edge by tying into the total customer satisfaction movement. (Should Total Customer Satisfaction fade away in importance, grab on to the next major movement or fad.)

BE COMPOSED UNDER PRESSURE

Successful people are typically composed under pressure. One aspect of being composed under pressure is to avoid an emotional tirade during an altercation on the job. An occasional emotional outburst adds to charisma, but too many outbursts leads to a reputation of emotional immaturity. A hothead reputation does much more damage in a large bureaucracy than it does in a small, entrepreneurial firm. The reason is that large firms value a veneer of politeness and cordiality.

Another aspect of being composed under pressure is more likely to give positive thrust to your career. The person who presents a logical plan during a crisis or under other heavy pressure gains the edge. The ability to create order out of chaos is intuitively recognized as exemplary leadership behavior.

Len Ashton was the customer service manager at an American distributor of low-priced Asian cameras. Thousands of automatic 35mm cameras were placed with dealers, to be sold at a suggested retail price of $65. The cameras came with a warranty, backed by an 800 number for customer and dealer complaints. A mysterious defect arose with the camera under field conditions. When the temperature rose above 90 degrees Fahrenheit, the back would sometimes pop open, thus exposing and ruining the film.

Approximately one month after the cameras were shipped to dealers, the customer service phone lines were jammed with irate customers. Some customers wept as they described how their precious graduation photos were ruined. Within an hour after the first fifty calls were received, Len developed a crisis plan that was immediately approved by top management. Each caller would be offered three free rolls of film, a five dollar gift certificate toward photo equipment purchases, and a camera repair within 30 days. Customers who were still not satisfied were offered a full refund and one roll of film.

Within forty-five days almost all the complaints were handled, and only one dealer was lost. Len emerged as a corporate hero because he was able to resolve a crisis calmly. The edge he gained was a sizeable year-end bonus and assurances of a future promotion.

MAKE A DELIBERATE SHOW OF ETHICS

Ethical behavior can be self-rewarding because self-esteem is enhanced for many people when they behave ethically. Being ethical can give you the edge for an additional reason. Glorifying ethical behavior is another current corporate trend. Being conspicuously ethical will enhance your reputation as having high integrity. Paradoxically, ethical behavior is looked upon favorably even in firms where members of top management are unethical themselves. For example, an investment banking firm duped many of its clients by artificially inflating the price of several of its new offerings. Nevertheless, the principals of the firm claimed that they insisted upon the highest standards of ethical conduct for its employees.

Mary Chambers, a payroll supervisor, made a conspicuous display of ethics that impressed top management. While conducting an audit of her operations, Mary discovered that employees had been overcharged for medical insurance by an average of 30 cents per pay period for sixteen months. The amount of money per paycheck was hardly noticeable to each employee. However, these small incorrect deductions gave the company approximately $11,500 in additional cash.

Mary brought the problem of the excess deductions to the company controller's attention. Mary's remedial plan was to notify each employee about the error through a pay-envelope stuffer. The company would apologize and deduct the total owed each employee from one insurance payment. The company controller thanked Mary for her ethical solution to the problem. He noted that many people in Mary's position would have suggested that the company correct all further deductions, but keep the $11,500 as miscellaneous earnings.

WORK HARD AND PLAY HARD

Part of the philosophy of many people who consistently gain the edge is to work hard and play hard. Such people are devoted to their work but are also are passionate about nonwork activities, including family, friends, hobbies, or community activities. Successful people who work hard may not necessarily work longer hours than anybody else, but they do work smarter. They tend to concentrate their efforts on projects that will either make money or save money. The same people value time as a precious resource and invest time wisely as much as possible, both in work and personal life.

Learning to work hard and play hard often is a matter of striving to eliminate nonproductive use of time. A breakthrough person, for example, is unlikely to spend thirty minutes at a morning rest break with co-workers. The same person, however, might invest those thirty minutes if he or she were attempting to build relationships with others or to tune into the office grapevine.

At home the person who works hard or plays hard minimizes activities that yield little pleasure or that are done with low intensity. The parent who works hard and plays hard, for example, is unlikely to shuffle through office paperwork while interacting with a child. The work hard/play hard type is more likely to devote separate time to office paperwork and to interaction with children. The result is paperwork handled more accurately and more joyous interaction with children.

Many people who have gained the edge in their careers also gain the edge in their sex life. Being energetic people, they can pursue both work and sex with intensity and enjoyment. An attorney commented, "I like a woman with a career of her own as a sex partner. Since she has learned how to concentrate on the job, she can concentrate in bed."

The edge gained from working hard and playing hard is higher rewards and more intense satisfaction. A career that brings above-average income and status is usually more fun than is one of lesser pay and status. Similarly, intense personal relationships and well-developed hobbies yield more fun than do bland relationships and failed hobbies.

LOOK UPON ADVERSITY
AS A CHALLENGE

Adversity almost inevitably strikes at some point in a person's career. Among these adversities are being fired, being laid off, losing a major account, having one's budget reduced, or falling into political disfavor. Long-term edge gainers do not surrender when adversity strikes. Instead, they look upon adversity as a challenge that must be handled in the way that all major business problems are solved. After getting over the emotional sting, the resilient person explores multiple options to find one workable escape route.

Engineering manager Pete Chan illustrates deftly the importance of looking upon adversity as a challenge. At one time, General Electric decided to move its semi-conductor division from Syracuse, New York, to North Carolina. Pete, the head of the reliability engineering section, did not want to relocate for personal reasons. He and his family were happily ensconced in their community.

Pete's survival plan was to attempt to merge his group with the electronics laboratory in Syracuse. The lab was conducting exciting research in radar, lasers, infrared cameras, and high-speed semiconductor devices. Pete wrote a report to division management explaining how his group would be more effective working with the electronics laboratory than by relocating.

Much to Pete's delight, division management listened to his suggestions and incorporated his group into the lab operations. Several members of his group who wanted to relocate to North Carolina were disappointed, but others felt relieved about not having to struggle with relocation. Pete's group is now a very important part of lab operations. Other departments within the lab depend on his support.

Pete gained a double edge because he was able to keep his work and personal life intact. He overcame adversity by developing a sensible survival plan and selling it to management. His suggestion of merging his group into the electronics laboratory was especially good because it saved money for General Electric.

COMBAT SELF-DEFEATING BEHAVIOR

Lurking within us are tendencies that can work against our own best interests and that can bring about significant setback and defeat. To maintain an edge you have gained, it is necessary to recognize these self-defeating behaviors and get them under control. Soliciting feedback from others is effective in detecting self-defeating behaviors. You might ask a spouse, a close friend, or a former boss: "What behavior of mine have you noticed that if repeated often could damage my career?" Following is a list of some widely observed self-defeating behaviors. Think through which ones might be part of your repertoire.

1. If I don't do a perfect job I feel worthless. _____

2. I am my own harshest critic. _____

3. I drink well beyond healthy limits. _____

4. My use of illegal drugs goes beyond experimentation. _____

5. My tendency to procrastinate is sometimes severe. _____

6. I do many things that could be classified as sexual harassment. _____

7. I waste a lot of time. _____

8. I have trouble focusing on what is really important to me. _____

9. I have trouble taking criticism, even from friends. _____

10. Many times I have rejected people who treat me well. _____

11. When I have an important project to complete, I usually get sidetracked, and then miss the deadline. _____

12. I frequently misplace things, such as my keys, and then get very angry at myself. _____

13. People describe me as the "office clown." _____

14. I have an insatiable demand for money and power. _____

15. I seek revenge for even the smallest hurts. _____

16. I try to get away with as much as I can on the job. _____

17. Time and time again, I come out a loser in situations. _____

18. I often fight with people who try to help me. _____

19. I am often late for important appointments. _____

20. People have often said that I am my own worst enemy. _____

The more of the above behaviors and thoughts you have, the more likely it is that self-defeating behavior can prevent you from gaining the edge and breaking through. If you are unable to overcome most of your self-defeating behavior on your own, talk over the problem with a mental health professional.

VISUALIZE YOURSELF STANDING OUT

Visualization is a primary method for achieving many different types of self-improvement. It is therefore an essential component of a master plan for breaking through to important career accomplishments. To apply visualization, program yourself to stand out in work situations. Imagine yourself engaging in self-enhancing, winning actions and thoughts that allow you to stand out and gain the edge.

Picture yourself achieving peak performance when good results count the most.

Visualization is much like watching a video of yourself doing something right. A starting point in learning to use visualization for gaining the edge and breaking through is to identify a challenging job situation you will be facing. Imagine yourself mentally and physically projected into that situation. Imagine what the room looks like, who will be there, and the confident expression you will have on your face. Think of yourself answering intelligent questions and overcoming objections to your ideas.

Think of key people in the meeting congratulating you for having fully met their expectations. Imagine how proud you will feel when you are asked when is the next most convenient time to work out the agreements reached during the meeting.

SELECT AN EDGE-GAINING TACTIC TO FIT THE SITUATION

The ultimate task for gaining the edge and breaking through in your career is to size up each situation and then select the edge-gaining tactic most likely to achieve the results you want. Before choosing from among the 330 or so tactics mentioned in this book, first establish a realistic goal for every work situation. For the goal-oriented, edge-gaining, breaking-through, standing-out person, every situation has a purpose. At lunch next Tuesday, your goal might simply be to relax and get to know this refreshing new person in your network. If this is your goal, show the soft side of you. Back off on a tactic such as impressing him or her with your expertise.

Perhaps next Friday you will be attending a meeting with an executive who dislikes flunkies and docile people. Your goal is to impress that executive that you are an independent thinker. The edge-gaining tactic you are most likely to choose is "avoid being a yes-person."

Virtually every work situation you face requires self-confidence or good negotiating skills, or deals with superiors, co-workers, lower-ranking people, customer prospects, customers, network members, or prospective employers. Our edge-gaining tactics, plus the master plan, can therefore provide tactics for you to enhance your effectiveness in most work situations.

Following judiciously what we have prescribed is not designed to make you independently wealthy within thirty days or to make you a major corporate vice president within five months. Yet if you establish a realistic goal for each situation, and then select an appropriate stand-out tactic, you will be on the road to breaking through. Good luck and let me know what happens.

❖
─────

REFERENCES

─────
❖

CHAPTER 1

1. Jay T. Knippen and Thad B. Green, "Building Self-Confidence," *Supervisory Management*, August 1989, pp. 22–27.

2. Wolf J. Rinke, "Maximizing Management Potential by Building Self-Esteem," *Management Solutions*, March 1988, p. 6.

3. Adapted from James R. Baehler, "Appearance and Reality," *Success*, May 1987, p. 24.

4. Several of the ideas here are from "Body Language," *Executive Strategies*, April 17, 1990, p. 4; *Body Language for Business Success* (New York: National Institute of Business Management, 1989), pp. 28–29.

5. Work cited in Michael Rozek, "Can You Spot a Peak Performer?" *Personnel Journal* (June 1991), p. 77.

CHAPTER 2

1. Mark Gill, "Unstoppable," *Success*, November 1988, p. 54.

2. "Negotiating: A Master Shows How to Head Off Argument at the Impasse," *Success*, October 1982, p. 53.

3. Gilda Dangot-Simpkin, "Eight Attitudes to Develop to Hone Your Negotiating Skills," *Supervisory Management*, February 1992, p. 10.

4. "Master Tactics to Negotiate and Win," *Working Smart*, August 1991, p. 1.

5. Howard Raiffa, *The Art and Science of Negotiation* (Cambridge, MA: Harvard University Press, 1983), p. 306.

6. "Master Tactics to Negotiate," p. 2.

7. "Master Tactics to Negotiate," p. 1.

CHAPTER 3

1. Many items on this list are from Eugene Raudsepp, "Exercises for Creative Growth," *Success*, February 1981, pp. 46–47.

2. Adapted from Sandy J. Wayne and Gerald R. Ferris, "Influence Tactics, Affect, and Exchange Quality in Supervisor-Subordinate Interactions: A Laboratory Experiment and Field Study," *Journal of Applied Psychology*, October 1990, p. 494.

3. "Get Ahead at PepisCo," *Executive Strategies*, September 18, 1990, p. 6.

CHAPTER 5

1. Andrew J. DuBrin, "Sex Differences in the Endorsement of Influence Tactics and Political Behavior Tendencies," *Journal of Business and Psychology*, Winter 1989, pp. 1–15.

2. "Career 'Insurance' Protects DP Professionals from Setbacks, Encourages Growth," *Data Management*, June 1986, p. 33.

3. Teresa Brady, "Effective Small Talk Makes for Big Success," *Supervisory Management*, January 1992, p. 3.

4. *Ibid.*

CHAPTER 6

1. Sheila Murray Bethel, *Making a Difference* (New York: G. P. Putnam's Sons, 1989).

2. R. Bruce McAfee and Betty J. Ricks, "Leadership By Example: 'Do as I Do!'" *Management Solutions*, August 1986, pp. 10–17.

3. *Ibid,* p. 16.

4. Jay A. Conger, *The Charismatic Leader: Beyond the Mystique of Exceptional Leadership* (San Francisco: Jossey-Bass, 1989).

5. Charles C. Manz and Henry P. Sims, Jr., "Super Leadership: Beyond the Myth of Heroic Leadership," *Organizational Dynamics*, Spring 1991, pp. 23–30.

6. Kenneth Blanchard, "How to Get Better Feedback," *Success*, May 1985, p. 6.

7. Merril E. Douglass, "Standing Saves Time," *Executive Forum*, July 1989, p. 4.

CHAPTER 7

1. William Zikmund and Michael D'Amico, *Marketing* (New York: John Wiley, 1984), p. 534.

2. Mark B. Roman, "Gold Rush," *Success*, March 1987, p. 50.

3. David J. Rachman and Michael M. Mescon, *Business Today,* 3rd edition (New York: Random House, 1982), p. 307.

4. "Psychology at Work," *Working Smart,* October 1991, p. 8.

CHAPTER 8

1. Jenny C. McCune, "The Perfection Principles," *Success,* April 1991, p. 27.

2. Joan Koob Cannie, *Keeping Customers for Life* (New York: AMACOM, 1991), p. 137.

3. Merrill Douglass, "Learning How to Give a Positive 'No,'" *Supervisory Management,* November 1990, p. 5.

4. Saul W. Gellerman, "The Tests of a Good Salesperson," *Harvard Business Review,* May-June, 1990, p. 65.

CHAPTER 9

1. "Your Office: It Should Reflect Stature, Workload, and Corporate Culture," *Executive Strategies,* August 6, 1991, p. 4.

CHAPTER 10

1. Several of the ideas in this list are based on Julie Griffin Levitt, *Your Career: Making It Happen,* Second Edition (Cincinnati: South-Western Publishing Co., 1990), p. 191.

2. "Moving Up," *Executive Strategies,* November 7, 1989, p. 4.

3. J. I. Biegeleisen, *Make Your Job Interview A Success,* Third Edition (New York: ARCO/Prentice Hall, 1991), p. 118.

CHAPTER 11

1. "Flattery Works," *Executive Strategies,* September 4, 1990, p. 4.

❖

INDEX

❖